Praise for

PATRIARCHY INC.

'Both entertaining and enraging, this is a brilliant resource for any woman who has been told "it's not really a gender pay gap" or been faced with inclusion policies which tell her she's the one in need of fixing.' Victoria Smith, author of *Hags*

'With her trademark command of theory, marshalling of social scientific evidence, and ear for le mot juste, Fine makes a powerful case for a new approach to gender in the workplace, one that would make work fairer, more secure, and more rewarding for all of us.' Professor Nick Haslam, School of Psychological Sciences, University of Melbourne

'Why do women still earn so much less than men? If you thought it was just the playing out of biological differences or the judgements of the market, Cordelia Fine's excellent new book, erudite, witty and always a pleasure to read, will set you straight.' Professor John Dupre, Egenis, The Centre for the Study of Life Sciences, University of Exeter

'*Patriarchy Inc.* is informed, nuanced, penetrating, written with understated passion but wonderfully free of leaden moralising.' Professor Kim Sterelny, School of Philosophy, Australian National University

'Cordelia Fine has done it again! Somehow, she is able to take a serious topic, decant decades of research into informative and persuasive prose, all whilst bringing a wry smile to the reader's lips.' Professor Rosie Campbell, King's College London

'Fine is a superb science writer. . . . If you have ever wondered why WWII code-breaker films are full of women typing away at proto-computers and nowadays programming is the domain of tech bros read this book.' Michael Jennions, Professor of Evolutionary Ecology, Australian National University

'In *Patriarchy Inc.*, Cordelia Fine once again demonstrates her remarkable ability to provide a fresh and critical view, this time to tackle the persistent problem of gender inequality in the workplace. She skillfully dismantles both the "Different But Equal" defense of workplace inequality and the corporate-friendly DEI approach, offering instead a compelling new framework for understanding how gender hierarchies persist in modern workplaces. Fine's characteristic wit and incisive thinking make this essential reading for anyone interested in creating genuinely fair and productive workplaces.' Professor Daphna Joel, author of *The Gender Mosaic*

'*Patriarchy Inc.* provides a timely analysis of how problematic patriarchal structures are negatively impacting our lives. It offers a comprehensive examination of prevalent myths and misconceptions surrounding gender equality issues in contemporary society, supported by robust scientific evidence. Cordelia Fine doesn't shy away from taking on some of the established notions around gender and gender roles. This book is an essential resource for anyone interested in gender equity.' Professor Heejung Chung, director of the King's Global Institute for Women's Leadership and author of *The Flexibility Paradox*

CORDELIA FINE is a professor in the History & Philosophy of Science programme in the School of Historical & Philosophical Studies at the University of Melbourne. Her previous book, *Testosterone Rex*, won the Royal Society Insight Investment Science Book Prize. Cordelia was awarded the 2018 Edinburgh Medal for her work on gender, and was recently named as a living legend by *The Australian* newspaper.

Also by Cordelia Fine

Testosterone Rex
Delusions of Gender
A Mind of Its Own

PATRIARCHY INC.

What We Get Wrong About Gender Equality—and Why Men Still Win at Work

Cordelia Fine

W. W. NORTON & COMPANY

Independent Publishers Since 1923

For information about permission to reproduce selections from
this book, write to Permissions, W. W. Norton & Company, Inc.,
500 Fifth Avenue, New York, NY 10110

For information about special discounts for bulk purchases, please contact
W. W. Norton Special Sales at specialsales@wwnorton.com or 800-233-4830

Manufacturing by Lakeside Book Company
Production manager: Gabi Montgomery

Library of Congress Cataloging-in-Publication Data is available.

ISBN 978-1-32406-474-9

W. W. Norton & Company, Inc., 500 Fifth Avenue, New York, NY 10110
www.wwnorton.com

W. W. Norton & Company Ltd., 15 Carlisle Street, London W1D 3BS

10 9 8 7 6 5 4 3 2 1

For Carsten

CONTENTS

A NOTE ABOUT LANGUAGE

THIS BOOK DRAWS ON DECADES OF DATA AND centuries of discussion that use the terms 'women' and 'men' to refer to people based on their sex. I do the same here, but in acknowledgement that a person's gender identification as a woman, man or non-binary can be distinct from their sex.

INTRODUCTION

WHAT'S YOUR VISION OF GENDER EQUALITY?

Whatever it is, it needs to take a stand on divisions of labour. Work – who does what tasks in society, and what they get in return – is at the heart of social justice. Among those concerned with social hierarchies, in which certain groups enjoy higher status and more power than others, there is a long and distinguished tradition of turning a beady eye on divisions of labour attached to the social identities people are born into. *You be the serf, I'll be the landowner*, for example, does not offer fertile ground for egalitarian relations between those two social categories. Little wonder that in the general scheme of things, these are matters that can inspire philosophical treatises and political manifestos, strikes and protests, campaigns and cries of 'Oil the guillotine, Pierre!'

When it comes to the gendered division of labour, just about everyone is familiar with the basic statistics. We know that along the 'vertical' dimension of prestige and pay, men remain firmly installed at the top. For example, in 2022 men

1

still held more than 80 per cent of the top 'C-suite' roles in North American and European financial services firms.[1] Among the world's 40 largest banks, all but one had a man as chief executive officer at the beginning of 2024. Men also took up 78 per cent of roles as finance ministers and 87 per cent of those as the heads of central banks in OECD countries.[2] (These are the countries, including the world's richest, that are committed to market economies and democracy and are members of the Organisation for Economic Co-operation and Development.) But men are also overrepresented in jobs on the bottom two rungs of the occupational ladder, in roles like caretaker, garbage collector, and process, plant and machine operative.[3]

Clear 'horizontal' divisions of labour also remain. These divisions only partly line up with our stereotypes about differences between women and men in terms of traits, abilities, values and motivations.[4] Females' (modest) advantage in language abilities and supposed keen interest in people rather than things are sometimes used to explain their lower representation in science, technology, engineering and mathematics (STEM) occupations.[5] Yet turn to film screenwriting, a job seemingly custom-built for stereotypical feminine skills and interests, and you will find that 81 per cent of screenwriters are men – an even steeper gender imbalance than is seen among people with PhDs in computer and mathematical science.[6] Less often commented on is that these horizontal divisions are linked to men's much higher rates of fatal work-related injuries compared to women.[7]

Finally, we all know there are marked differences between

women and men when it comes to the amount of time spent in paid work in the market versus unpaid work taking care of the home and its occupants.[8] The average woman in the UK spends about 24 hours per week doing unpaid childcare, adult care and household chores, and 21 hours per week in paid work or education. For the average UK man, the priorities are reversed, with about 27 hours of paid work or study per week and 18 hours of unpaid work. He also enjoys 3 more hours of leisure every week than his female counterpart (which gives him plenty of spare time to read this book).[9] Unpaid domestic labour takes gendered patterns too. Women are more likely to do the time-sensitive chores-without-end like cooking, grocery shopping, cleaning, laundry and routine childcare. In contrast, men are more likely to do more sporadic, time-flexible activities, like playing with the kids, and tasks like mowing the lawn or mending the gate that can be held off until a convenient moment, such as the weekend, the new year or the end of time.[10]

These divisions are both cause and consequence of the sex-based hierarchy of status and power over resources, aka patriarchy, that we see in the advanced economies of the Global North that are the focus of this book.[11] But our progress in dismantling these arrangements has been stymied by two false visions that pervade mainstream debate and discussion.[12]

The first is what I call the Different But Equal perspective. This reframing of gender equality emerged in the 1990s, when the steady erosion of the gender traditionalism of the 1950s hit a wall.[13] The 'Equal' part holds that women and men now rightly enjoy equal opportunities in education, work

3

and family life. They are therefore both largely free to fully develop their skills, talents and other potential as they choose. This human capital can then be fairly exchanged in the labour market, in return for status, income and other rewards, via the gender-neutral market mechanisms of supply and demand.

The 'Different' element of this perspective assumes that women's and men's choices about how to realize their potential, such as whether to invest more in career or family, or what kinds of occupations to pursue, are strongly shaped by inherent sex differences in personality. Different But Equal-ers often draw on ideas from Evolutionary Psychology,[14] which holds that biological effects of sex on the brain, honed over millennia by evolution, mean that males and females are born with programmes for the development of importantly different abilities, motivations and decision-making processes. These evolved because they gave ancestral males and females an advantage over others of the same sex in the struggle for survival and reproduction.

Different But Equal-ers don't subscribe to rigid biological determinism. They readily acknowledge that non-biological factors shape development and behaviour. They are typically careful to draw attention to the fact that average sex differences still allow for plenty of overlap in personality (a term I am using here in the broad sense of traits, abilities, motives and values). But they think that in countries that boast wealth and gender egalitarian norms, the gendered division of labour is approaching a just and natural state in which women and men are able to freely and fully develop and express their potential, preferences and choices. Then, as adults, they neatly slot

4

themselves into forms of work that best match their evolved personalities.

The Different But Equal perspective is not a niche view. According to a national survey of Australians in 2018, about a third of respondents were quite comfortable with traditional gender roles, and half agreed that the sexes have different skills and talents. About a fifth of respondents thought that men make better leaders and are more ambitious. Almost a third thought that women don't aspire to leadership positions because of their family responsibilities, and a substantial minority approved of women prioritizing home over career.[15] Even though, at the time of the survey, more than three quarters of Australia's most senior justices and judges, private-sector CEOs and federal government ministers were men, only six out of ten respondents agreed that Australia should have more women in the top echelons. Nor, it's important to say, were these kinds of views exclusively clustered among the older generations, and therefore destined to die out.

Half a decade later, another survey of Australians found that 58 per cent agreed that men are naturally suited for some jobs, women for others, with another 29 per cent unsure either way. Only 22 per cent of respondents firmly disagreed that some areas of study are naturally suited to boys and others to girls. A quarter thought that traditional families and children function best when fathers do the breadwinning and mothers do the caring, and a further 38 per cent were on the fence.[16]

It's not difficult to see why the Different But Equal viewpoint is an obstacle to tackling inequalities relating to the gendered division of labour. According to this vision of gender equality, *there is no real problem to solve.*

The second major obstacle to dismantling patriarchy is the vision offered by the business-case Diversity, Equality and Inclusion (DEI) approach. I'll be using the acronym DEI when referring to this package, and the terms 'diversity', 'equality' and 'inclusion' when referring to the concepts themselves. (Sometimes, particularly in the US, the 'E' is for Equity.) Corporate communications teams tend to write about their companies' DEI values and commitments as if they were being paid by the platitude. However, they boil right down to a handful of points. Most obviously, the DEI approach values diversity. It affirms a positive orientation towards a workforce with many dimensions – gender, ethnicity, viewpoint and experience are often offered as examples. The main reason to value diversity, according to the contemporary DEI approach, is because it can create more competitive, profitable, high-performing, innovative businesses. Therefore, in order to foster these business benefits, we need to treat everyone fairly (the 'equality' or 'equity' part), and cultivate environments that ensure all employees feel welcome and able to make their business-enhancing contributions (the 'inclusion' part).

The DEI approach has taken the business world by storm. In *Seven Steps to Leading a Gender-Balanced Business*, published by the prestigious Harvard Business Review Press, a leading gender consultant designates the end goal of mere equality as an outdated, twentieth-century framework. In *this* century, the 'end goal is competitive advantage'.[17] Along similar lines, the recent book *All the Brains in the Business: The Engendered Brain in the 21st Century Organisation* seeks to replace 'the argument for equality' with one for 'organizational advantage'. The co-authors, a business academic and a consultant, recommend leaders reap this gain from a fuller appreciation of 'feminine energy' within organizations, which they refer to as the 'emergent quality of women'. They even coin the term 'e-quality' to refer to this promisingly under-leveraged female human capital, as if to emphasize the end of demand for the unamended version of the word.[18] The message is getting through. A recent analysis of the organizational diversity cases of the Fortune 500 (the 500 US companies with the largest annual revenue) found that these business-case arguments were first and foremost in 81 per cent of the diversity cases offered by these companies on their websites. Only 1 per cent argued for diversity in terms of fairness.[19]

The problem with the DEI approach is that it pivots away from what most of us believe is the most important reason for caring about the equality and inclusion of marginalized groups – that we want to create a fairer society. The DEI approach may well be successful at making a profit out of women's labour. It has failed to create workplaces that offer genuine gender equality for women (or men), *because that was never the goal.*

The DEI approach has not won everyone's hearts and minds. This is perhaps not surprising, given the apparent popularity of the Different But Equal perspective. The 2019 Ipsos global survey, in conjunction with the Global Institute for Women's Leadership, found that 40 to 44 per cent of respondents in Great Britain, the United States, France and the Netherlands disagreed that 'employers doing more to promote women to senior leadership positions' would have a positive impact.[20] Their 2024 survey found that among those same countries, approximately one in two men agreed that 'We have gone so far in promoting women's equality that we are discriminating against men' (ranging from 46 per cent of men in France to 59 per cent in Great Britain). Nor can we simply chalk up these attitudes to male-privilege-induced blindness, given that about a third of women from these countries reported feeling the same way.[21]

These dissatisfactions can also be found in the higher ranks of management and white-collar work. In 2021, an Australian survey of professional men, conducted by a DEI consultancy company, found that one in four agreed that 'men and women aren't supposed to be equal' and that 'gender initiatives actually do more harm than good'. Forty-four per cent thought that women and men were already treated equally and they didn't know what the problem was. Forty-five per cent agreed with the statement that men are not to blame for women lagging behind in society or the workplace, since 'sometimes women are less driven or motivated'. Just over half thought that men 'are now suffering from reverse-discrimination, to the point where they are missing out on opportunities'. Almost one in two men were also fed up with the issue – 'I'm tired of hearing about it'.[22]

I am tired too. We have had more than enough of this unproductive clash between one vision of gender equality that obscures the problem, and another that doesn't really care about it. It is time for a new vision, grounded in a deeper understanding of the social processes that give rise to the gendered division of labour, and the inefficiencies, harms and injustices that this division creates.

The starting point of the Patriarchy Inc. account is that humans have been using sex to divide labour for at least tens of thousands of years, and perhaps much longer. Whether the contribution to keeping society functioning is hunting big game, boatbuilding, caring for toddlers, writing computer code, sewing clothes, assisting with childbirth, building houses, or selling complex financial products that will bring the global financial system to its knees, even children soon understand whether it is typically women's work or men's work.

Key to understanding why these divisions are so persistent is the special importance for our species of cooperation, social learning and culture for meeting the challenges of survival and reproduction. Whether the setting is a hunter-gatherer community, a household or a global investment bank, reaping the benefits of complex forms of cooperation, like divisions of labour, involves working out who will do which tasks, and what they will get in return. (*You dig up the tubers, I'll hunt the elk, and we'll share the spoils equally. You work in the home, I'll work in the market, and I'll take the greater share of status, control over family income and leisure time. You work on the reception desk, I'll do the merging and acquiring, and I'll work double the hours but take home ten times the pay.*)

How did we create and work out these complex arrangements? Cultural evolutionary perspectives on human behaviour and social life offer an alternative to Evolutionary

Psychology, and a quite different answer to that question: with distinctively human capacities for acquiring, curating and passing on culture. We have evolved both minds and culturally constructed niches that shape us into social roles. We are sensitive to norms, imitate some but not others, and are adept learners and teachers, alert to the matter of *what it means* to be *someone like me*. We create social categories and load them with cultural baggage concerning the skills and knowledge *these kinds of people* should have, how they should behave, their status, and their rights and responsibilities.

These same processes, acting on and through individuals, interactions and institutions, also explain the gendered division of labour.[23] My analysis centres on sex: a fundamental biological category, and human societies' most ubiquitous way of dividing both people and labour. But as we'll see throughout, gender intersects with the other major social hierarchies around which societies often organize labour, most commonly race and class, deepening disadvantages. Crosscutting with race and class, these processes shape women and men into different gender roles (*who does what*) and maintain the gender hierarchy of men's greater status and power over resources (*who gets what*). In its post-industrial form – the focus of this book – this gender system is what I name Patriarchy Inc.

The idea that the gendered division of labour is at the heart of a patriarchal gender system is hardly novel. But the Patriarchy Inc. account does offer something new for everyone, from the gender-fatigued sceptic to the weary foot soldier of social justice. First, it sets out an argument that the gendered division of labour is *both* a product of evolution *and* socially created. These two positions are normally pitted against each other, and accusations that social explanations of gender inequality are 'blank slate-ist', eager to deny sex, biology and evolution for political reasons, are always at fever pitch. Clearly, it would be false advertising to claim that this book will bring together supporters of warring scientific worldviews to find consensus, peace and harmony. Still, I hope there will be a constructive element to seeing how well the two perspectives fit together.

This book also makes a very abstract concept – the gender system – more concrete. It's easy to throw out accusations that 'patriarchy' is to blame for this, that and the other. It is much harder to get a handle on exactly how, when and where it operates – particularly since one important aspect of the system is the ideologies (sets of values and assumptions that we are sometimes barely conscious of) that we and others use to justify and rationalize our social arrangements. I hope this book will help you to really *see* the problem, and recognize Patriarchy Inc.'s handiwork in workplaces, households and government, and even within your own mind.

Finally, this book serves as an intervention to prevent the important concept of gender equality from becoming what the nineteenth-century political philosopher John Stuart Mill called 'dead dogma'. By this, he meant a doctrine for which, 'Instead of a vivid conception and a living belief, there remain only a few phrases retained by rote; or, if any part, the shell and husk only of the meaning is retained, the finer essence being lost.'[24]

I wrote this book because Patriarchy Inc. continues to perpetuate real harm and injustice for both sexes. It limits what we can do and who we can be, and its fat thumb unfairly tips the scales when it comes to what we get in return. It creates gendered distortions of competence and productivity, and irrational resistance to reforms that would make our workplaces not only more productive but also fairer. In workplaces where it is given the loosest rein, Patriarchy Inc. destroys organizational cultures, by corrupting those at the top of the ladder and creating upside-down value systems that 'pass off vices as virtues and condemn virtues as if they were vices', as one philosopher puts it.[25] But Patriarchy Inc.'s effects seep well beyond workplaces, contributing to economic insecurity, undermining health, putting pressure on family life and preserving females' second-class status. My hope is that a deeper understanding of how Patriarchy Inc. really operates will make gender equality once again a 'vivid conception and a living belief'; dispel the false visions that distract us; and inspire effective, common-sense reforms that will make workplaces and society fairer and freer for everyone.

I

DIVISIONS

IN 1976, AN AUSTRALIAN WOMAN CALLED DEBORAH Lawrie applied to become a trainee pilot with what was then a major Australian airline, Ansett Airways.[1] Despite her irreproachable qualifications, her application was rejected. As the general manager of Ansett helpfully explained, 'We have a good record of employing females in a wide range of positions within our organization but have adopted a policy of only employing men as pilots.'[2]

Lawrie (who soon thereafter married and changed her surname to Wardley) promptly took up a discrimination claim against the company – a bold move that was possible thanks to freshly minted equal opportunity legislation that made it illegal to discriminate on the basis of sex.[3] In its legal defence against Wardley's claim, the company didn't make any attempt to deny her competence. A letter to the secretary of the Women's Electoral Lobby from the general manager of Ansett even described her as 'a very nice person, highly intelligent and undoubtedly a good pilot'.[4] Instead, Ansett drew on an argument that twenty-first-century organizations now routinely use as a rationale *in favour* of hiring women – the business case. The company argued that it simply was not economically efficient to hire Wardley given that she was likely to get pregnant and have to take extended leave. This, they argued, wasn't *sex* discrimination.[5] They had nothing against women per se. They'd make the same decision about any male candidate who was likely to be off the job for a lengthy stretch.

There's a certain logic to it. If you are piloting Ansett-ANA Flight 325 from Sydney to Canberra, you will not be available at home to mash bananas and feed them to a baby. Conversely, if you are wiping mashed banana off hands, face, highchair, floor, your clothes and, perplexingly, the kettle on the other side of the room, it is not possible for you also to be located 40,000 feet in the air, calmly warning passengers of upcoming turbulence.

Divisions of labour yield efficiency boons.[6] As Scottish philosopher and economist Adam Smith famously observed in *An Inquiry into the Nature and Causes of the Wealth of Nations*, where one man could perhaps not even make a single pin in a day, ten men working on distinct parts of the process could make more than 48,000.[7] There can be gains if one group of people learns to exploit one resource while another group learns to make use of another. You do the hunting and I do the gathering; you make the pots and I'll carve the weapons; you cook and I clean. In contrast, if we *both* clean, we will be hungry. If we both cook, we will live in squalor. True, everyone could try to do a bit of everything. But that strategy may lead to us eating burnt food out of greasy pots. Dividing labour in an organized way becomes particularly beneficial when it comes to work that takes some skill and practice to do well, that has to be done in particular locations, and there are more and more *kinds* of work to do as households and societies become more complicated, and work becomes more specialized.

So, dividing labour in an organized way is likely to leave everyone better off, even if some people end up getting less desirable jobs than others. But how do we decide who does what? And why, across all human societies (from hunter-foragers to our own post-industrial economies), is this division of labour so often organized by sex?

Two standard answers to this question have locked horns for decades. The first explanation comes from Evolutionary Psychology. According to these accounts, at least some aspects of gendered divisions of labour are best understood as a downstream effect of genetically evolved sex differences in personality that promoted reproductive success in our ancestral past.[8] Evolutionary Psychologists acknowledge the existence of gender roles – culturally shared beliefs about what women and men are (and should be) like. But they think that the important core of these gender roles largely *tracks* and *tweaks* evolved sex differences in personality, rather than insidiously creating them. As two Evolutionary Psychologists have put it: 'culture-level gender roles may serve to amplify or attenuate fundamental sex differences in evolved biology'.[9]

The second explanation, from what is known as Social Role Theory, reverses the chain of command.[10] Psychologists

Alice Eagly and Wendy Wood propose that sex differences in personality are mostly a downstream effect of gendered divisions of labour. According to them, these divisions are shaped by social, economic and ecological factors, in combination with enduring physical differences between the sexes – most importantly, that men are typically stronger and faster, while only women get pregnant and breastfeed. Gender roles track what work men and women do. If women do the childcare, we assume they are caring. If men do the leading, we assume they are authoritative and decisive. These cultural expectations then help create their own reality. Behaviour that fits the gender role is rewarded, while nonconformity is punished. We internalize at least some of the cultural expectations attached to our own gender identity. And our biology offers a helping hand too, such as when testosterone rises or falls depending on whether the circumstances call for competition or nurturance.[11]

Evolutionary Psychologists regard Social Role Theory as an implausible 'blank slate approach' to understanding sex differences in personality.[12] But as we're about to see, the theory fits rather nicely with alternative evolutionary accounts of what's on that slate. This chapter suggests that socially created gender roles evolved not just because physical differences between the sexes mean that some tasks are easier for one sex than the other, but also because gendered divisions of labour help solve the problem of coordinating *who does what.*[13]

I realize that to some, the idea that we *evolved* cultural gender roles, rather than sex-differentiated personalities, might seem fantastical. Even as I write, I imagine my sternest critics from Evolutionary Psychology shaking with mirth as they gleefully announce to each other that Cordelia has really surpassed herself this time. The Evolutionary Psychologist David Schmitt recently argued that 'It would defy everything known about evolution by sexual selection to maintain that selective forces have continuously and completely "wiped the gender slate clean" of psychological sex differences during the long path of human evolution.'[14] Two important questions are packed into this short quote. One has to do with our evolutionary history – 'the long path of human evolution'. What were the selective pressures that, by weeding out less successful individuals, brought about the evolution of the human mind (including sex differences)? That is, what were the challenges our ancestors faced? The second matter is what kind of creatures we have become – what minds have we evolved? – as a result.

Researchers interested in human evolution have offered many different answers to both questions. Evolutionary Psychologists have long favoured the view that over the course of the Pleistocene, a relatively stable period between 2.5 million and 11,700 years ago, we fixed on adaptations to help solve many challenging day-to-day problems: evade predators, find mates, raise children, maintain a good reputation, detect social norms, cooperate with others without getting swindled, and so on.[15] Evolutionary Psychologists do recognize the importance of learning. But, they say, our minds are not blank slates. By this they mean a mind that comes without any inbuilt information to assist with navigating the complexities of survival and reproduction, beyond a domain-general capacity to learn associations provided by the environment. Instead, they argue that learning is channelled and shaped by pre-existing content. This content is packaged in hundreds, if not thousands, of genetically bestowed adaptations – mechanisms that furnish abilities, motives and processes for making decisions.[16] Each mechanism is highly specialized – it evolved to solve a specific problem. And because some of the challenges facing our ancestors differed depending on their sex, for these problems sex-specific adaptations evolved, prefigured to generate somewhat different abilities, motives and decision rules. These can operate in ways that are sensitive to context, but it is a prefigured range of plasticity, limited to what was adaptive for Pleistocene environments rather than novel ones.

Hopefully it is clear from this brief sketch that Evolutionary Psychologists aren't just committed to the uncontroversial idea that human minds have evolved. They are committed to a particular story about *how* our minds evolved, and *what* our minds are like. We'll come back to their ideas in chapters 6 and 7. But at this point, allow me to condense the lengthy and sometimes testy exchanges that have taken place over decades down to a brief sentence of understatement. Not everyone agrees with Evolutionary Psychologists on these matters – including those who instead back one of a suite of cultural evolutionary perspectives that, as the term suggests, put much greater emphasis on the role of cultural processes.

For example, everyone agrees that our minds are not entirely blank slates, ineffectually trying to pick up patterns like a useless aristocrat who has learned little more than that when he rings the bell, someone brings a cocktail. But other evolutionary scientists have quite different views on the initial starting state of the slate. A view termed 'cultural evolutionary psychology' proposes that our 'starter kit' is little more elaborate than genetically inherited warm feelings and tolerance towards our fellow humans, a bias to attend to other people (especially faces and voices), and extra-powerful general-purpose mechanisms for learning and processing information.[17] Other cultural evolutionary perspectives on offer think instead that our slates come with prefigured biases about what, when and from whom to hoover up information.[18]

Some advocates of cultural evolutionary approaches also think that selective pressures acting on us during the Pleistocene were too irregular – too rapidly changing – for highly specific inbuilt psychological adaptations to be useful.[19] One reason for this is just how fast we evolved, as philosopher Kim Sterelny has persuasively argued.[20] As evolutionary scientists like to point out with justified awe, our hominid precursors split off from the chimpanzees just six to seven million years ago. About three million years later, we started undergoing what from an evolutionary perspective can only be described as a whirlwind transformation. We started walking on two legs. We developed technology and cooperation and became dependent on both. We adapted to climatic variation, spread geographically and worked out new ways of feeding ourselves.

We also revamped our social organization. Fathers cast aside the neglectful ways of their chimpanzee forebears and started investing in their children. We evolved cooperative breeding: a flexible arrangement of 'mothers and others', as evolutionary scientist Sarah Hrdy put it.[21] The extra childcare help provided by this more communal approach was accompanied by the evolution of bigger, smarter brains that develop over the course of an extended childhood.[22] Whether cooperative breeding evolved before, simultaneously or subsequently to becoming a highly cooperative species in other domains remains a matter of debate.[23] But here we are now. We have language, adolescence and postmenopausal grandmothers graciously helping out with the kids. Our social and sexual lives have continuously adapted to shifts in family organization, social hierarchies and divisions of labour. As we raced our way to becoming the literally singing and dancing modern human – music and rituals being yet another addition to our repertoire – we charted an entirely unique path.

And as our ancestors changed, so the ecological, economic, social and psychological environments – and selective pressures – also altered. The pace and novelty have implications for the kind of minds we could have evolved, says Sterelny: 'As humans have lived in such variable environments, many . . . [informationally demanding] problems cannot be solved by prewiring information into human heads. Our genes cannot predict the kind of world in which we will live. That has been true for at least 200,000 years, probably longer.'[24] One adaptation that was called for, he argues, is a profound capacity for developmental plasticity.[25] Like many others, Sterelny contends that the reason humans have been able to rapidly and successfully adapt to such a diverse range of environments, including by *changing* those environments, is that we increasingly relied on, and enhanced, three processes that have precursors in other animals: cooperation, social learning and cumulative culture. Cooperation refers to groups of individuals working together for mutual benefit. Social learning refers to when we learn from other people, rather than through our own individual efforts. Cumulative culture refers to 'culturally constructed niches filled with artifacts, skills, beliefs, and practices that have been inherited, accumulated, and modified over generations.'[26]

To help you get the feel for the concept of the 'culturally constructed niche', let me offer an incomplete survey of my own. My artifacts include, in no particular order of importance, a house, a cup of coffee, a laptop (running off electricity), a diary, books, flip-flops, a table and chair, and a fan (the kind that creates a pleasant current of air on a hot day, rather than the kind that tells you how much they love your books). My skills include reading, writing and typing. Less tangible, but no less powerful, are the beliefs and practices shaping my behaviour: such as the education I received, conventions about clothing, the ideas I have encountered, and my daily routine as a professor at a university.

Cumulative culture is important because it 'is a system that fairly quickly evolves novel solutions to novel problems. In this respect, Cultural Evolution is like a faster version of genetic evolution, and, like genetic evolution, generates design and functionality in traits.'[27] But also, by changing the environment, we potentially alter what it takes to successfully survive and reproduce. These cultural innovations can therefore also create their own selective pressures, including on our genes over a long enough timescale. (When this happens, it is called gene–culture coevolution.)[28]

Herein lies the trifecta of our success, with the total being bigger than the sum of its parts. Cooperation helps us with social learning and accumulating cultural capital; culturally constructed niches help us to socially learn and cooperate; social learning helps us cooperate and construct our cultural niche.

These three interlocking processes provide the social structure within which gender roles, including the gendered division of labour, occur.

Certainly, in line with Social Role Theory, ethnographic surveys of non-industrialized societies find that work that requires strength (particularly upper body strength), travelling far from home, or that would be especially dangerous for people who are smaller, weaker or pregnant – tree cutting, smelting of ores, metalworking and big game hunting – is done exclusively or predominantly by men.[29] Collecting wild honey, another male-typical activity, is also physically demanding – not because the jars are hard to open, but because reaching the source involves cutting steps into trees with an axe and climbing them.[30] Meanwhile, cooking, laundering and dairy production – activities that are safe, close to home, don't require intense concentration, and can be interrupted by a nursing infant and then resumed – are mostly performed by women.[31] Similarly, in small-scale hunter-gatherer societies, there is a 'broad patterning' whereby 'men tend to spend much more time hunting for large prey, women in gathering plant foods and caring for young children'.[32]

But what neither Social Role Theory nor Evolutionary Psychology can explain is why there are also many examples of sex being used in diverse and arbitrary ways to divide labour.[33] Some activities, like building houses, hunting small animals, crop planting and harvesting, are done mostly by women in some societies, and mostly by men in others. And even when it comes to activities that are usually strongly sex-patterned, there are sometimes exceptions to the rule, such as societies in which men are the launderers or the gatherers, or in which women are the land clearers or the wild honey collectors.[34] In some communities, women are also regular hunters of middling-sized animals such as deer, antelope, reindeer or forest pigs.[35]

To set ourselves a reverse-engineering exercise, why would human societies universally create gendered divisions of labour, including designating jobs as for women or for men in arbitrary ways? And how do these cross-culturally diverse arrangements, including occasionally counterintuitive ones, come about?

Philosopher of science Cailin O'Connor argues that we should expect gendered divisions of labour to emerge in any human society, even when neither sex has a physical or psychological advantage for performing the work. This is because divisions of labour offer a solution to a problem – *who does what* – posed by forms of cooperation in which people have to coordinate their behaviour by taking complementary roles.[36] Dancing the tango offers a nice example: things run more smoothly and efficiently if everyone knows that *these people* lead and *those people* follow. If there were some ubiquitous and obvious method for creating these social categories, we might well expect the benefits for everyone to mean that the practice spreads through a population. And of course, there is.

Sex categories offer a universal and easy basis for creating social categories that can be used to organize labour (or tango dancing). Every society has both sexes, usually in roughly equal numbers. The sexes are readily distinguishable, and certain vital tasks are already done by women (childbearing and breastfeeding) due to different reproductive roles. Using mathematical models, O'Connor shows that groups that use sex to coordinate divisions of labour will often be more successful than those that ignore it, leaving everyone better off. The sheer efficiency of using sex to assign roles means that we can expect groups 'via social learning or cultural evolution to . . . take advantage of existing biological sex differences to create . . . gender roles and conventions'.[37] In other words, the gendered division of labour evolved as a *cultural adaptation* – a culturally inherited practice that increased survival and flourishing. To keep it going, we needed people to categorize themselves and others as men or women (and boys or girls) based on their sex, ideally emphasizing the distinction through artifacts such as clothing and other adornment. We needed culturally shared norms about which sex should do what and how they should behave, and we needed members of the society to notice, conform to and enforce those norms. In short, we needed gender roles that gradually emerged and were passed on and modified via cultural evolution.

The gendered division of labour might well have been adaptive overall in populations in which fertility is high, in economies in which many forms of labour require considerable physical strength, and in cultures in which tradition trumps autonomy and self-expression comes rather low on the list of cultural values.[38] But none of these features apply to post-industrial economies, rendering the drifting-on of the gendered division of labour a problem rather than a solution.

We are not the only species to have evolved divisions of labour. Social insects, such as ants, bees and termites, organize their communities around this principle. A termite is not simply a termite, but a reproducer (makes the baby termites), a soldier (defends against ants and other intruders), or a worker (in charge of food, grooming and tunnel building).[39] But compared with other specializing species, the scale and novelty of our cooperative activities, and the demographic complexity of who we cooperate with, is beyond compare.

The US Bureau of Labor Statistics classifies human workers into no fewer than 867 different occupations, including banquet cooks, egg graders, log ropers, radio time buyers, aircraft instrument mechanics, flower arrangers, morgue attendants and, thank goodness, career counsellors.[40] How do we achieve these specialities? Obviously, the environment doesn't activate one of 867 prefigured psychological mechanisms. One is not born, but rather becomes, an egg grader.[41]

A concept called 'mindshaping' is helpful for understanding this process of becoming. Developed by the philosopher Tadeusz Zawidzki, mindshaping refers to processes such as imitation, education and norm enforcement, which shape our minds and behaviour to become more like those around us.[42] Mindshaping is a crucial evolutionary lynchpin of human cooperation, because we can only effectively cooperate when we behave in ways that are similar, predictable and acceptable to the people we interact with. We have therefore evolved to become fervent imitators, teachers and learners, exquisitely sensitive to norms, and to create and curate cultural niches that provide extensive and forceful information about what shape our minds should be taking, and thus how we should behave.

For example, like chimpanzees, we imitate. Both chimps and human children will copy the actions an adult takes to get into a box in order to retrieve a reward. But if the chimp can work out a more efficient way than the one modelled by the adult, she will use it. All she cares about is getting into the box and grasping the treat inside it. Children, in contrast, carry on breaking into the box in just the same way the adult did it – including gratuitous and silly rituals.[43] The standard explanation of this human penchant for over-imitation is that for us, instrumental goals aside, there is also something *intrinsically* rewarding about matching the behaviour of a model. As one academic observed: 'All my children, from the time they could wriggle, would pull books out of the bottom shelf of the nearest bookcase and then flip through the pages intently, pausing only to giggle to themselves every once in a while. As they were the offspring of academics, their behavior was transparent. They were doing, to the best of their ability, what their parents did.'[44] This proclivity for faithful imitation is an important channel for cultural inheritance – a non-genetic route for passing on useful knowledge and skills, including about how to behave, to the next generation.[45]

Cultural learning is also actively propagated through what Sterelny calls 'master–apprentice' relationships.[46] Those in the 'master' role are predisposed to offer guidance, while 'apprentices' are receptive from an early age to what others might teach them. For example, evolution has surely genetically gifted us with parental motivations to care for our infants. But we also have the ability to learn the culturally tuned specifics of how to tend to babies' cognitive, emotional, social and bodily needs (alongside plenty of tearful individual trial-and-error learning).[47]

Parents then pivot from being learners to teachers. Emotions, for instance, are arguably mindshaped from birth, helping to curate development and expression in culturally approved ways. Caregivers mirror certain patterns of babies' facial expressions in an exaggerated way, while ignoring others. They help infants to regulate their emotions. They positively reinforce culturally valued emotional expressions, while responding negatively to, or ignoring, others. Caregivers also structure interactions in ways that draw attention to (or away from) certain emotionally charged features of an unfolding situation. As one emotion expert has put it: 'Socialized norms and prescriptions about emotions affect caregiver responses to infants (including attentiveness, reward, and punishment), and shape the development of their emotions long before infants internalize these norms and prescriptions explicitly.'[48]

Indeed, as parenting guides like to ominously warn, we are often teaching our children even when we don't realize it.[49] Words of admiration at a valiant attempt to tidy up the toys is 'teaching by evaluative feedback'. Helping a child sweep up leaves with a broom twice his size is 'opportunity provisioning'. Drawing a child's attention to the task at hand is 'teaching by local and social enhancement'. Telling a child to say thank you when they receive a present, a meal or decades of selfless parental service is an example of 'direct active teaching'. Performing traditions or rituals with your toddler nearby is yet another pedagogical style – 'teaching by social tolerance'. Meanwhile, complex human societies set up 'institutions of formal education and sanctioning to shape group members to play highly specific roles in very complex social structures', as Zawidzki observes.[50] These are all ways of helping children and young people pick up the know-how to be successful cooperators.

Knowledge of norms is a crucial part of this. 'Almost everyone who has written on the evolution of norms and normative guidance', says Sterelny, 'has argued for a funda-mental connection between human cooperation and norms.'[51] Particularly once cooperation became more complex, and involved people we didn't know and to whom we were unre-lated, norms were essential to effectively police defectors and prevent lazier members of the group from free-riding on the hard work of others. Norms also reduce ambiguity as to what *counts* as free-riding – an uncertainty that would only other-wise intensify as the social world becomes more complex.[52] The group can sanction the norm violators, and the would-be exploiter knows it. (Nonetheless, one interesting feature of norms, as Sterelny points out, is that many have no obvious and direct connection to cooperation, and even seem to under-mine smooth relations.[53] As Freud might have said, sometimes a norm is just a norm.)

Then, in 'larger and more complex environments', Sterelny suggests, individuals 'regulate their interactions and expecta-tions of one another through recognition of social role and function, rather than through specific individual knowledge'.[54] When I walk into a university lecture hall to teach, I don't have to explain how it all works. ('You sit quietly in those seats over there, while I stand here at the front and upload knowledge into your mind. If I ask a question, continue to sit quietly, but now avoid all eye contact.') Mindshaping is so effective that nobody needs to know what's going on in anyone else's mind (and it's frankly perhaps as well that these contents remain obscure). Students don't direct their attention towards the PowerPoint slides because they know that I have an internal desire that they do so. I don't disseminate my wisdom because, surveying the young people slouched and drooping before me, I intuit a powerful thirst for a fuller understanding of the observation summarized in bullet point three. We each do what we do because they are the students, and I am the lecturer, and these are the socially learned expectations for how to behave in these roles.

We receive both formal and informal training in norms throughout life. From birth, we are steeped in normatively loaded cultural clues – stories, songs, myths, rituals, role models, codes of conduct, laws and much more. We have social institutions, like families, religions, schools and organizations, that are hotbeds of norms. Even young children are sensitive to clues as to whether they are watching actions that are simply about achieving a particular goal, or behaviour that reflects social norms, and tend to more slavishly imitate the latter.[55] There are rewards for those who conform to those social norms. Conversely, when we fall short, family, peers, co-workers, employers, fellow citizens and the state are often very happy to let us know, via penalties that run the gamut from a coldly raised eyebrow to state-sanctioned execution.[56]

From an early age, these norms and cultural expectations become incorporated into the way we think of ourselves and plan our lives. Some philosophers consider our sense of self, and our lives, as 'in some sense story-like', as one such advocate puts it.[57] These 'self-constituting narratives' are, according to Zawidzki, another evolutionary innovation to foster mindshaping. (Another possibility is that this was a helpful adaptation for foraging economies, in which simply living in the moment was a bad approach – we instead needed to plan for and invest in the future.)[58] Importantly, these self-narratives are shaped not just by our unique personal identities, but also by our identities as members of social categories (like 'lecturer' or 'student'). 'For example,' Zawidzki suggests, 'one's self-regulating narrative might include one's status as a responsible parent. This immediately generates a set of culturally determined expectations that guide one's behavior and others' responses to it.'[59] While everyone's life story is unique, its meaning and arc and the underlying intentions, desires, aims and motivations that guide our behaviour and decisions are informed by broader shared cultural understandings and expectations.

Meanwhile, our capacity for complex language means that our minds are shaped not only by the flesh-and-blood individuals standing before us, but also by absent, fictional, mythical or abstract archetypes: the ideal worker; the eccentric genius; the great leader. Again, this sets us apart from other species. Our family dog, Günther, is a well-meaning animal, eager to please. However, I am pretty sure he has never handled a tricky situation by asking himself: *What would Lassie do?* Suppose, however, you are an egg grader, faced with some kind of egg-thical dilemma. (Sorry.) Your awareness of what an egg grader would do – abstracted out of policies, codes, observations of others and personal experience – will factor into your decision-making.

This returns us to the question of how one *becomes* an egg grader, tasked with ensuring that the breakfast egg neither disappoints nor overwhelms. The answer, as we have now seen, is: with a vast amount of mindshaping. This evolutionary innovation, unique to us, is how genetic propensities for social learning, cooperation and cumulative culture enable us to find diverse and flexible collective solutions to the challenges of life.[60]

By now it should be easy to see how mindshaping can give rise to gender roles, including gendered divisions of labour. All the mindshaping ingredients are present in abundance. Social learning of gender roles starts at birth. Painstakingly rich observations of hours of North American caregiver– infant interactions reveal that from a very young age, care-givers provide visual, auditory and tactile inputs that differ by sex. Unsurprisingly, there's plenty of variation in how parents care for their babies. But amidst this diversity in the quality and quantity of care, there are divergences in how parents respond to boys versus girls in patterns of face-to-face com-munication, physical play, responses to their child's coos and gurgles, help with infants' fine motor skills and fussing over the child's appearance.[61]

On the other side of the equation, infants become attuned to sex from a very early age (at least in the Global North populations where this research takes place). At three months of age, infants with a female caregiver prefer female faces (and vice versa for a small sample of babies with a male primary caregiver).[62] By eight months, babies can discriminate between male and female faces, and at ten months show evidence of categorizing faces on the basis of sex.[63] Around this time they also start showing knowledge of gender stereotypes, and at about two years of age, toddlers start explicitly using gender categories to carve up the social world, including themselves.[64]

This brings us to the concept of gender identity – a term used in many (and often confusing) ways. Here, I do not refer to knowledge of a biological fact about oneself, or to an affinity with male or female gender roles (or with both or neither). I'm using the term as it is often used by social cognitive psychologists, for whom gender identity, like other social identities, 'involves the self-representation of a gendered self' as part of 'a broader conception of the self'.[65]

As with all such self-conceptions, gender identity is partly constructed from social experiences and interactions. If sex were not an important category in the social world, if it didn't reliably shape the way people respond to and treat us across a wide range of social situations, it's possible we would no more have a gender identity than we do a 'breakfast identity', based on whether we eat cereal or toast, a 'belly button identity', grounded in whether we are an innie or an outie, or a 'hair colour identity'. (Whether it's plausible that sex could ever lose its significance as a social category, given the reproductive differences between the sexes, is another matter.) The fact that a small percentage of the population – namely transgender and non-binary people (and, in non-Western cultures, people who belong to third or additional gender categories) – *don't* identify as a member of their sex (despite sex-typical genes and hormones) shows that the endpoint of this constructive process is not a given. Gender identity has to *develop*, and the fact that it so very reliably does (and so early in childhood) is testament to the salience of social categories based on sex – that is, gender categories – in everyday life.

One way to understand gender identity is as an ongoing process – a story, if you will – of oneself as a woman, man, boy or girl (or some other gender category). It is shaped throughout the life course by continuous interactions between personal factors ('biological proclivities, self-conceptions, goals, behavioral and judgmental standards, and self-regulatory processes associated with gender identity'), the individual's own behaviour, and social influences, which include culturally constructed niches saturated with gender norms.[66] Nobody internalizes all of them, but there is backup enforcement via laws, policies, traditions and customs, as well as through more informal social, economic and physical rewards and penalties dealt out by parents, siblings, peers, family or co-workers. From an early age, children start to anticipate whether others will approve or disapprove if they engage in gendered activities.[67]

The importance of gender categories in social life, and the heavy baggage of gender norms they carry, means that children do not treat their membership of one or other gender category as a mere fact about themselves, like their height or shoe size. Young children become so motivated to know more about what it means to be a boy or a girl that developmental psychologists have described them as 'gender detectives', in search of clues as to what is 'for men' and what is 'for women'. Children also display in-group favouritism and out-group prejudice when it comes to gender categories, including the copying of same-sex models and a favouring of clothing, toys, playmates, occupations and activities labelled as being for their gender.[68] For example, if you tell a boy that a job he's never heard of before (a chandler, for instance) is typically performed by men, he will be significantly more interested in it than if he thinks exactly the same job is usually done by women – and vice versa for girls.[69]

Along similar lines, hunter-gatherer forager children play in ways that emulate their future gender roles in their community's division of labour. These activities include making little huts, pretending to set traps and play-hunting with spears, pretending to collect mushrooms and to dig tubers, making dolls and then caring for them, pretending to collect honey, pretending to make bows, baskets and other objects, and pretending to fish. In fact, from a remarkably early age, it is not mere make-believe. In one striking account, an anthropologist working in Melville Island in northern Australia in the 1950s was invited by two girls aged about eight to join them on a water cruise. Having made the wooden rafts more seaworthy with strips of bark and set off, the girls plunged into the water and up trees to collect eggs, returning to the safety of the raft in the later afternoon when failing light made it harder to spot the crocodiles.[70]

Sex differences in these childhood activities match the local gendered division of labour in adults. For example, boys from the Hadza (northern Tanzania) and BaYaka (northern Congo) hunter-gatherer societies spend more time play-hunting than girls (in keeping with this being men's role in both societies). Conversely, girls from both societies spend more time than boys playing house. This includes *building* the house, since constructing shelter is women's work in both societies. However, it was only in the Hadza societies that sex differences in doll play and pretend-foraging appeared – reflecting the more gender-egalitarian divisions of labour among the BaYaka.[71]

A cross-cultural study of children's nurturing behaviour towards infants – sampling mostly from rural horticulturist and pastoralist subsistence societies – found that the most consistent sex difference in behaviour was that girls were more often in the company of infants, interacted with them more, and in most but not all communities were more nurturant towards them. But why? The researchers proposed what is in effect gendered mindshaping as the explanation:

[I]nvolvement with infants is an important source of sex-typed behavioral development in children. The system of self-socialization is founded on attractedness to like-sex community members, followed by identification. Girls are predisposed in their development to maintain proximity to adult females, where they receive maximal opportunity to attend selectively and maintain proximity to infants, with the result that they

35

gain knowledge and practice in nurturing styles of interaction. As they gain knowledge and practice, they become more skillful caregivers, with the result that nurturant interaction becomes differentially rewarding to them.[72]

In other words, the female caregiving role is a culturally inherited trait.

For those used to thinking of evolved gendered traits as *genetically* inherited, the idea that they are instead *culturally* inherited might seem like a strange juxtaposition. But there is nothing particularly outrageous about the proposal that for some traits, we biologically inherit a neural capacity for social learning, but it is the environment that furnishes most of the information about what is learned.[73] For example, North American moose usually display an adaptive anti-predator response when they encounter the sound or smell of wolves or bears: they become vigilant and aggressive, they stop eating, and they will abandon the feeding site. However, among some populations, human eradication of wolves and bears means that moose have been enjoying largely predator-free lives. After just a handful of generations of living predator-free, moose show a striking reduction in this anti-predator behaviour. But if predators re-colonize the local ecology, mothers whose infants have been killed quickly learn to be astute and wary around the sounds and smells of those animals, and seem to transmit this wariness to their young.[74] In other words, if mother moose quivers and then moves swiftly from the scene at the first whiff of wolf urine, and moose junior has sufficient genetically endowed neural capacity to pick up the gist of the routine, that will more or less do.[75]

Pointing to cultural evolutionary perspectives, Daphna Joel, John Dupré and I have argued for the potential importance of *cultural* rather than biological inheritance of at least some components of gender roles. What's nice about this cultural evolutionary explanation is that it can account for both the considerable variation we see in gender roles *and* the remarkable stability and persistence of the gender system.[76]

Applying this explanation to gender roles in the division of labour also readily accommodates tentative suggestions that these are only a few tens of thousands of years old in our species' lineage. The evidence relating to social arrangements in human prehistory is sketchy, and the more so the further back in time one goes. It is only in the last 15,000 years or so that anthropologists find clear evidence of gendered divisions of labour 'in the acquisition and processing of food, in the caretaking of the young, in the production of technologies, and in the social, political, and economic hierarchies of societies'.[77] These years roughly mark the transition from mobile hunter-gatherer foragers to agriculture and settlements, a period in which birth rates were increasing and societies were becoming more complex and hierarchical. Also pointing to a later arrival of gendered divisions of labour, one analysis of burial sites in the Americas dating from within that period concluded that 'female participation in early big-game hunting was likely nontrivial'.[78]

But other anthropologists quite reasonably believe that gendered divisions of labour extend back much further (eighty to a few hundred thousand years).[79] If so, there would have been time for selective pressure to give rise to gene–culture coevolution: the *cultural* adaptation of gendered divisions of labour giving rise to *genetic* selection for fitness-increasing traits. One possibility, suggested by cultural evolutionist Joseph Henrich, is that we aren't just mindshaped into copying same-sex individuals, but genetically evolved 'to preferentially hang around, attend to, and learn from' others of the same sex.[80] This is an intriguing idea, although hard to test.[81]

Henrich has also suggested that selective pressures might have led to genetically inherited sex differences in personality that made it more likely that boys and girls were successfully socialized into their roles. Girls who had a greater interest in infants and boys who were more interested in projectile objects (to facilitate becoming hunters) might have had a competitive advantage.[82] Fair enough, and maybe so. But there isn't much in the way of empirical support for these ideas. For instance, studies *don't*, overall, find that female newborns, compared with boys, are especially interested in social stimuli.[83] Nor is there currently uncontested evidence of greater male interest in propulsive toys.[84]

So, while gene–culture coevolution may play a minor role, the gendered division of labour is best explained as a cultural adaptation. It is part of an evolving and cross-culturally variable package of culturally inherited gender roles that helps us to solve an ever-present problem of human life – *who does what*. Like any other evolutionary process, it doesn't infallibly lead to optimal solutions.[85] Traits can drift in random directions. And evolved forces such as 'morality, social norms, and social institutions . . . often act against immediate biological or material interests of individuals, promoting instead the interests of the society as a whole', as one trio of cultural evolutionists argue. Or, they add, 'of its powerful segments'.[86] Deborah Wardley may have had the skills, ability and desire to be a pilot, but the general manager of Ansett felt that the airline would be better served by maintaining the status quo. Stay tuned for a good deal more on this point as, in the next chapter, we see how another cultural adaptation – status hierarchies – helps to 'solve' the problem of *who gets what*, turning gender roles into gender hierarchy.

2

SEX AND STATUS

TWO WOMEN — ONE A BLACK AMERICAN ANALYST OF emerging markets, the other an Asian American senior vice president in structured finance — are discussing other women working on Wall Street who wear sneakers for their commute into Manhattan. These other women then change into their less comfortable heels on arrival at the office. Listening to this exchange is a Princeton University ethnographer, Karen Ho, herself working on Wall Street as an analyst at the time. When Ho asks the two other women if they do the same, the women affect horror. Both agree that the 'look', which typically combines a skirt, pantyhose, white socks and sneakers, is 'tacky' and 'unprofessional'. These women invariably wear leather pumps with a medium heel, from the start of their commute to their return home.

Later, one of the women admits to Ho that she too did the 'shoe-change-thing' in the first few months in her job, but she soon stopped. As she reflected on that decision, the underlying rationale became clear, Ho writes. '[S]ocks and sneakers over hose is a marker, albeit imprecise, of a lower-class status.'[1] Female back-office and administrative assistants – support staff to the male-dominated front office – both tended to wear higher heels and to live further away from their offices than higher-ranking front-office professional women. Wearing trainers during commutes was therefore tied to a critical social distinction.

> Front-office women, then, make sure to distinguish their dress from that of administrative staff: they wear body contouring suits that are not too tight, heels that are not too low or too high, hair that is coiffed but not too high or too hair sprayed. Because women in general are often treated similarly as a class and are 'feminized' as support staff, female investment bankers must constantly guard against class slippage: being mistaken for assistants or 'admins'. Thus, they must police themselves and each other for such class infractions as wearing socks over hose. This concern is even more pronounced among women of color, as racial hierarchies threaten to 'deprofessionalize' them even further.[2]

The setting in which these women work, global finance, conveniently demonstrates a 'fundamental tension in the human condition', as Stanford University sociologist Cecilia Ridgeway has put it. In her book *Status: Why is it everywhere? Why does it matter?*, Ridgeway starts with a recurring theme of the Patriarchy Inc. account – that one of the defining features of human existence is our interdependency. 'Survival itself requires entering into social relationships and coordinating efforts with others to produce what is required and desired in life.'[3]

As I described in the previous chapter, cooperation becomes particularly challenging as societies grow more complex, with specialized divisions of labour performed by people who don't necessarily know each other very well. The cut-throat world of international finance is a prime example, involving the coordinated activities of traders, salespeople, financial analysts, financial engineers, research and development engineers, back-office support, risk control, IT, accounting and human resources, just within a single organization. We solve the problem of *who does what* with the assistance of social roles, together with mindshaping processes that mould individuals into behaviour that is predictable and appropriate for their role.

But how do we recognize a stranger's social role? This happens through a process called 'social categorization'. Ho's recounting of the wardrobe dilemmas facing professional women in finance nicely illustrates the fact that our species are experts at drawing distinctions between people. We don't look around, declare everyone a marvellous creation of Mother Nature and leave it at that. Around 380 BC, Plato proposed three groupings of types of people – warriors, workers and philosophers – and we've been developing his list ever since. Modern human society is absolutely saturated with social categories. Society-wide categories (like *woman*, *man*, *white*, *black American*, *Asian American*, *working class*, *middle class*) interleave

43

with more locally specific categories (*analyst, administrative assistant, senior vice president*). Even as babies we are already parsing faces into categories, and by the second year of life, children have developed expectations that category members have social obligations to each other.[4]

The categories we use *stick* because they have meaning. Even if someone *were* to propose the concept of, say, *plants above and below thirty centimetres high*, or *brown animals and not-brown animals*, the chances of it taking off would be slim. The distinctions we draw between things track our interests and goals (or *some* people's interests and goals, at least). We categorize some animals as companions, and others for food. We like to put some plants in a nice vase, toss others in a salad bowl and rip out yet others from garden beds with a cry of satisfaction.

So too when it comes to social distinctions between types of people.

Categories are incredibly useful. 'With the help of categories,' one team of social psychologists explain, 'the mind transforms the world from chaotic complexity into predictable order.'[5] Social categories, which carve up humans into different kinds of people, bring the same benefits. (Context helps too, of course, since people belong to multiple social categories.) It is not difficult to see the advantages of categories when it comes to social life, particularly for cooperation. As the psychologists go on to point out:

Whether on the basis of demographic features, social roles, kinship networks, shared tasks, or other social

44

cues, identifying an individual as belonging to a particular social category enables inferences about a range of relevant and important issues. We can infer, for example, what the person's goals and intentions might be, what skills and knowledge she might possess, and what general personality traits are likely to characterize her. These sorts of inferences can be exceptionally useful in determining whether and how to interact with other people.[6]

Of course, inferences about what a person is like and how they will behave are only helpful inasmuch as they are accurate. As any DEI trainer will tell you, in exchange for a handsome fee, these inferences can lead to biased expectations, as well as unfair penalties when double standards are violated. Of course, people in the same role aren't completely interchangeable – we tend to care quite a lot about *who* our boss is, for instance. But it's also the case that most of the time when we are cooperating, people don't surprise us at all.

As we've seen, mindshaping creates the behaviour patterns that permit such largely seamless cooperative interactions, including between individuals who are not familiar to us personally. We imitate others 'like us', we teach and learn the art of behaving as a member of a particular social category, we enforce norms based on other people's membership of social categories, and our social identities as members of those categories play a role in our self-regulation. If you are a female front-office worker in an American global financial services firm, you learn to wear the right shoes.

But not all categories are created equal. Karen Ho's vignette reminds us that social distinctions often mark out hierarchies: front-office workers are a higher 'class' than back-office workers. Degrees of discomfort with this situation may well vary. To some, the rank ordering of individuals and groups is the path to order, merit and efficiency. To others, it is a tool of oppression. It's therefore worth pointing out that there are different kinds of hierarchies. Take, for instance, a very obvious hierarchy at play within my own household. This is the hierarchy between our dog, Günther, and our cat, Pippi, renewed afresh at the start of every day. Following their morning pees in the front yard, the pair form a dignified procession down the corridor towards the breakfast bowls: the cat at the head, setting a despotically leisurely pace; Günther following subserviently behind at approximately one thousandth of his normal speed of travel. Whatever the resource in question – the dog's kibble, the dog's bed, the dog's water – the cat helps herself first. And although Günther hardly needs reminding, every so often Pippi will assert her dominant role with a hiss and a swipe of her claws.

This is an example of a *dominance* hierarchy, in which dominant animals make others defer to their will through displays of physical or social power. As Ridgeway points out, dominance hierarchies are effective, albeit in a rather brutal way, if the task is simply to distribute resources. Hens, for instance, don't fight it out every time the corn appears, to decide who gets to go first. The establishment of a literal pecking order means that everyone knows their place.

But unlike hens, humans must first work together to *produce* the resources, before they are distributed. This makes classic dominance hierarchies of limited use for a cooperative species like ourselves. In accounts of how hominins broke away from our closest ape relatives to become the hyper-cooperators we now are, Sterelny and others have argued that a key early change in social organization was the suppression of the dominance hierarchies inherited from the great apes, about 1.8 million to 800,000 years ago.[7] Dominant bullies destabilize cooperation, as Sterelny explains. What fool is going to work up a sweat bringing back food for everyone to share, or spend many laborious hours carving tools, if there's a good chance some big bully will just grab the lot? Little wonder that chimps, who 'live in a social world of bullying . . . with a quite marked dominance hierarchy', only cooperate in quite minimal, immediate and low-risk ways.[8] The suppression of dominance hierarchies in humans set the stage for the flourishing of 'a form of foraging that depended on collective action', Sterelny argues — an important stage in the hominid evolutionary path.[9]

Social arrangements organized around dominance hierarchies clearly haven't disappeared altogether from human life. But at some point in that journey towards ever more complicated and committed cooperation, a different form of hierarchy evolved, based on *prestige*, according to Henrich and others.[10] Group members defer to those with apparently superior expertise and information, in exchange for a chance to pick up vitally useful tips themselves, such as how to build an intricate fishing net. Consider another hierarchy within my own household, where I am affectionately referred to as the

Matriarch. Unlike the cat's reign of terror over the dog, my own status is not based on threats and intimidation. Instead, it has been accrued in recognition of my great wisdom on matters both practical and esoteric: such as when best-before dates on food labels can be safely ignored; if instant noodles are an appropriate meal for breakfast, lunch or dinner; and whether one's knees should be visible at the dinner table.[11]

But there is another challenge for successful cooperation, which neither dominance nor prestige hierarchies can solve. On the one hand, we need to cooperate. But there is also a strong element of competitiveness in this interdependence. As Ridgeway puts it: 'Everybody has an unavoidable interest in forming cooperative endeavors with others, but everybody also has an interest in maximizing what they get from those endeavors.'[12] In her view, we have developed a third kind of hierarchy for handling this tension between cooperation and competition: *status* hierarchies of esteem, honour and respect. High-status individuals are those who contribute the most to the group as it works cooperatively on a task (not just the individuals with the most knowledge and expertise). To the extent that status hierarchies are genuinely based on competence, it's an effective solution to achieving shared goals. Even though we might all, as individuals, want to sit at the top of the chain and enjoy the greater rewards of that position, we also want the most competent member of the group – the one most likely to lead everyone to success – to be in charge.

These kinds of hierarchies may well 'be laid on evolutionary residues', Ridgeway suggests. '[S]tatus is something like language in that it is a social form that is deeply cultural and socially learned, but also something to which we may be predisposed to learn and respond.'[13] Alternatively, status hierarchies may simply result from our desire to identify and conform to community norms – in this case, status-related norms.[14]

Either way, it is certainly notable how early in development Western children absorb information about social hierarchies: 'children are sensitive to a range of cues to wealth, power, and status differences' among individuals, as one team of developmental psychologists have summarized it.[15] This includes even very subtle cues, like a person's posture, or who sets norms. But children aren't just attuned to differences in status among their co-workers in the sandpit. They also quickly identify group-based *patterns* of status, including gender groups. '[B]y the early elementary school years,' the psychologists note, 'both boys and girls view boys as having greater decision-making power, more resources, and higher-status positions compared to girls.'[16] (This is despite the in-group bias that pushes girls towards seeing their own group more favourably.)

Status differentials shape cooperative behaviour by encouraging members of a group – even demographically similar strangers – to defer to the person perceived to be the most competent. As Ridgeway explains: '[I]f I really want us to succeed at our goal and I think that person over there has much better ideas about how to do that than you do, then I want you to be quiet and let the person with the good ideas talk, and I am likely to pressure you to do that. But of course, you and all the other group members have the same sort of interest in my own deference behavior and may pressure me in the same way.'[17] Ridgeway and others see these norms playing out in groups created and observed in lab studies. Even when a group member's high status is artificial and arbitrary, they enjoy more opportunities to contribute, their contributions are evaluated more positively by others, they have greater influence over how things are done, and they enjoy more admiration and attention than lower-status individuals.[18]

Status hierarchy norms mean that even if you personally doubt someone's competence, you will have to navigate the fact that, so far as you know, everyone else accepts their legitimate authority. Group censure of those who fail to 'know their place' helps to keep people in line. The English novelist Dorothy Whipple humorously captured this dynamic in her 1939 novel *The Priory*. She describes a scene in which Aunt Anthea is left alone to care for her baby niece. When the baby starts to howl with hunger, her distraught auntie gives her a bottle of milk. Unfortunately for Anthea, this goes against the firm instructions of her brother-in-law, a distinguished doctor: 'It was the end. After a dreadful interview with her brother-in-law Anthea left the house that night and had never re-entered it. No one had any sympathy with her. All were amazed that she should set herself up against a specialist. A *specialist*, they repeated.'[19] In addition to the stick, there is also a modest carrot: deference on the part of lower-status group members is rewarded with the 'dignity of being deemed reasonable' by the rest of the group.[20]

Despite the obvious potential downsides of status-based group norms, they do at least seem to curb dominance hierarchies. One study found that a stooge (planted by the researchers), who persistently presented their own mediocre ideas in a domineering fashion, was quickly shut down by other members of the group.[21] (Sadly, the mechanism isn't infallible, as most of us will have experienced first-hand.) Cross-cultural anthropological research points to the same benefit.[22] This makes sense: everyone except the would-be dominator has a collective interest in preventing aggressive but incompetent assholes from being in charge.

What happens when an individual's status is somehow tied to their membership of a group? Remarkably, even when a group is completely artificial, and the link to status is implicit, we nonetheless rapidly develop shared beliefs about the competence of *members of that group in general*.[23] In fact, there are just three simple steps for creating a sense of shared reality that *these kinds of people* are more competent and status-worthy than *those kinds of people*. And it works even when, as is standard in these experiments, the people are same-sex undergraduate students.

Step one is to create arbitrary social distinctions. To begin, randomly assign people to one of two groups. Give each newly created group a label. You don't even have to drop heavy hints with the labels, like *Goodies* and *Baddies*. Following the research, let's call the new social categories *S2s* and *Q2s*. All you have to do is tell people that these categories differentiate between two types of people, with distinct and stable variations in the way they think. (In the research, the two groups are ostensibly based on modern art preferences.) The second step involves giving one group – the *Q2s*, say – a bit of an advantage in a group decision-making task. What you need here is a dynamic whereby the *S2s* tend to defer to the *Q2s*: the former are hesitant, uncertain and deferential; the latter are confident and assertive. There are a few options here. One is simply to plant subtly sycophantic stooges into the group, who hang on every word of *Q2s* but interrupt *S2s*. But it's also possible to get these dynamics to arise 'naturally', by exploiting the fact that we seem to unconsciously assume that people get what they deserve. Just casually let it be known that *Q2s* are being paid a bit more than *S2s*, and let false inference do the rest. The third step is simply to repeat the second.[24]

Note that at no stage has there been any explicit claim that *Q2s* are more competent than *S2s*. But when researchers follow these steps and then quiz participants afterwards, it becomes clear that participants have put two and two together and made five. They tend to agree that *Q2s* are higher in status, more respected, more leaderlike, more powerful and more competent. What's more, they also say that 'most people' would think the same – although participants also say that *S2s*, bless them, are more considerate. In short, a few uncharged, low-stakes encounters involving a novel, arbitrary social category is enough to make 'participants think that there was a socially valid reality here – those with one style type clearly were more status-worthy and competent than the other and would be rated that way by most people'.[25]

We all know what happens next. Before you know it, *Q2s* are controlling most of the wealth, running all the institutions, and perhaps also producing dubious scientific research explaining why these inequalities are the natural outcome of biological differences between *Q2s* and *S2s*. As influential sociologists have long argued, for inequalities to really stick, to be *durable*, they need to be linked to social categories that can provide some sort of explanatory fig leaf for why *S2s* are cleaning *Q2s'* gold bidet, and not vice versa.[26] Ridgeway explains the general principle: '[T]he development of shared status beliefs about a group difference transforms *individual* advantages in the resources and power possessed by individuals in the richer group into a superior right to those advantages based on their *group identity* as a certain type of person.'[27] At this point, some readers might be reminded of the famous *Punch* boardroom cartoon by Riana Duncan. It depicts the male chair responding to a suggestion made by the lone woman at the table with the comment: 'That's an excellent suggestion, Miss Triggs. Perhaps one of the men would like to make it.'[28]

Nobody knows exactly how, when or why a patriarchal relationship between the sexes emerged.[29] But once it did, it's easy to see why it has been so durable. Status hierarchies are based on culturally shared understanding that members of some social categories are more competent, more worthy of esteem and more deserving of material rewards than others. Once one group enjoys an edge over the other, it is very hard to stop the train.

For men, the status hierarchy between the sexes casts a pall on female-typed jobs – how skilful and important can they be if *women* do them? Interviews of men who had chosen female-typical occupations found that they had to 'overcome [the] associated discomfort' of being in a female-typical occupation. To that end, they deployed strategies of relabelling the job ('I say I look after business information, that sounds more impressive,' said one male librarian); re-casting job content in a more masculine fashion ('It's anything but a service job – we are there for safety and security,' said one man of his job as cabin crew); and distancing from women, by stressing their own cool heads, specialist skills or the less menial nature of *their* work compared with female colleagues.[30]

For other men, the status-undermining presence of too many women in an occupation remains an ever-present threat. An important but overlooked contributor to occupational sex-segregation is men's tendency to flee jobs that are becoming too popular with women. An analysis of representative longitudinal data from the UK, spanning from 2000 to 2008, estimated that between 19 and 28 per cent of sex segregation is caused by men *leaving* occupations as women enter them. As the researcher points out, this dynamic poses a challenge to Different But Equal explanations of occupational segregation as 'the outcome of voluntary choices and individual freedom' that reflect inherent differences. Rather, occupational segregation is 'substantially produced' by workers' sensitivity to the gender balance of occupations, 'regardless of work content'.[31]

Status beliefs are likely held particularly fervently by those who enjoy the power to *define* what being competent, esteem-worthy and deserving looks like. The ability to define *what competence is* shapes all our important institutions. The supposed superiority of the attributes and competence of the higher-status group, and the legitimacy of their interests, is embedded in the laws, policies, practices, norms, habits and traditions that govern our lives – including what kinds of work are paid, and how much.[32]

Two centuries ago, in the robustly titled *Appeal of One Half of the Human Race, Women, Against the Pretensions of the Other Half, Men, To Retain Them in Political, and Thence in Civil and Domestic, Slavery*, political writers drew attention to the fact that because women are the ones who bear children, and typically take care of them (as well as other family members), their 'peculiar efforts and powers for the common benefit of the race' put them at a distinct disadvantage in a capitalist system that financially rewards only those who can or do work for a wage. The authors even pointed out the false inference that underpins status hierarchies – namely the tendency to assume that those who end up with greater power must somehow be superior. The economic dependence of wives on their husbands begged the false conclusion that they weren't really doing anything of value. Their work was 'looked upon as an additional badge of inferiority and disgrace', even as '[s]uperiority in the production or accumulation of individual wealth will ever be whispering in to man's ear preposterous notions of his relative importance over woman'.[33]

Fast-forwarding through two centuries of feminist campaigners, politicians, activists, economists, political scientists, philosophers and others pointing out remedies for these unfair arrangements, that disadvantage persists today. The gender pay gap is largely a 'motherhood wage penalty', whereby mothers earn a lower hourly wage than women without children. Whether you are looking at Sweden, Denmark, Germany, Austria, the United Kingdom or the United States, the birth of the first child brings about a drop in wage from which mothers' pay cheques never fully recover,[34] with British data finding that it hits the lowest-income households the hardest.[35]

Part of the motherhood wage penalty seems to be due to straightforward maternity discrimination – that is, paying a mother less than she would otherwise earn for no other reason than that she is a mother. Even in countries that have long made such practices illegal, things have only progressed so far since Ansett Airways declined to employ Deborah Wardley as a pilot. Half of the mothers surveyed in a 2014 Australian review reported experiencing discrimination during their pregnancy, parental leave or on return to work. Of these women, nearly one in five lost their jobs, and nearly a third resigned or looked for employment somewhere else.[36] Submissions to the review included reports from human resources professionals of decision-makers openly discussing not recruiting or promoting a woman because she had young kids or might get pregnant. In the UK, a survey of about 500 managers of small and medium-sized businesses found that nearly a third avoided hiring women who might get pregnant.[37] But a hefty proportion of the motherhood pay gap can be attributed to the fact that spending less time on paid labour results in lower and stagnant wages.[38]

Over the years, it all adds up. In Australia, the estimated difference in lifetime earnings between men and women without children was about $300,000.[39] (This figure is modelled on someone aged 25 in 2017 dollars.) But this far-from-trivial discrepancy paled in comparison to the estimated lifetime earnings gap between fathers and mothers. That weighed in at $2 million.

Cumulative effects over time transform the earnings gulf into a gender wealth chasm. To see why, we can start with how things are 'supposed' to work. Well-behaved, rational actors of traditional economic models sensibly accumulate wealth during their working years, by saving and investing. Thanks to the magic of compound interest, their wealth grows at an ever-increasing rate, particularly during the prime earning years. If all goes as planned, it reaches a lofty peak at retirement, ready for decumulation in order to fund winter years of well-earned ease. Mothers, however, are excluded from this time-honoured plan. Because mothers earn less (or nothing at all), particularly in the prime wealth-building years, they have less to save and invest – and that 'less' compounds over time.

In Australia, an earlier, far-sighted government recognized that the ageing population was a ticking time bomb. (This is because state pensions for retired workers are funded through tax revenue generated from current workers. The greater the proportion of retirees relative to the working-age population, the less tax revenue there is to be distributed among more pensioners.) To defuse the situation, in 1992 the government introduced the superannuation system ('super').[40] In essence, the super scheme involves deputing employers to act as the frontal lobes of their workers. The employer diverts a certain minimum percentage of wages into a retirement savings account.[41] The idea is that by the time the worker retires, they will have a nice big super nest egg to supplement an ever more miserly government pension.[42]

I'm told that Australia's superannuation system enjoys considerable cachet among the bureaucrats and professionals whose life's work is to worry about their citizens' financial futures. However, you might have spotted a problem for a certain demographic. For those approaching retirement, the superannuation gender gap in Australia ranges from 22 to 35 per cent, according to a 2021 KPMG report.[43] Why was this flaw in the system not obvious to the persistently male-dominated Senate Select Committee on Superannuation?[44] Perhaps thanks to 'the male bias of a wilfully gender-blind system that persistently fails to value the gendered distribution of unpaid caring labours', as one scholar has put it.[45]

Other countries handle retirement differently – earnings-based pensions are a common approach – but the problem is universal. For instance, across the OECD, the gender gap in pension benefits is 26 per cent, ranging from under 10 per cent in the Slovak Republic and Estonia to about 40 per cent or more in Japan, Mexico, Austria, the UK, Luxembourg and the Netherlands.[46] (These statistics don't include women who, because they never participated in the labour market, receive no pension at all.)

Other aspects of the gender wealth gap tend to get little attention. The gap varies quite widely from country to country (probably due to differences in women's labour market participation, divorce laws and state support of caring work in the home). But a comprehensive analysis of 15 Eurozone countries (based mostly on survey data collected in 2010/11) found that a gender wealth gap in favour of men was virtually universal.[47] Across the Euro area, the median woman owned just 62 cents for every dollar owned by the median man, from a surprising low of 28 in the progressive Netherlands, to a high of 97 in the Slovak Republic (also the country with the lowest net wealth).[48]

Even within a single country, the pattern looks quite different depending on age and marital status. Take France: a country with a middling overall gender wealth gap. There is almost no gap in the youngest age bracket (25- to 34-year-olds). But for French women from their mid thirties to mid forties, things have gone *poire*-shaped. Single women who have never married own 82 cents to the man's dollar, widows just 61 cents and divorcees a measly 38 cents.[49] (Given the censorious times in which we now live, I will refrain from making a tasteless joke about what, purely from a financial perspective, these statistics suggest about the best way to be rid of an unwanted husband.)

Romantics may wonder whether a gender wealth gap really matters all that much. After all, when couples share a household, we expect some endowing of worldly goods upon each other. When my partner sits on the antique IKEA sofa that I bought with my own hard-earned cash, I don't coldly ask him to either remove his backside from my cushions or pay me a usage fee. In long-term relationships, regardless of whose salary pays the mortgage, both parties typically live in the same house. But as Mariko Lin Chang and others have pointed out, this line of argument doesn't work particularly well in contemporary society.[50] We are marrying later or never, divorce rates are high, and husbands tend to die before wives. In the US, the target of Chang's analyses, this results in nearly

40 per cent of households being single-headed.[51] (In the UK, people living alone make up 30 per cent of all households, and another 16 per cent of households are lone-parent families.)[52] This 'makes the wealth gap between men and women a reality for a large percentage of people'.[53]

The gender wealth gap hits some women harder than others. Data based on the nationally representative US Survey of Finances in 2004 indicated that even though women were earning 78 per cent of men's wages, unmarried women owned only 36 per cent as much wealth as unmarried men. But the situation was especially dire for Hispanic and black women. More than half of single Hispanic women and a third of black women had zero or negative wealth (i.e., debt), compared with about a quarter of single white women. The median wealth of single Hispanic women was a grand total of $0. By comparison, it was $1,700 for single Hispanic men and $53,500 for single white men.[54]

Along similar lines, a detailed analysis of the wealth of older single black American women painted a bleak picture. Despite consistently stronger participation in the labour market compared with other women,[55] 'average widowed, divorced or never married black women have virtually no net financial assets at age 51, and do not accumulate any as they age. Overall, results suggest that most black women experience chronic asset poverty characterized by persistently low and flat trajectories of net worth and net financial assets.'[56]

Single parents – the vast majority of whom are women – are especially likely to lack adequate economic resources. In Australia, even several years after divorce, mothers are much more likely than divorced fathers to experience financial stress, such as being unable to access emergency funds, afford a one-week holiday, or pay for items like school clothing, leisure activities or school trips for their children.[57] In the UK, half of lone-parent families, which are mostly headed by mothers,[58] were in poverty in 2021/22, contributing to the just over one in three children in that predicament.[59] As one scholar has summarized it: 'In all countries, single-parent wealth is at the lower end of the wealth distribution with a non-negligible share of negative and zero wealth.'[60] In other words, they are raising the next generation with nothing, or less than nothing.

We might want to look at that.

It might be true that the best things in life are free. However, many dimensions of well-being – such as shelter, education, leisure time, mobility and physical and mental health – often come at a price. Wealth is a 'financial cushion' that softens economic blows such as job loss, illness, divorce, a broken-down car, or emergencies. Wealth is also access to (superior or faster) medical treatment, a holiday or a day off, a fresh start, a parachute with which to escape a soul-destroying, exploitative or unethical job, or an escape hatch through which to flee an abusive or miserable relationship. Wealth is freedom from constant, corrosive anxiety about paying rent, putting food on the table or escaping debt. It's political influence. It's having enough money to be able to participate in mainstream society with dignity, and provide opportunities and security for your children.[61]

The gendered division of paid and unpaid labour offers a particularly stark example of the connection between *who does what* and *who gets what.* Currently, men do less unpaid care and enjoy more income, wealth, job opportunities, social status and leisure. It is not very surprising that they haven't been falling over themselves to increase their share of unpaid labour contributions to the economy.

But some people say that even if the division is currently unfair, it is natural. Throughout the history of the feminist political movement, there has always been a strain of 'difference feminism' that accepts the 'Different' part of the Different But Equal perspective — agreeing that natural personality differences between the sexes help explain the gendered division of labour. This political group just considers that the 'Equal' bit rings rather hollow. Their arguments can't be dismissed out of hand. After all, unlike social categories such as *emerging markets analyst*, or *vice president in structured finance*, social categories like *mother* and *father* are also biological categories — and evolutionarily fundamental ones at that. Nonetheless, elaborating the arguments from chapter 1 about the importance of social identities, social learning and norms for moulding us into social roles, the next chapter argues that mindshaping offers a better explanation of the division than biology.

3

(RE)PRODUCING FATHERS

WHEN THREE WORKPLACE GENDER INEQUALITY EXPERTS were commissioned by a prestigious global consulting firm to help them with their 'women's problem', everyone the researchers spoke to understood the problem in the same way. The researchers, Irene Padavic, Robin Ely and Erin Reid, came to refer to this shared understanding as the 'work–family narrative'. This story, which they heard over and over from different people across the firm, had two 'plot elements'. First, success in the job required gruelling hours and constant availability. As one consultant put it, 'shoot me something on Saturday by 10 p.m., and I'll work on it from 10 to midnight. Because I don't have a life'.[1] The second plot element was that women's family commitments prevented them from meeting these time demands.

This was not just some convenient account asserted only by men to explain why they held most of the top jobs. Women themselves endorsed the explanation. As one consultant, also a mother, explained to the researchers: 'There's no overt sexism.

63

Once you've proved yourself, people work with you. No one would hold me back from being on a hard-core partner track if I were willing to work 70-hour weeks and get on a plane every week. The issue is that women are choosing to have kids and be their primary caregiver.'[2] As a result, the work–family narrative continued, women were more likely to leave the firm. Or, if they stayed, were less likely than men to advance to the highest rungs of the occupational ladder. How, the management wanted to know, could this 'women's problem' be solved?

The work–family narrative draws on one dimension of the gendered division of labour to explain another. Because men typically prioritize paid work over unpaid work in the home, while women do the reverse, men are more likely to put in the long hours required for better-paying and higher-status jobs. Many people find this a compelling explanation. A 2012 survey of Harvard Business School graduates found that nearly three quarters of the men, and even more of the women (85 per cent), invoked women's prioritizing of family over work as the primary reason why women tend not to advance as far as men in their careers (even though their own ambitions didn't reflect this stereotype).[3]

Support for the work–family narrative came from a research study that recruited a broader sample and probed a little deeper. In a series of nine surveys of a total of more than four thousand US participants, from high-level executives to everyday working adults, the researchers found women less willing than men to sacrifice other life goals for career progression. As the authors summarized their findings: 'compared to men, women have a higher number of life goals, place less importance on power-related goals, associate more negative outcomes (e.g., goal conflict and tradeoffs) with high-power positions, perceive power as less desirable though equally attainable, and are less likely to take advantage of opportunities for professional advancement'.[4]

This simple idea underpins an influential theory developed by a sociologist called Catherine Hakim at the turn of the twenty-first century. Women have different preferences from men about how to balance work and family (on average). They then try, often successfully, to arrange their lives accordingly. While to the outsider this idea might not seem particularly controversial, it proved contentious among the many sociologists who felt that social forces weren't being accorded due respect. These sociologists are concerned with societal norms that allow selfish men to take it for granted that staying at home with the baby is their partner's responsibility, expensive or oversubscribed formal childcare, societal disapproval of 'working mothers', inflexible workplaces, and managers who look at a capable, ambitious young woman and see a uterus, a hefty maternity-leave bill and major disruption to project timelines.[5] In other words, these are sociologists who, on hearing the word *choice*, instantly reach for the scare quotes with a frown. It was in this context that Hakim, by christening her thesis Preference Theory, lit an intellectual touchpaper.[6]

Hakim's argument is an optimistic one. For the first time in history, she contends, the majority of women in rich, post-industrial economies enjoy real choice about how to combine paid and unpaid work. This freedom is the happy culmination of several major shifts in society and the labour market, starting

65

in the late twentieth century. Women have much greater control over their fertility, thanks to the availability of reliable contraception. The rolling-out of sex discrimination legislation has given them 'equal access to all positions, occupations, and careers in the labor market'.[7] An expanding service sector has offered them plenty of non-manual work opportunities, including jobs suitable for 'secondary earners', who need to be able to fit their paid work around family commitments. Finally, rigidly enforced traditional gender roles have given way to an open-minded philosophy of 'you do you'.

Presented with this new wealth of choice, women do not all make the same decision about how to divide their time and energy, argues Hakim. About one in five choose, like men, to be work-centred. A similar percentage are home-centred and would rather do no paid work at all. This leaves the largest share of women, about 60 per cent, who prefer an 'adaptive' approach of pursuing a less demanding career, with limited work hours.[8] These are the supposedly less committed working mothers who play a starring role in the work–family narrative.

Of course, people's work–family preferences aren't necessarily fixed. Hakim is agnostic about their origins, and acknowledges that social, economic and institutional factors continue to shape women's decision-making – the percentages of women reporting home-centred, work-centred and adaptive preferences vary somewhat across countries and time.

The importance of these external factors has been well illustrated by the work of Nobel Prize-winning economist Claudia Goldin, in her comparison of five cohorts of female American college graduates.[9] Every woman graduated with a college degree. But what each cohort aspired to and achieved in terms of paid work (job, career or neither) and family (marriage, children or neither) changed markedly over time. (Roughly, the difference between a job and a career is that only the latter is 'long-lasting, sought-after employment for which the type of work – writer, teacher, doctor, accountant – often shapes one's identity'.)[10]

The first cohort, born between 1878 and 1897, typically faced the choice of *either* family *or* career. Almost a third of this cohort never married and half had no children. The second cohort (born between 1898 and 1923) tended to have a job then family, thanks to a relatively late age of marriage and the dismal economic context of the Great Depression. The third cohort, born between 1924 and 1943, was characterized by the pattern of family then job. These women returned to (highly constrained) job options once they'd finished raising their families. The fourth cohort, born between 1944 and 1957, graduated college between the mid 1960s and the late 1970s. This group was the first that aspired to high-status professions in large numbers and tried to establish their careers before having families. The last cohort, born between 1958 and 1978, graduated college in the 1980s and 1990s. They are the ones valiantly attempting to 'have it all' simultaneously: career *and* family.

Preference Theory proposes that for this latter cohort, a genuine increase in the availability of choices for women means that their 'motivations and aspirations are independent factors with causal powers'.[11] That is to say, released from gender norms that curtail their choices, women now enjoy much greater freedom to meld the pattern of their lives as they personally prefer. Based on analyses of survey data from Britain and the US, Hakim argues that women's preferences about how and whether to combine paid work with caring for family are good predictors of their actual pattern of workforce participation.

What about fathers? We might assume that they were always free, and still are. But data from ten countries, drawing on the European Social Survey for 2004, found that the 'vast majority of fathers . . . wanted to reduce hours substantially and believed that reconciling employment with family is a high priority'.[12] (The exceptions were fathers from economically insecure post-socialist countries.) Dads from Denmark, Sweden, Germany and the Netherlands, for instance, all on average wanted to work at least five hours less per week, taking them to less than forty hours per week, even if it would reduce their earnings.[13]

It may be that loosening gender roles have given mothers wriggle-room to curate their work–family priorities in ways that suit them, while fathers remain straitjacketed by both the societal expectations and economic necessity of uninterrupted, full-time devotion to paid work.[14] Even as changes in gender norms have given women more freedom to pursue paid work, the 'Inc.' part of Patriarchy Inc. has eroded the 'standard employment relationship' – a secure job with predictable hours and decent wages and conditions.[15] This has put incredible strain on some women, because insecure jobs can be particularly hard to combine with caring responsibilities. One researcher observed the chaos created by unpredictable shifts for the mostly female workers at a Canadian call centre. The women were unable even to advance-schedule personal commitments, like medical appointments or a child's birthday party. 'Children's homework could be supervised (or not) by as many as eight different people over a two-week period.' Likewise, health-care aides working in a seniors' residence had little control over their shifts, giving rise to 'an exhausted 100 per cent female workforce trying to survive in a rats' nest of backbiting and competition for decent schedules'.[16]

But men have been negatively impacted too, and a growing gap between good- and bad-quality jobs has made many men feel less economically secure and therefore less able to balance work and family.

For example, in the aggressively competitive construction industry, project contracts set tight deadlines for completion of work, and apply heavy penalties for not meeting them. Adding to the stress is the rise of job insecurity for construction workers, in the form of increased subcontracting and self-employment. As one interviewee observed: 'they have this pressure that if they have any time off, then you know, it's gonna affect their home life, so they'll just soldier on through, through aches and pains and then they'll probably drink more to ease the aches and pains and it's just like an ever-decreasing circle of poor health'.[17] In circumstances like these, conformity to norms of overwork that interfere with family life are effectively obligatory. Interviewers of professional construction workers at Australian sites heard stories of sleepless men, rigid with worry throughout the night, or suffering anxiety and panic attacks on their way to work.[18]

Interviewees also reported that the job demands created considerable work–family conflict. One man described how he worked six days a week for sixteen months of a project, and seven days a week for the final two months. 'I didn't see my kids for like eight weeks. You know, and the point where your wife gets sick and pneumonia, and ends up in hospital because she's just constantly with them and can't cope.' Although he remained in the industry, he was far from happy about it. 'I was like, "I don't care how much you pay me, I don't wanna do that anymore."'[19] Interviewees also reported detrimental impacts on relationships, including breakdowns and divorce.

Indeed, men also face increasing uncertainty when it comes to family life, as household formations have become more diverse and less stable.[20] As a result, men's confidence has been undermined. '[H]aving lost their status as breadwinners and resident fathers, many men find themselves a little lost', observes boys' and men's advocate Richard V. Reeves.[21] Meanwhile, women continue to do the majority of the unpaid caregiving and continue to be underrepresented in leadership roles.

As sociologist Kathleen Gerson points out:

> If concerns about a stall in women's progress seem inconsistent with worries about a decline in men's status, they actually reveal that a more complex and multi-layered social landscape has emerged. Uncertain employment prospects face contemporary workers, including men whose college-educated and unionized fathers could depend on a steady job . . . These widespread

economic and family transformations pose unprecedented challenges for women and men alike.[22]

To gain insights into how midlife adults are handling these
conflicts, Gerson interviewed 120 women and men from
diverse racial, economic and educational backgrounds, living
in Silicon Valley and New York metropolitan areas. Her
interviews revealed four major responses to the conflicting
demands of simultaneously building a family and maintaining
job prospects (in very roughly equal proportions).

One response was to form 'hyper-traditional arrangements':
fathers worked 'long days, nights, and weekends to assure their
employers of their outsized commitments to their jobs', and
mothers devoted themselves to child-rearing.[23] Neither ended
up with much time to themselves, or together as a couple,
and more than half wanted a more egalitarian arrangement.

Another common arrangement was 'dual-earner' couples,
where the bulk of the caregiving responsibilities were dumped
on the mother. Predictably, this 'left most of these women
feeling tired, disheartened, and unappreciated'. Less than one
in five of dual-earner women preferred this arrangement to
alternatives, and 70 per cent said they wanted responsibilities to be divided more equally. More surprisingly, almost half
the men in this uneven situation 'also expressed frustration,
saying they wished to be more involved in caregiving but
feared that taking the necessary time would endanger their job
security and long-term work prospects'.[24] A third of the dual-
earner men also expressed a preference for being in an egalitarian relationship.

A third group were dubbed the 'sidesteppers'. They avoided work–family conflict by staying single and childless. While this group contained both women and men, they tended to have sidestepped family for different reasons. Contrary to stereotype, the women often described valuing their independence and autonomy too much to take on what they perceived as the burdens of family life, and more than half were quite satisfied with their situation. In contrast, less than a third of the single childless men were content. Poignantly, they often felt that their difficulties finding steady work meant that they didn't feel they could *afford* a family life. Over half desired an egalitarian relationship in which work and caregiving responsibilities were shared, and just a quarter desired a relationship based on the traditional breadwinner/homemaker model.

A fourth way of navigating contemporary pressures of work and family was showcased by the 'egalitarians', who tried to blend work and family in equal ways. Just under half did this by forgoing having children, looking instead 'to relatives, friends, and pets' for intimate and rewarding personal relationships. But the remainder were parents who, attempting to combine paid work and caregiving equally, were following 'a path of *most* resistance', given the lack of support in the form of family-friendly work policies or affordable childcare.[25] Nonetheless, this was the only group in which the majority thought their approach was better than the alternatives (88 per cent of the women and 81 per cent of the men).

One thing that is notable across all these groupings is that the majority of men, regardless of their personal circumstances, expressed a preference for involvement in caregiving. It's often forgotten that industrialization wrought huge changes in men's lives, as they moved out of household economies, away from their families and into manufacturing and services in the market sphere. In fact, this shift has been described as 'just as revolutionary as the more recent changes for women'.[26]

Human fathers are interesting. Not necessarily as individuals, of course – who hasn't come close to losing consciousness while in the conversational clutches of a proud dad? – but as an evolutionary phenomenon. Paternal care is a minority arrangement among mammals, and scientists don't quite know how it came to evolve in our species. One suggestion is based on evidence that wild mountain gorilla males who do more babysitting as youngsters go on to have more reproductive success in later life.[27] Perhaps then female human ancestors were more likely to mate with males who 'babysat' children in the community, and this dynamic gradually ratcheted up via sexual selection. (This is quite a radical departure from the claim by Evolutionary Psychologists that a central feature of evolved human female mate choice is a preference for men who seem well placed to acquire resources.)[28]

Another noteworthy feature of human fathers is that certain features of their physiology are more like birds' (in which both parents care for young) than like other primates'. As I discussed in *Testosterone Rex*, men's hormones change with fatherhood and fathering. The best-studied change is a reduction in testosterone production, but there seem to be additional hormonal changes, roughly parallel with those seen in mothers. This 'plastic male psychobiological profile' seems to result from triggers like sensory cues from the pregnant

73

partner or infant, the development of a social identity as a father, and plain old falling in love with the baby.[29] As one dad, interviewed for the *Working Fathers* podcast, put it: 'I was in awe of the fact that we humans can create this human being. And for me it wasn't real until I held each child – I burst out in tears.'[30]

In keeping with the importance of contexts and conditions, anthropologist Barry Hewlett found that Aka Pygmy fathers among hunter-gatherer foragers in the western Congo Basin in Central Africa behaved quite differently to their US counterparts. Where the latter largely played the role of economic provider and occasional rough-and-tumbler: 'The Aka father's role can be characterized by its intimate, affectionate, helping-out nature, rather than by its playfulness. Aka fathers spend 47 per cent of their day holding or within an arm's reach of their infants, and while holding the infant, father is more likely than mother to hug and kiss the infant.'[31] The day-to-day closeness of Aka fathers to their children and wives serves as a good reminder that the norm of the male breadwinner and the female homemaker, which to us seems 'traditional', is culturally created and maintained with social identities, beliefs, norms, practices and the rest.

So where did the breadwinner dad come from?

Wages play a central role in the story. In telling the British version of this tale, historian Wally Seccombe asks us to imagine the wage as Janus-faced: one face pointing forwards towards the workplace where commodities are being produced; the other looking backwards to the household that generated the worker's labour power. In theory, these could be seen as complementary, rather than competing, conceptions of how the wage is earned. But in practice, Seccombe argues, there was a struggle as to which became the dominant understanding. In the end, the perspective that prevailed was the workplace as the site of production and the household as the site of consumption. The wage became a price: 'payment for labour performed in capitalist production during a definite time period, and nothing else'.[32]

But the wage also gradually came to be a key part of a new gender order: male breadwinners and 'dependent' female homemakers. In Britain, the 'initial response . . . to women working for wages was overwhelmingly *positive*', says Seccombe. Indeed, '[i]t was widely remarked that no working man would marry a woman who was economically dependent'.[33] But here and in the US a shift occurred – 'from a positive, indeed insistent, attitude to women's work in industry in the eighteenth century to a negative, stigmatizing one by the late nineteenth century'.[34]

Helpful to understanding why there was an initially positive response to women being wage earners is that the work was readily understood as part of a family unit, or family labour team, headed by the man of the house. For example, in early-modern mining communities, the mine owner's agent would hire a man as a hewer (to loosen the rocks and minerals in the mine), and he would recruit a team of labour to get the coal out of the pit. Men would hire their own kin wherever possible, including women and children, to maximize family income.

But from the start, the situation was different for relatively well-paid skilled tradesmen. Here, conditions were ideal for male breadwinner ideology to flourish, because these men earned enough to forgo contributions to the family income from their wives and children. Moreover, there was 'normally a strong separation of men's work in the workshop from women's in the house and yard', helping to create a conceptual division between 'his work' and 'her work'.[35] Young women were also increasingly excluded from apprenticeships in the skilled trades, compared with in the eighteenth century. An added push towards the breadwinner ideal came from the potential for sex-based competition, when family-based earning opportunities were increasingly replaced by women being hired as *individuals*, mixing and competing with men in an open market and earning their own personal wage. Not *my* wife, thank you, was the perspective of higher-earning men sitting atop their patriarchal perch. And not *your* wife, either, was the view of men facing the threat of being undercut by cheaper competition.

Indeed, that threat was an important driver of the breadwinner ideal, as Seccombe explains: '[I]f men could earn a living wage, then women would not have to work for pay; they would cease competing for scarce jobs and bidding the price of labour down.'

Not all male breadwinners had dependents, not all women had access to a breadwinner's wage via a working husband, and many breadwinners continued to earn too little to support a wife and children. Nonetheless, rather than organize all workers, regardless of sex, in their fight for better pay and conditions, most unions prioritized employment rights for men, and made the male breadwinner ideal 'their ideological armament'.[36] To this end, trade unions systematically deployed two strategies of segmentation: excluding women altogether from certain kinds of employment ('freeing' them to devote themselves to their 'proper role' of homemaker); or segregating them into lower-paid jobs. This often placed unionists in tension with the interests of capitalists (who were generally keen to employ cheap, largely unorganized, female labour), as well as with women themselves.[37]

As Seccombe explains, with a hat-tip to feminist theorists before him, conceiving of wages as a price for labour performed in the workplace had a string of consequences. One was that the wage was earned by the worker alone, not also the family who produced and supported his labour power. From this, it followed that it also *belonged* to him alone, with no obligatory disbursements to be made to his spouse. This, in turn, made his wife economically dependent. Because it was officially unwaged, work in the home became conceived of as 'care' rather than 'work': 'No wage is paid for this labour, and it is therefore difficult to take it seriously as real work, lacking as it does the general signifier of work in capitalist society: the wage. It appears as a *natural* service, a simple act of caring, a labour of love, with all the attendant mystification that this involves.'[38]

One interesting illustration of this shift is the fact that while obviously there have always been mothers, the modern sense of mothering as a moral calling, requiring devoted focus by a home-bound mother, is a product of industrialization. Working-class women transitioned into wage labour during this period, and there was an emerging women's rights movement. But overwhelmingly, social, cultural and economic momentum pushed women towards unpaid labour in the home.[39] Maternity was redefined as motherhood. Caring for children was no longer something mothers unsentimentally slotted in alongside shared household production; rather it became a cultural ideal, 'a vocational path and exclusive calling', observes motherhood expert Petra Bueskens.[40]

Class by class (starting in the middle), women became economically dependent on a husband, particularly if they were mothers. In pre-industrial societies, unmarried or widowed mothers could rely on subsistence from a family farm. Mothers of dependent children continued to contribute to household production alongside the many other members of the household, including multigenerational family members, servants and apprentices. But industrialization slowly changed all this. Even waged working-class women were mostly young and single and, thanks to the unions, restricted to a small set of low-paid occupations (such as in the textile industry). The breadwinner ideal meant that women without access to a male wage, and especially those with dependent children, faced destitution.

In reality, many families could not survive on a husband's earnings alone. Nonetheless, marriage was reconceptualized. In the US, the shift was from a partnership in joint economic production to 'an exchange of material sustenance for spiritual sustenance', as one legal scholar put it.[41] Here, too, this was an ideal based on arrangements in wealthy families, in which wives delegated physically demanding, and not especially spiritual, household chores, like handwashing soiled laundry or thwacking a rug with a carpet rod, to women in servitude or slavery.[42]

Academics have painstakingly documented how the gendered division of labour is the accumulated result of 'round upon round' of tussles between the forces of capitalism, unions and guilds, patriarchal interests at home, the state, and feminist activism.[43] In an analysis of UK history that spans from the 1800s to the 1980s, sociologist Sylvia Walby passes through two world wars, the dismantling of laws restricting married women's employment, the Equal Pay Act and the Sex Discrimination Act, as well as the post-war expansion of service sector jobs. She argues that the endpoint of the 1980s, which arrived at a common pattern of a full-time male bread-winner supplemented by part-time female paid labour (and plenty of unpaid domestic labour), can be understood as: 'the new form of the compromise between patriarchal and capitalist interests . . . Women's labour was made available to capital, but on terms which did not threaten to disrupt the patriarchal status quo in the household, since a married woman working part-time could still perform the full range of domestic tasks.'[44]

As those compromises and tussles continue into this century, researchers have begun to pay more attention to 'working fathers'. How do men understand what it means to be a father? What expectations and responsibilities do they take upon themselves in that role?

Unsurprisingly, 'provider' continues to be a common feature of men's identities as fathers. For one Australian 39-year-old father, a senior lecturer at a university, the internalization of that norm felt deeply biological. As he told a researcher interviewing him: '[Your] instinct is that . . . you need to go out and earn money, and so as soon as the baby was born my work hours actually kicked up again and so I probably went back to working, 50 55 60 hours a week again.'[45]

Yet even if such an 'instinct' were to exist, it would be redundant. The expectation that men will remain strongly committed to work and constantly available – the so-called 'ideal worker' norm – is built into workplace interactions, and into male-typical jobs themselves.[46] For women, who are expected to be devoted mothers, the ideal worker norm puts them in a double bind if they become mothers: if they are good workers, they are bad mothers; if they are good mothers, they are bad workers. But traditional norms of good fathers and workers tend to push in the same direction – towards work.[47]

Little wonder, then, that flexible work arrangements, deemed by many to be the solution to work–family conflicts, are typically understood as being for women. Consider a series of interviews conducted with upper-level managers in large, male-dominated Australian organizations. These were chosen specifically because they had proudly trumpeted the slogan that flexible work arrangements were important 'for all, from the CEO down'. Yet discussions with managers soon revealed that 'for all' really meant 'for women'. The interviewers had to explicitly ask about the potential benefits of flexible work arrangements for *men*, since the topic didn't come up spontaneously. When directly prompted, managers agreed that these policies could indeed be useful for the male of the species, but only in the event of rare combinations of calamities, such as the conjunction of divorce and a sick child. The managers were also quite clear about the stigma attached to using these arrangements on a more permanent basis. Said one: '[that] manager is quite traditional and men are concerned that if they work from home they'll be seen to be slacking off and it will reflect in their performance reviews'.[48]

Even taking paternity leave after the arrival of a baby violates the ideal worker norm. In Sweden, for example, a qualitative interview study of 56 employees from both white- and blue-collar private companies identified no fewer than seven significant obstacles to fathers taking up their paternity leave entitlements.[49] At the time of the study, fathers were entitled to two months of 'use it or lose it' paternity leave, compensated at 80 per cent of their salary. In addition, they could share another nine months of parental leave, also generously paid, with mothers. But the fathers faced both cultural and structural barriers to taking up those opportunities. In the words of one blue-collar manager: 'The culture concerning fathers' parental leave? We don't have one (laughs).'[50] It was simply *not normal* for men to take up their full two months of daddy leave. Managers themselves took the least leave (a third took no leave at all), sending a clear signal: work first, family second. This left both white- and blue-collar men anxious about the possible consequences of taking their full leave entitlements. For some, the prospect seemed so outlandish that it was not so much rejected as barely even considered in the first place.

The interviews also revealed an expectation that men who *did* take parental leave would do so in a way that disrupted the workplace as little as possible. Regardless of when they might be most useful at home, it was preferred that the men took their leave at Christmas, in the summer, or part-time. Men also perceived it to be their responsibility to work out how their jobs would get done while they were away. That was easier said than done. The structure of work – particularly the high degree of specialization and intense workloads – meant that workers were often considered indispensable. Moreover, companies and human resources teams had put little thought into how to solve these problems. In short, the assumption that men would not take parental leave for more than a few days was built into the very culture of the organization, inter-actions between managers and workers, the structure of work, and the meaning of jobs themselves.

While this study looked at common pressures facing white- and blue-collar men, there are also differences between the two groups. For blue-collar men, jobs are often a means to fulfilling their role as providers for their family. But for the professional classes, work can become 'a totalizing identity'.[51] For example, a detailed comparison of two groups of working men in the US, physicians and emergency medical technicians (or EMTs, providing emergency medical care from ambulances and fire departments), found that the groups 'did' fatherhood in quite different ways.[52] The physicians engaged mostly in what the researchers call 'public fatherhood'. They were there for the dance show or the ball game, but not for the everyday 'private fatherhood' of day-to-day care. More than half had a family member who wanted them to work less. But several factors limited their participation in family life. Long hours were the norm in their profession, and the men reported a sense of obligation to be there for patients, as well as a reluctance to hand them off to others. The physicians also felt responsible for maintaining a certain standard of living; and there were often steep medical school debts to pay off. Only a few seemed willing to earn less to find more family time.

For EMT dads, on the other hand, fathering took place in both public and private. Many nudged a 60-hour work week (once you added on the second jobs many worked) and had little control over their rostering schedules. They too felt a sense of duty towards their jobs and patients (although they felt more 'interchangeable' than did the surgeons). And with considerably lower salaries than the physicians, taking overtime was a financial draw. But unlike the far better-paid physicians, the EMTs 'routinely turned down overtime in exchange for time with their families'.[53]

One apparently important difference between the two groups was that the EMTs' wives worked an average of 30 hours per week; more than twice as much as the physicians' wives. This contributed to a much smaller spousal income gap in the EMT households: $32,000, compared with a difference of $177,000 in the physician households. Likely thanks in part to this lower inequality of earnings, the EMTs' wives successfully negotiated that their husbands arrange their work in a way that enabled them to also contribute to daily family care. The researchers describe an exchange in the fire station in which 'one EMT responded to the question, "Do your families ever ask you to not come in?" by laughing and saying, "No they tell you: You're not going in." The other EMTs sitting around joined in the laughter and nodded in agreement.'[54]

Life in EMT households was clearly more of a juggle, involving informal negotiation of shift swaps with fellow workers, and prevailing on extended kin to help with last-minute childcare emergencies. Yet 91 per cent of EMT fathers said they were happy with their current schedules and, in interviews, cited the fact that they could spend time at home with their children as a key reason. 'I love the fact that I can be home with my kids a lot, because it's long hours at times, but honestly, I get four days off in a row with my kids. How many people get that much?'[55]

But for the professional classes, long hours can be a badge of manhood. Take the fascinating case study of three US hospitals between 2002 and 2004, amidst the introduction of new regulations mandating a reduction in work hours for surgical residents, from a standard of 120 hours per week to a maximum of 80.[56] Defying reason and common sense, many senior doctors were vehemently opposed to the policy. Their identities had been forged in the 'Iron Man' model of surgery that helped draw clear social distinctions between themselves, the surgical gods, and those lower in the hospital hierarchy. *Those* mere mortals needed sleep and lived at home rather than at the hospital. In often tellingly gendered language, colleagues in favour of the new rules to restrict work hours were derided by the senior surgeons as 'weak', 'softies', 'part-timers', 'wusses', 'pantywaists' and, of course, 'girls'.[57]

Similarly, a study of engineers working in Silicon Valley, undertaken by sociologist Marianne Cooper, unearthed the same hypermasculine norm of relentless work hours. Cooper described this culture as giving birth to a 'new masculinity' in which 'men compete in cubicles to see who can work more hours, who can cut the best code, and who can be most creative and innovative'. One engineer explained the logic: 'He's a real man, he works 90-hour weeks; he's a slacker, he works fifty hours a week.'[58] Cooper describes ways in which 'ideas, norms, and expectations about what is and is not masculine have a regulating effect on the thoughts, choices, and actions of fathers'.[59] So thoroughly did this 'new masculinity' culture of the 'turbo-capitalism' of Silicon Valley seep into men's self-narratives that even their personal lives became suffused with market language. Engineers talked in terms of only managing to go out on a date with their wives 'once a quarter', failing to 'execute' on going out more regularly; of exercising work-life flexibility not being fair to shareholders; and of pressure to lead an 'emotionally downsized' life.[60]

Some Silicon Valley fathers found ways to 'pass' as upholders of the ideal worker norm, even while surreptitiously finding flexibility. Cooper identified three strategies deployed by Silicon Valley fathers 'to personify and embody the public aspects of the new masculinity'. One was the 'silencing' of work–family conflicts. Dropping work for anything less than a full-scale family emergency was hidden. Even paternity leave was 'secretly arranged through managers'.[61] A second strategy was to rely on women. Most obviously, these men were dependent on their wives to cover the considerable care gap. But these wives were useful in another way too: by insistently calling or paging to remind them to come home, they provided the men with an 'excuse' to leave work.

Finally, some men paid a 'tremendous personal cost' to

meet the demands of their workplace, sacrificing all rest and leisure time to be more present as fathers and husbands. 'I'm continually feeling like I'm not quite doing what I want to be doing in either place [job and home] and I'm doing absolutely nothing else that isn't one of those two things. I mean the concept of free time or hobbies, well it seems kind of laughable at this point.'[62]

This complaint, which we tend to associate more with the experiences of working mothers, brings us back to the work–family narrative circulating within the professional consulting firm with which this chapter opened. Recall how, according to that well-rehearsed story, women weren't advancing because they alone experienced work–life conflict and resolved it by stepping back from their careers. However, this didn't quite stack up with the evidence. For example, the firm's leaders wanted to know how to address the higher turnover rate for women: yet the turnover rates for men were virtually the same. Nor was work–family conflict something that only women experienced. Among the interviewees, two thirds of the firm's associates who were fathers commented that they were experiencing work–family conflict. As one father put it, 'I wouldn't characterize myself as unhappy. It's more overworked, and under-familied. If I were a betting man, I'd bet that a year from now I'm working somewhere else.' And he was.[63]

But even though both women and men experienced work–family conflict, only women took up work–family accommodations, in the form of internal, non-client-facing roles. Ostensibly, the purpose of these roles was to help women to successfully combine work and family. But in keeping with ideal worker norms, in which only those who put work first are seen as truly committed and fit for the job, these accommodations were strongly stigmatized. Rather than saving women's careers, they derailed them, serving to *entrench*, rather than solve, the problem of women's lack of advancement.

The researchers identified another strange inconsistency in the interviews. Many interviewees stated that long hours and constant availability were simply an inescapable fact of the kind of work they did – there was no way around it. Yet in these very same interviews, associates would draw attention to 'the firm's practices of overselling and overdelivery'.[64] Associates complained about account managers piling on work that added little real value – like presentations with hundreds of slides – and that came at a steep price for associates' family life and health. 'We heard many stories of partners who, as one associate put it, "promise the client the moon" without thinking of how much time and energy it takes to deliver on such promises. The pitch goes like this, he explained: "We'll do X, Y, and Z, and we're going to do it all in half the time that you think it should take." Clients are wowed and can't wait to sign up, he told us.'[65] Although many associates had the same complaint, with everyone else overworking to overdeliver, each of them had to do the same just to keep up.

Padavic and her colleagues took these insights to the leadership team, explaining that the work–family narrative was an unhelpful simplification. What was being perceived as a 'women's problem' was, they suggested, better understood as an overselling and overdelivering problem. This culture was crushing everyone, but while men either persevered or left, women often shunted themselves into career-stifling accommodations. The researchers proposed a new path that might not only alleviate the so-called women's problem, but could reduce employee burnout and turnover across the board, while minimizing low-value work and reducing the risks of failure to deliver on projects.

These conclusions and recommendations fell on deaf ears. The firm's management reasserted the work–family narrative when they spoke about the topic, and the project fizzled out. This left the researchers curious. Why the refusal even to consider the potential benefits of changing the long-hours work culture? Why would leaders of a top consultancy firm, who prided themselves on basing decisions on data and analysis, ignore the evidence presented to them? They were intrigued . . . and suspicious: 'The widely shared nature of organization members' belief in a questionable proposition – one that had the insidious effect of pointing to remedies that derail women's careers – together with the intensity of leaders' reactions when presented with data that challenged it, suggested to us that leaders' resistance might be a smoking gun – a tip-off that something profound was at play.'[66]

And of course, something *was*: fundamental social identities – as good bosses, workers, men, women, fathers and mothers – were at stake. The researchers suggested that the work–family narrative served as an unconscious 'social defense' against conflicts that would otherwise give rise to painful emotions. For men, the narrative enabled their neglect of their families – which clearly troubled them – to be justified as an inevitable price of the job. For mothers, it helped soothe the sting of a ramped-down career because, according to the narrative, that was inevitable, too. The firm's leaders, meanwhile, could shed responsibility for the brutal trade-offs they were imposing on their employees, and the persistence of male dominance at the top of the firm. According to the tenets of the work–family narrative, what else could they reasonably be expected to do?

But under the surface, when the researchers scrutinized not just *what* was said, but *how* it was said, they found evidence of emotional conflict in the form of contradictions, changes of subject, hesitations and revealing metaphors. The firm's demand that associates be constantly available was the source of greatest angst: namely, 'the internal conflict arising from that demand that daily forces a choice between love (family) and work, undermining individuals' sense of human whole-ness'.[67] The researchers examined how the interviewees *handled* those conflicts – 'how they mobilized specific unconscious defense mechanisms to deal with them'. Fathers, for instance, split off their feelings of love for their family and projected them onto women. In one particularly moving example, an associate spooled out a version of the work–family narra-tive, citing 'some biological imperatives' as being responsible for the special challenge faced by women in balancing these two dimensions of life. But he then went on to describe his *own* experience of becoming a parent in exactly those terms: 'When my first child was born, I got to carry her from the delivery room to the nursery. It's almost like I could feel the chemicals releasing in my brain. I couldn't imagine a world without her. I mean, here it was in [just] the first eight minutes of her life.' As the researchers shrewdly observe, he then abruptly distanced himself from these strong, biologically rooted emotions, and redirected them back onto women. 'So I can understand, "How can I possibly give this up and go back to work?"' But give it up he did, and 'back to work he went'.[68]

The overworked associate's newborn daughter should remind us of an often overlooked set of interests when it comes to how economies, workplaces and parents arrange paid work and care: children.[69] A survey of 10- to 13-year-old Australian kids (from a large, nationally representative sample) found that 35 per cent thought their father worked too much, and 17 per cent wished he didn't work at all. The fathers whose children felt most deprived of their dad's time were those who worked on weekends, were time-pressured, had no control over when they worked, and who worked long hours. These are the fathers in both the time-greedy good jobs and the poorly paid and insecure bad jobs.

When my eldest child was born, over two decades ago, his father – a civil engineer who was working as a project manager in the construction industry – asked the owner of the business if he could work part-time. Although this was an unprecedented request, the company agreed to give it a try. The catch, however, was that this highly abnormal violation of the ideal worker norm was not to be disclosed to clients. Human fatherhood is not a mere biological fact: it is a tapestry of cultural expectations, woven out of policies, practices, standards, traditions and norms at work and at home; a social identity; a role in complex and specialized divisions of labour. The previous chapter emphasized the unequal consequences of *who does what* in the division of unpaid domestic and care labour this mindshaping maintains.

But what about the world of paid work? Surely, at least in theory, we should expect equitable pay-offs in a rational, efficiency-focused labour market. As we'll see in the next chapter, that really depends on the theory.

4

BEYOND MARKET-THINKING

WHEN IT COMES TO *WHO GETS WHAT* ON THEIR PAYSLIP, some numbers can seem hard to justify. In 2019, about three and a half thousand bankers working in the UK earned more than one million euros a year. Twenty-seven bankers were paid more than ten million.[1] Why?

In his book about profit, wages and bonuses in the financial industry, the French sociologist Olivier Godechot invites readers to question some of the rationales offered to deflect outrage triggered by these astronomical sums. Such explanations include that it 'is the game of supply and demand', that these employees possess unparalleled human capital, that they work incredibly hard, or that the huge bonuses they receive are economically justified because they incentivize performance and profit-making. But, Godechot writes, '[t]hese ready-made responses in turn give rise to a number of questions'.

a) Why, in the finance industry, have wages remained so high in comparison with other sectors? b) What are these people so 'good' at? Are they better than aeronautical or nuclear engineers? What are their skills? Why are skills worth more in finance than elsewhere? c) Do they really work more than professionals in the industry (for example, 20 times more)? d) Why do people need such strong incentives in finance? Why do incentives cost so much? Are workers in gold or diamond mines offered comparable incentives?[2]

As Godechot's research shows, simple explanations in terms of rewards for performance or incentives are easily felled by the facts. For instance, variations in bonus size are mostly due to global economic fluctuations, for which individual bankers can take no credit. Sometimes a large bonus serves as a reward for outstanding performance; other times as an inducement for retention. Some workers wind up with larger bonuses not because of their superior human capital, or contribution to their firm's profits, but because they manage to assert tacit property rights over clients, products and teams, and leverage that de facto ownership in never-ending politicking and negotiations.

The sky-high earnings of financiers may seem a far cry from the more pedestrian wages earned by everyday working men and women. However, the very same 'simple ideas'[3] used to justify the high wages in finance – supply and demand, human capital, contributions to productivity – are used by some to reassure us that the sexes really are equal, despite significant gender gaps in *who gets what* at work.

These ideas reliably enjoy an airing whenever gender pay

gap statistics are released. In Australia, reporting requirements came into effect in 2024, requiring companies with 100 or more employees to publicly report their gender pay gap. This move inspired an article in the conservative national newspaper *The Australian*, declaring it 'basically nonsense'. The journalist and economist Judith Sloan argued that the pay gap exists because women are much less likely to be interested in well-paid 'greedy jobs' that take over one's life. The government agency's new report, she surmised, was based on 'misguided reasoning'.[4] 'Let's face it,' she has also written, referencing well-paid jobs in remote Australian mining regions, 'it doesn't suit everyone to have a fly-in, fly-out job in the Pilbara. The pay may be great but the sacrifices to family life may be too high for some women (and men) to contemplate.'[5] And with a touching faith in the power of the market to weed out prejudice and bias, she wrote that '[i]f there were really a comparative advantage for companies in paying women more, it would happen of its own accord, without the meddling of a bossy, naïve government agency'.[6]

The centre-right National Party senator Matt Canavan, also trained as an economist, declared the new gender pay reporting 'useless data' that would function as 'the annual Andrew Tate recruitment drive', thanks to a 'divisive and clearly incorrect gender narrative' that herds men into the arms of the world's most famous misogynist.[7] Canavan called for a comparison of like with like, objecting in particular to the lack of separation of part-time and full-time workers (even though, for the purposes of calculating the pay gap, part-time earnings are 'annualized' to what they would be based on full-time work). 'In what world are there lots of part time CEOs?' he rhetorically asked on the social media platform X. 'If you want to be paid a big salary, you have to work full time.'[8] His concluding argument was a video of men handling some heavy drilling machinery, together with the comment, 'I wonder what the gender pay gap is at this workplace?'[9] (The answer to his rhetorical question is 15.1 per cent.)[10]

Canavan and Sloan are looking at the gender pay gap through a lens informed by mainstream (neoclassical) economics that I call Market-Thinking. According to this viewpoint, wages are set by the neutral market mechanisms of supply and demand, with three factors playing the most important role in determining the price for labour supplied.[11] The first factor is how much market demand there is for the employer's products or services. This naturally sets an upper limit on wages, because if wages and other costs outstrip revenue, the employer will go bust.

The second input determining the worker's pay is his or her 'marginal productivity' – that is, how much value they add to their employer's products or services. According to another popular economic concept, human capital theory, a worker's contribution to productivity can be gauged by human capital characteristics like education, experience, job tenure, job-related skills, work hours and so on.

The third ingredient, according to the supply-and-demand framework, is a competitive labour market. Workers naturally search out the employer offering the best wage for their human capital. Conversely, employers search for the worker who can offer the skills they need at the lowest price. In a competitive market, wages therefore move towards an 'equilibrium', supposedly also creating a mechanism that weeds out bias (as Judith Sloan assumed). A woman or minority worker offered less remuneration by an employer than he or she deserved would vote with their feet and go to work somewhere else for better pay. Conversely, an employer who overpaid men and white workers would eventually be outdone by market competitors who cleverly put profit before prejudice.

Economists recognize that things are more complicated than this in the real world.[12] In various ways, markets are not perfectly competitive. Employees don't always have accurate knowledge of what other employers might offer. Finding out what pay might be available elsewhere and switching jobs is costly. In the absence of perfect information about employees' productivity, employers may draw on cultural stereotypes. In a less than perfectly competitive market, tastes for discrimination may take time to be weeded out. But for many economists, this discrimination is seen as a distortion of the underlying market mechanisms that would otherwise spit out the true 'price' of a wage.[13] The rest of the gender pay gap is 'explained' by differences in men's and women's human capital, the jobs they do, the industries they work in, the hours they put in, and so on. Not much to see here, according to commentators like Sloan and Canavan.

In contrast, supporters of these reporting measures say that the 'explaining' is far from complete. For them, these 'raw' pay gaps, unadjusted for sex differences in human capital, occupations and industries, show us how far we still have to travel in terms of *who does what* – the first of our big problems of coordination in the division of labour. As one women's advocacy report put it: 'Gender pay gaps reflect women's under-representation in senior roles, over-representation in low-paid and insecure work, the unequal distribution of unpaid caring work and the impact of bias and discrimination.'[14]

But we also need to dig much more deeply into the second problem of coordination — *who gets what.*

Supply-and-demand market mechanisms are certainly part of the reason some people earn higher pay than others. However, these factors are far from being the *whole* story. 'Like the practitioners of every other discipline, economists of every stripe can only "see" what their chosen theoretical categories permit to be seen', as two practitioners of that discipline have noted.[15] Economists' models are simplifications that neither attempt nor claim to represent all the rich complexity of economic behaviour. Instead, economists devise mathematical models that incorporate some basic assumptions and highlight whatever aspects of the situation they as economists deem most important, useful and relevant.[16] As a general principle, that's fair enough. You can't blame an economist for not being a psychologist, anthropologist or sociologist. Every social scientist emphasizes the variables most pertinent to the theories favoured by their discipline. But for those trying to understand and fix inequalities, there will be problems if we gather and interpret data using a model that overlooks important factors, or that makes assumptions that deviate too wildly from reality.

As it happens, economists are notorious among the social scientists for not letting the mess of the real world get in the way of mathematically convenient axioms. So much so that there is even a well-known joke about it. A geologist, a physicist and an economist are marooned on a desert island. As they sit there, despondent and hungry, a tin of soup washes ashore. Following the very practical suggestions for getting into the tin made by the geologist (smash it with a rock) and the physicist (heat it until it explodes open), the punchline has the economist proffer the solution 'Assume a tin-opener.' Some economists I know find this joke funny; others don't. But they all *get* it.

A key feature of this real-world mess are social relationships between people, positions and organizations. These relationships are central to a rival lens to Market-Thinking, offered by an account called Relational Inequalities Theory. I'll call this lens Relations-Thinking. The authors of this theory, sociologists Dustin Avent-Holt and Donald Tomaskovic-Devey, argue that if we want to understand how we wind up with inequalities in *who gets what* at work, we can't just look at people's human capital and assume that everyone involved is making rational choices about what to ask for and what to give. The way that revenue *actually* gets parcelled out among workers in the form of wages or salary is not, in fact, the outcome of 'abstracted, disembodied market forces', say Avent-Holt and Tomaskovic-Devey. Managers are not passive rubber-stampers of wages, calculated and handed down by the invisible hand of the market. Instead, these distributions are the result of 'flesh-and-blood human beings negotiating organizational life'.[17]

One important insight of Relations-Thinking is that the very conditions of the market are negotiated by people in ongoing relationships with each other. These negotiated market conditions make a big difference to the resources an organization can get its hands on (and therefore how much it can pay its workers). We often think of differences in net profit as being the outcome of differences in productivity and efficiency. If Company A can produce more widgets in a set period than Company B, and with fewer resources, it will turn a bigger profit. But productivity and efficiency are not the only factors shaping net revenue, nor even perhaps the most important. For instance, organizations and industries with greater market power can charge customers and clients more, screw down suppliers on price, and lobby politicians for more favourable regulations and conditions. Organizations make claims on governments for subsidies, tax breaks and regulatory forbearance. This contributes to considerable inequalities *between* organizations that have nothing to do with a natural law of the market but are politically and legally created.

For example, part of the reason wages are low in the female-dominated care sector is because work in these industries involves activities that are usually face-to-face and labour-intensive.[18] This leaves relatively little scope for increasing productivity or efficiency without this simply being a euphemism for reducing the quality of the service and/or increasing staff workloads. There is also the inconvenient fact that those most often in need of care-sector services, such as children, their parents, students, the elderly, or those with disabilities, are often not well placed to pay handsomely for it. Another downward pressure on wages comes from the fact that care work is a public good. When a kindergarten teacher helps develop her young charges' physical, emotional, social and cognitive capabilities, every future employer of those children benefits. So do their future colleagues, friends and partners. Yet none of them pay directly for these benefits. Kindergarten teachers don't get a trailing commission as the children they have taught make their way through life. Often, then, the revenue available to pay for wages depends at least in part on how much cash the government of the day is prepared, or able, to stump up. These are political and legal decisions: of taxation, public-sector funding and centralized wage setting (when wages and conditions are set by the government). They are not natural laws of the market.

At the opposite end of the spectrum from the often poorly resourced care sector are winners-take-all information technology markets (think Apple, Google, Facebook, Microsoft and Amazon). 'In their relatively short lives,' Tomaskovic-Devey and Avent-Holt observe, 'these companies have generated some of the richest people on the planet.'[19] The financial sector has also enjoyed a meteoric rise since the 1970s, becoming a much larger and more important part of national and global economies. (For example, the share of corporate profits reaped by the US financial sector doubled between 1980 and 2000, from approximately 20 to 40 per cent.)[20]

Where there is growth, there is opportunity galore. But who is on site, cap in hand, to reap these benefits? In the US, men hold nearly three quarters of jobs in computer and mathematical occupations (such as computer programming and software development).[21]

Over in finance, analysis of population-representative

survey data collected between 1975 and 2009 found that much of the wage premium associated with working in the finance sector since the 1980s was scooped up by elite white men (and especially fathers).[22] As mentioned in the introduction to this book, the vast majority of senior leaders of financial services firms are men (no doubt helping to explain why some of the biggest gender pay gaps are seen in that sector).[23] Women make up just 12 per cent of portfolio managers on Citywire's global database of 6,000 companies, and white male portfolio managers handle nearly 99 per cent of US assets, despite evidence that, if anything, women overperform.[24]

Things get particularly homogenous at the intersection between tech and finance. A Deloitte diversity survey of 315 US-based venture capital firms found that women made up just 19 per cent of investment partners.[25] These mostly male decision-makers give funds to mostly men: women-founded start-ups secured just 2 per cent or less of venture capital funding in Europe and the United States.[26]

An excellent illustration of the indulgently forgiving approach extended to both sectors was provided in March 2023, when the US government announced a $175 billion bailout for Silicon Valley Bank (SVB), a bank specialized for the financial needs of tech start-ups.[27] (Contrary to wild claims that its failure was caused by excess focus on diversity and socially and environmentally responsible investments, experts attribute the collapse to 'a bank run precipitated by a decline in start-up funding, rising interest rates and the firm's sale of government bonds at a huge loss to raise capital'.)[28] SVB's share price fell by over 60 per cent and depositors started to withdraw funds in large amounts, pushing the bank towards insolvency and triggering the government decision to step in. As the economist Paul Krugman remarked in the *New York Times*: 'Just a few years ago, SVB was one of the mid-size banks that lobbied successfully for the removal of regulations that might have prevented this disaster, and the tech sector is famously full of libertarians who like to denounce big government right up to the minute they themselves need government aid.'[29] At the risk of sounding like a stuck record, it was political decisions, not some natural law of the market, that enabled both industries to enjoy private profits from their risk-taking gains, while 'socializing' the costs of the losses. (Exhibit B: the global financial crisis.)

Bailouts are a specific example of a more general phenomenon, sometimes referred to as corporate welfare. This can be loosely defined as various public services and state benefits on which private businesses depend or demand (thus running counter to common claims that businesses would do better without government 'interference').[30] These services and benefits include direct grants, subsidized loans, research services, insurance and tax concessions and, *in extremis*, bailouts. For example, at the time of writing the website Good Jobs First has so far as of this writing tracked $6.7 billion of government services and benefits given to tech giant Amazon.com and its subsidiaries.[31] (Amazon.co.uk has done pretty well out of corporate welfare too.)[32]

And unlike their *social* welfare counterparts, when things get desperate for the powerful beneficiaries of corporate welfare, they can call a government minister for assistance. Alastair Darling, the UK's Chancellor of the Exchequer when the global financial crisis was unfolding, recalls a phone call with the chairman of the Royal Bank of Scotland (RBS): 'I came out [of a high-level meeting] to take a call from Sir Tom McKillop, the RBS chairman. He sounded shell-shocked. I asked how long the bank could keep going. His answer was chilling: "A couple of hours, maybe." If we didn't act immediately, its doors would close, cash machines would be switched off, cheques would not be honoured, people would not be paid . . . And what, its chairman asked me, were we going to do about it?' The answer: put together a financial rescue package of more than £1 trillion.[33] Analyses of the effects of the following ten years of austerity policies found that women – particularly single mothers and single female pensioners, and low-income black and Asian women – were the most severely affected.[34] In other words, the bailout handed over massive funds to the male-dominated finance sector, and lower-income women disproportionately helped pay for it.

What about relationships *inside* organizations, and their effect on wages? An interesting feature that emerged from Australia's first mandatory gender gap report was just how much variation there is among companies when it comes to the size, and even the direction, of the gender pay gap. Overall, every single industry had a pay gap favouring men. But this gap was bigger in some industries than in others. Moreover, 30 per cent of *organizations* had a minimal pay gap (no more than 5 per cent in favour of either sex), while 8 per cent had a pay gap in favour of *women*. This figure rose to 15 per cent in the female-dominated education and training sector.[35] This is interesting. Why is a woman's work worth less than a man's in most companies, the same in a minority, and more in a very few?

One of the ideas from chapter 2, that inequalities are most entrenched whenever status is attached to group member-ship, suggests an answer. Modern organizations are hotbeds of socially created categories – *administrative assistant, financial engineer, human resources, security guard* – that draw distinctions between jobs, roles and people. Some of these are higher-status than others. These assessments of status are based on percep-tions of the skill and competence attached to those people, positions and roles. (*Jack earns more than Joan because he is a better fund manager. Doctors earn more than nurses because they are more highly trained.*) People and groups who are deemed to be more skilled have an easier time making claims on organizational resources.

So far this would have economists nodding along. 'In the human capital model,' write Avent-Holt and Tomaskovic-Devey, 'employers are treated as calculators of merit who are able to recognize individual productivity. If they fail to recog-nize value produced, they are disciplined by the market until they properly reward skill or go bankrupt.' But there's a catch. The 'coupling' between markets and what happens in firms is much weaker than this in real life, and this 'loose coupling allows imperfect information and biases to creep into evalu-ations of productivity and thus who is more or less skilled'.[36]

This scope for bias is where the tightness of the link between organizational status and gender status (i.e., maleness) becomes important when it comes to understanding the gen-der pay gap. An already high-status role, like manager, takes on an additional status-shine if the majority of people in that role are men. In the resolving of *who gets what*, their demands will seem especially reasonable. Conversely, if most of the workers in a lower-status role, like core worker, are women, that role will sink a little further in estimations of skill. Or so suggested an analysis of US and Australian workplaces by Donald Tomaskovic-Devey and colleagues. Unsurprisingly, they found that managers on average earned more than core workers – although somewhat more so in the US, likely due to its history of weaker worker protections. The researchers then went on to test Relations-Thinking predictions. These analyses revealed that in both countries, and especially for workplaces in the US, this 'class inequality' between managers and production workers was bigger when workers were primarily women and managers were primarily men.[37] The status-boosting effect isn't restricted to gender. The researchers saw similar patterns when managers were largely composed of other higher-status groups (such as being white in the US, a native language speaker in Australia, and permanent employees in both countries).

Along similar lines, consider a meta-analysis of gender gaps in job evaluations on the one hand, and financial rewards such as salary and bonuses on the other. Overall, this found that men were being much more generously rewarded than women, even though this couldn't be explained by superior job performance. The bias was pronounced in more male-dominated occupations, as well as in jobs where there was higher ambiguity over performance. But in those rare organizations with a high proportion of female executives, the performance and reward gaps were *reversed* and now favoured women.[38]

As these studies suggest, biases can pervade assessments of *jobs themselves*. When widely shared, they can become embedded in the labour market. For instance, although Canavan took it for granted that an hour's work performed by someone who works a 30-hour week is worth less than an hour from someone pulling a 60-hour week, employers have not always paid a premium for 'overwork' (that is, more than 50 hours per week) as they do now, and it's far from obvious that long hours always equate to greater productivity per hour.[39]

Biases in jobs themselves can also include the importing of broader cultural bias due to society-wide status hierarchies, such as of gender, race and class, and historical assumptions can have a lasting legacy on wages. For example, the systems used to evaluate jobs were developed at a time when there were literally 'men's jobs' and 'women's jobs', and the ideology of the male breadwinner took it for granted that men deserved and required a bigger wage. As one sociologist explains: 'Valuable job content was intentionally designed to be associated with high-paying (male) jobs. Since women's work was especially low-paying at the time of the development of these systems, this method of constructing job evaluation systems assured that the characteristics associated with female jobs would remain uncompensated.'[40]

Thus, an edition of the *Dictionary of Occupational Titles* from the 1970s reveals that working at a dog pound or as a parking lot attendant was considered more complex than being a nursery school teacher. The job of nurse-midwife was supposedly less complex than that of hotel clerk. No doubt foster mothers would have been interested to learn that, according to the *Dictionary*, their work was simpler than pushing a horse-drawn cart.[41] It's sometimes assumed that the rise of demand for so-called 'soft skills' benefits women in the economy. However, the very fact that sociability, empathy and communication are assumed to come 'naturally' to women serves to make such work seem 'unskilled' – at least when performed by women. Social astuteness, emotional regulation and other stereotypical feminine qualities are seen as a natural state rather than an achievement.[42] Despite the demand for such skills, jobs that require them come with 'a rather sharp wage penalty', according to analysis of US labour market data.[43]

As the Center for Nursing Advocacy has observed of the metaphor that nurses are 'angels of mercy':

> Although the Center appreciates positive comments about nurses, we believe that the image of the 'angel' or 'saint' is generally unhelpful. It fails to convey the college-level, knowledge-based, critical thinking skills, and hard work required to be a nurse. And it may suggest that nurses are supernatural beings who do not require decent working conditions, adequate staffing, or a significant role in health care decision-making policy. If nurses are angels, then perhaps they can care for an unlimited number of patients and still deliver top-quality care. To the extent nurses do seem to suffer in such working conditions, it may be viewed as merely evidence of their angelic virtue, not a reason to alter the conditions.[44]

Self-sacrificial sainthood has not always been part of the nursing job description. A common practice in eighteenth-century European societies, particularly France, was for parents to send their babies to 'mercenary wet nurses'. One estimate is that a sixth or more of Parisian infants were boarded out in this way. (Common clients included urban mothers and the wives of small shop owners and artisans.) There, infants experienced freezing, overcrowded and filthy living conditions, neglect and abuse. Mortality rates were 'ghastly', according to historian Edward Shorter.[45] As for traditional nurses, tasked with caring for the many abandoned infants prior to 1820, 'as a rule [they] were indifferent beyond belief' when it came to the welfare of the foundling babies they took in.

> Children were commodities for them, just as, let us say, cocoa futures are commodities for the modern trader. And they acted invariably to maximize their profits, as a trader would with any standardized interchangeable unit in the marketplace. For the commodities dealer, one sack of cocoa is not intrinsically more marvelous or precious than any other given sack. So also for the mercenary nurses of the eighteenth century.[46]

For example, once a child reached the age of seven, nurses would routinely return them to the local foundling home or hospital to exchange them for an infant who came with a higher rate of pay. As Shorter observes, drolly comparing the nurses' decision-making to that of commodity traders: 'Attached though you may be to Cocoa Lot 688, you unload it at the first opportunity if the price drops.' This market-minded approach was replaced by 'an almost maternal affection' over the course of the nineteenth century.[47] Today, this more compassionate ethos is the basis for the assumption that women doing caring work, however poorly paid, are nonetheless *richly* compensated. It's just that they 'choose to take a portion of their pay in warm feelings instead of cash', as one dissenting feminist economist has described these claims.[48] It has even been proposed that, were wages for that kind of work to be *too* generous, they might start to attract the wrong sort of person, just in it for the money. The possibility that the *right* sort of person might be deterred because of an awkward need to pay for food and rent appears not to enter into the equation.

Indeed, there seems to be an allergy to applying market logic to such roles. In the US, concerns about nurse shortages were first raised by hospitals in 1997. Yet nurses' wages remained stagnant for years, according to a 2006 report.[49] Indeed, hospital administrators instead turned to strategies that made the job *less* attractive, including mandatory overtime, hiring temporary agency nurses and understaffing. (Some hospitals were even investigated for collusion in setting nurses' salaries.) When salaries did at last temporarily increase, so too did supply. Yet as the report's authors point out, despite the persistent undersupply of nurses in hospitals, the majority of state commissions and task forces, industry groups and federal agencies routinely ignored the obvious solution: better pay. An almost comical scene springs to mind. Setting: a boardroom, located somewhere in the throbbing heart of free-market ideology, in which a dozen well-paid professionals scratch their heads over the seemingly insoluble problem of how to attract more nurses into hospitals.

None of this is to claim that supply and demand in the labour market plays no role in wage-setting. But whereas the supply-and-demand framework sees its see-saw dynamic as the central mechanism determining wages, in Relations-Thinking, supply and demand is also a cultural resource that individuals or groups can draw on, more or less successfully, to lend legitimacy to their claims. For the heavily female-dominated occupation of nursing, as we just saw, even urgent market demand might not be effective in raising salaries.

Conversely, for groups with enough cultural clout, these 'market claims need merely be plausible, not true, to be influential', as Tomaskovic-Devey puts it.[50] He and Avent-Holt point, for example, to research showing that the soaring rise in CEO pay in the US, starting in the 1990s, was largely due to compensation committees selecting 'aspirational peer groups' as benchmarks for appropriate pay. What looked like market logic was just a very expensive game of executive leapfrog.[51]

Something similar appears to have been going on with the salaries of university vice chancellors (equivalent to the CEO of a company) in Australia. The previous vice chancellor of my own university earned about AU$1.5 million, compared with about AU$550,000 for the man who runs the entire country.[52] Unlike corporations, members of the councils that set vice chancellor salaries aren't guided by financial self-interest, whereby an excessive VC salary reduces their own profits. Indeed, '[t]hey might even prefer to pay their vice-chancellor over the odds because it makes their university look more prestigious'.[53] Exactly this motive was revealed in an episode in which the incoming vice chancellor of the Australian National University – the Nobel Prize-winning physicist Brian Schmidt – effectively negotiated his salary *down*. (Admirably, he didn't think he deserved to earn so much more than the average rank-and-file academic.) 'The university council was very concerned about the signal it would send to the market about not paying me enough,' he recalled.[54]

Another example of the deployment of merely plausible market claims comes from a detailed analysis of four landmark pay discrimination cases in the US, by Robert Nelson and William Bridges. These were cases in which, back in the heady days of the second-wave feminist movement, plaintiffs argued that employers were discriminating against women by paying lower wages for female-dominated jobs, for no other reason than that they tended to be done by women rather than men. This promised to be a key pathway to greater pay equality between the sexes. (However, although it's sometimes claimed that the gender pay gap is largely due to the different occupations women and men hold, recent data from 15 countries finds that sorting of the sexes into different jobs, different workplaces *and* unequal pay for the same job all contribute to the gender pay gap.)[55]

But despite an encouraging initial win in the courts, these so-called 'comparable worth' claims were ultimately unsuccessful. Legal opinions coincided with the mainstream economic view: wage differences were the product of neutral market mechanisms and efficiency-minded employers. The courts accepted this explanation of pay differences despite there being very weak evidence to support it. In some cases, these propositions were even 'demonstrably wrong'.[56] The researchers' conclusion was not that market conditions were *irrelevant* to pay structures, but rather that these structures were *also* products of 'convention and tradition'. 'When we took the unusual step of looking at what organizations actually did in setting wages,' they add, 'we found considerable indeterminacy.'[57]

In the concluding chapter of their analysis, Nelson and Bridges wryly observe that the law has replaced one inequality-justifying ideology with another. Upholding the ban on women practising law in the late nineteenth century, the US Supreme Court 'cited higher authority: "The paramount destiny and mission of woman are to fulfill the noble and benign offices of wife and mother. This is the law of the Creator."' In the late twentieth century, the courts 'found a new deity to cite as the source of gender inequality: the market'.[58] Amen.

A fascinating series of interviews with senior managers of Australian residential and community aged-care organizations shows how low wages can be sustained even for skilled work that is in high demand. As the researchers explain, the systematic de-professionalization of the aged-care workforce has put managers in a tricky spot, whereby 'they need to show that in employing cheaper labour they are not allowing quality standards to drop'.[59] Managers achieved this by drawing heavily on two premises. The first was that *real* quality of care was not to be found in educational qualifications or professional certification, but in caring skills honed by years of unpaid care at home. However, in a neat illustration of the point that 'skill' is an ambiguous concept, shaped by cultural biases and political interests, workers were only considered skilled when managers were talking about the quality of care. When the conversation moved on to appropriate pay grades, the work turned out not to be so skilled after all. 'I think that predominantly it's not skilled work,' said one CEO. "I think a carer's job is an important one but a lot of the skills are time management and the really unmeasurable things of care and things like that and I don't think you learn those skills in a university degree or trained [*sic*] course.'[60]

The second premise was to deny that the people who tend to end up in this low-paid care work – typically mothers returning to the workforce after several years' absence, and newly arrived migrants – are in a weak position because they have few other better-paid options. Rather, the managers suggested, their workers are drawn to aged care because of the compensating emotional rewards from helping others. As one site manager put it: 'People come into aged care because they have a passion to help old people and to give something back to the community . . . not because they think they're going to make money . . . They are more driven by compassion and care.'

Putting these two premises together, the perverse conclusion drawn was that only by paying low wages was it possible for managers to ensure high quality of care. Presented with the observation that pizza delivery drivers earn significantly more than aged-care workers, one site manager 'expressed horror' at the comparison.[61] The logic seemed to be that were the wages of care workers for the elderly to scale the heady heights of those enjoyed by fast-food delivery drivers, one would be likely to attract workers with an orientation to their charges as lacking in compassion and commitment as that of a driver towards a thin-crust pepperoni with extra cheese. Perhaps unsurprisingly, workers themselves don't see it quite the same way. 'Virtually every aged care workforce planning document identifies poor wages as a primary problem for employee attraction,' the researchers point out.[62]

In 2021, a Royal Commission by the Australian Commonwealth government revealed an ugly picture of the state of the Australian aged-care sector, including the shocking statistic that nearly 4 in 10 residents of aged-care facilities experience elder abuse, in the form of emotional abuse, physical abuse and/or neglect.[63] Some of the recommendations for dragging up the sector to tolerable standards were to provide its workforce with more training and professional development, and to improve wages.[64]

As a happy coda to this story, in March 2024, Australia's Fair Work Commission (the national industrial relations tribunal) handed down a judgment of hourly wage increases of 18 to 29 per cent for direct aged-care workers, and an increase of 15 to 26 per cent for home-care workers.[65] An important context for the ruling was a change in legislation in 2022, which required the Fair Work Commission to ensure that its consideration of claims about the value of work to 'be free of assumptions based on gender' and to 'include consideration of whether historically the work has been undervalued because of assumptions based on gender'.[66] The Commission's historical excavation of this question went right back to Australia's legislation of the breadwinner wage in 1907, in which the typical worker was assumed to be a married man with three children. It concluded that the wages of direct aged-care workers reflected a 'continuation of the history . . . of treating the skills exercised in female-dominated industries and occupations as merely feminine traits and not representative of work value in the traditional, narrowly defined sense'.[67]

Only nine years earlier, the narrative being spun by the managers had been win-win-win: the state gets a cheaper aged-care bill, and private owners the benefits of lower wage costs; the elderly receive the tender ministrations that only the lowest wages and a de-professionalized workforce can buy; and the very special self-sacrificial workers enjoy the emotional rewards of 'the hard work that other people wouldn't touch', as one CEO of an Australian aged-care facility let slip, such as the handling of vomit, urine and excrement.[68]

It is certainly a far cry from the financial institutions inhabited by millionaire bankers, whose mistakes and greed are still being subsidized. Continuing the examination of workplaces through the lens of Relations-Thinking, the next chapter reveals some of the ways in which women are still being excluded from these and other lucrative opportunities.

5

BORDER CONTROL

IN SEPTEMBER 2016, WELLS FARGO BANK WAS FINED $100 million by the Consumer Financial Protection Bureau, for illegally creating more than two million deposit and credit card accounts without customer authorization.[1] Over the preceding years, rank-and-file employees had been put under immense pressure to meet unrealistic targets to sell additional financial products to customers — a practice known as cross-selling. 'I had managers in my face yelling at me,' one former employee in Houston told CNN. 'They wanted you to open up dual checking accounts for people that couldn't even manage their original checking account.'[2] One Florida branch manager, who ended up resigning, told the *Los Angeles Times* that employees who failed to meet daily quotas were forced to work weekends and evenings. The threat of job loss hung over anyone who persistently fell short of achieving their quotas.[3] According to one lawsuit, filed against Wells Fargo by terminated employees who failed to hit targets that were impossible to meet by ethical means, these workers were earning just $12 per hour.[4]

At first glance, this might seem like a peculiarly unprofitable kind of fraud. True, some unwitting customers paid unnecessary fees or penalties, but there were not great riches to be gained directly from these unrequested accounts. A few additional facts clear up the mystery, however. The fraudulent accounts inflated the metric tracking the bank's cross-selling success. In turn, announcements of Wells Fargo's triumph in meeting their cross-selling target boosted the share price. This, in turn, enriched its shareholders, as well as the top executives whose compensation was linked to the share price. Suddenly it all makes sense.

What, however, does this case of corporate greed have to do with gender? Received wisdom holds that women are generally nicer and more ethical than men, and that including more women in senior leadership teams therefore brings about nicer, more ethical organizations. While there is some evidence that female representation is associated with more socially responsible governance, it is not a simple matter of adding women and stirring.[5] Wells Fargo provides a good case in point. At the time the fraudulent accounts were proliferating, women were well represented on the board: they made up seven of the sixteen members.[6] Moreover, it was a woman, Carrie Tolstedt, who was the head of consumer and small business retail banking during the company's operation to set and meet the cross-selling metrics. In a triumph for female representation in corporate wrongdoing, in March 2023, Tolstedt 'agreed to plead guilty to obstructing a government examination into the bank's widespread sales practices misconduct'.[7] Although prosecutors wanted a 12-month prison sentence, in September

2023 she was sentenced to six months of home confinement, three years of probation and 120 hours of community service, on top of a $100,000 fine.[8] In a separate settlement with the government's Office of the Comptroller of the Currency, she consented to a $17 million civil penalty and a ban on working again in the banking industry.[9]

However, there *is* a gender story – one in which women have been described as facing a 'triple bind'. They are punished if they play by men's rules, punished if they *don't*, while their relative lack of interest and success in this rigged game reinforces it as men's terrain.[10] But we will continue our intellectual journey illuminating the intricacies of cut-throat corporate America in a more benign setting: specifically, my home.

One of my privileges as the matriarch of the household is to be brought morning tea in bed. According to family lore, it is more or less a natural right for female Fines to receive this benefit. Amidst the interdependency of domestic life, the arrival of a pot of tea on the bedside table in the morning, together with cup and little jug of milk, is as much a part of the status quo as the rising of the sun. All males who enter the family, whether by birth or choice, are inculcated into the system. To me, the arrangement seems quite natural and just. But to your average sociologist, it is an object lesson in how inequalities are created.

As we've seen, as divisions of labour become more complex, we rely on social categories and roles to manage expectations around who does what, and who gets what. But this creates a motivation to try to ensure that one's own group gets a generous helping of any scarce resources. For anyone trying to do this, there are essentially two top tips. The first is to draw boundaries around your group, to circumscribe who is eligible for those resources. The Fine family tea rule is not that *any Fine* or *anyone living in a Fine household* deserves to enjoy the first cup of tea of the day without stirring from their pillows, but that this is an entitlement of *adult female Fines*. Clearly, liberalizing the boundary would divert the flow of resources in unwanted directions.

The second vital move is closely related. Having created the relevant social identity, it is necessary to establish an in-group community that establishes one's own as having a superior claim to those scarce resources, and outsiders as ineligible. In the morning tea case, the three living generations of female Fines are all proud feminists who naturally abhor divisions of labour based on sex and bloodline. But we are also only human. Thus, each of us has asserted our case for special treatment and, on occasion, assisted each other in establishing and reinforcing these norms. For example, when it became known within the family that a partner was *showering and getting dressed* before making the tea, creating an intolerable delay, in a loving act of informal disciplinary action, the offender received a dressing gown for Christmas.

Sociologists refer to these 'processes of drawing boundaries, constructing identities, and building communities', in ways that wind up with one group enjoying superior access to resources, as 'social closure'.[11] Common labour market forms of closure are educational credentialling, licensing, certification, unionization and professional association.[12] Rightly, wrongly or imperfectly, each practice sets limits on who can be employed to do particular kinds of work. Sociologists sometimes risk giving the impression that they long for the day when *anyone* can offer to scoop that tumour out of your lung for you. But the point is rather that these practices, by limiting labour supply (or threatening to cut it off, in the case of unions), boosting and channelling demand towards a particular occupation, and signalling quality, give those included in the inner circle of social closure processes a leg up in negotiating wages and conditions.[13]

But there are also forms of social closure that elbow out potential contenders on the basis of social identities like sex, race, sexuality or religion. A simple and highly effective example of this approach is open and explicit exclusion. As we saw, Ansett Airways used it to great effect to close off piloting jobs from women. British Airways, in an earlier incarnation as Imperial Airways, achieved double closure by restricting airline pilot positions to members of the Royal Air Force, the Reserve, or the Auxiliary Air Force, which in turn excluded women.[14] (British Airways hired its first female airline pilot, Lynn Barton, in 1987.)

In today's workplaces, the exclusion is usually unconscious (or at least kept quiet about). One of the most familiar forms is gender bias in evaluations of competence. In general, men's higher status can give them a little edge in how capable they seem (all else being equal), but gender stereotypes do bestow women with an edge in specialist feminine realms. Just like the wage gap data discussed in the previous chapter, we should therefore expect differences across workplaces in manifestations of this kind of gender bias, depending on how strongly competence is correlated with maleness.

In line with these expectations, a large-scale study of professionals found that respondents who had a female manager, and who worked in an organization with a higher proportion of women in management, were less likely to show a preference for male managers. They also tended to have a more androgynous stereotype of the ideal leader.[15]

Organizational gender ratios also proved to be the most critical factor predicting bias against aspiring female apprentices in Germany. Economists sent 3,400 fictitious entry-level CVs for apprenticeships to 680 nationally representative German firms, and asked employers to rate how likely the applicant would be to reach the next stage of the application process.[16] Overall, there was clear discrimination against young women. Nor was it trivial. The benefit of being a man rather than a woman was equivalent to being one grade level higher at school. (Females were also two and a half times more likely to get the worst rating; and one and a half times *less* likely to receive the top rating.) However, the degree of gender discrimination varied across industries and occupations, with the most important source of that variation being the extent to which the firm was male-dominated. Across the eight industries sampled in the study, construction stood out as the most biased. Men weren't discriminated against even in the most female-dominated industries or organizations in this particular study, although others have found that male applicants are disadvantaged when it comes to applying for heavily female-dominated jobs such as data entry and waiting staff.[17]

However, gender bias is not inevitable, even in male-dominated occupations, according to a synthesis of the huge research literature investigating whether university scientists tend to favour men, published in 2023.[18] The researchers focused on six key contexts for academic science careers: hiring for continuing positions (these are the most desirable 'tenure-track' positions in research institutions); grant funding; teaching ratings; acceptance of articles by scientific journals; salaries; and letters of recommendation. They also restricted their search to evidence collected between 2000 and 2020, to ensure they were looking at the contemporary situation in science rather than a historical one. As they point out, their findings were more positive than the media tends to present. They found no evidence of bias against women in grant funding, acceptance of journal articles or the fulsomeness of recommendation letters. They also found bias against *men* in hiring, even in the male-dominated fields of physics, computer science and mathematics. This left only two domains of the six in which female scientists were disadvantaged. Women earned lower salaries (more than half of this difference was statistically 'explained' by women's overrepresentation in less well-paying institutions and fields, as well as lesser productivity and years of experience compared with men). Women also received more negative teaching ratings from students (including in well-controlled studies in which students only *thought* they were being taught by a woman).

As the researchers point out, 'institutions should get credit for progress they have made as a result of decades of efforts'.[19] Moreover, unlike students, the people rating applicants for jobs, and reviewing grants and journal articles, have both the expertise to perform those evaluations and the motivation to evaluate well. Committees, editors and journal reviewers also have a huge amount of information on which to base their judgements. These are all factors that militate against bias.

However, it is easier to be impartial when looking through the CV of a stranger than when interacting with colleagues and friends in everyday work life. The centrality of social categories and identities makes us susceptible to bias towards our own — so-called 'homophily'. This 'love of sameness' shapes many important workplace interactions, including mentorship, sponsorship, friendships and alliances, trust, feelings of obligation and the passing-on of useful information and opportunities.[20] These may all seem like positive things to be happening in workplaces. However, homophily can be a powerful mechanism for maintaining in-group advantages. Those with the most power, resources, insider knowledge and status offer a helping hand to others like them. All it takes is the repeated 'nonoccurrence of a helpful act' to give one group a systematic advantage over another.[21] When one sex (and race) dominates powerful, high-status positions, it's easy for fully 'equal opportunity' to fly out the window. Particularly when formal or informal opportunities and advancement depend on relationships, connections and networks, there is fertile soil for gender, class and racial inequalities to grow.

This is why the good news about the lack of bias against women in academic science hiring and grant evaluations isn't the end of the matter. Seemingly 'objective' measures of quality may have gender bias built into them, for instance.[22]

But also, success in science isn't simply about talent and hard work (though of course both are important). Behind every CV or grant proposal being scrutinized by a carefully unbiased selection committee are webs of relationships and networks of affiliations. Lab visits, collaborations, advice on research proposals, invitations to speak on panels, opportunities to contribute articles to journals or serve on editorial boards, access to equipment or specialist knowledge – all these things, and more, depend on relationships with senior scientists. A study of junior medical scientists, all of whom had won prestigious early-career fellowships, found that junior men mentored by senior men enjoyed the greatest number of enhancements to their CVs from those mentorships. Down the track, this parlayed into greater future grant success.[23]

In-group biases help explain why, as mentioned in the previous chapter, men scooped up such a large share of the meteoric growth in profits in the finance sector that started from the deregulating 1980s. A study of the career histories of 76 Wall Street financial professionals, like other classic studies of that time, helped answer a question we still grapple with today: why an avowed commitment to equal opportunities doesn't necessarily translate into equal outcomes. The female financiers began their careers with similarly elite educational credentials to the men, yet reported notably less in the way of opportunities, mentoring and networking. It was assumed, for example, that they would be best suited for clients 'like them' – but female clients tended to be less wealthy. As the researcher, Louise Marie Roth, explains:

Women workers — and remember, by objective standards, these women matched their male counterparts — described how managers did not assign them to the most important accounts or deals: managers promoted those who closely resembled themselves and/or their clients. By the same logic, managers deliberately assigned their female employees to work on accounts with female clients, but those accounts tended to be less lucrative. Senior male managers also sometimes took men under their wing because they shared common backgrounds and interests, and they gave them better access to lucrative accounts and deals. In these ways, opportunities to perform were distributed unequally by gender.[24]

Minority men, including one Southerner, also sometimes reported exclusion. But the environment was perhaps most heartbreakingly isolating and hostile for the single black woman in the sample of interviewees, Sabrina. A double-tick for diversity for her firm, once hired, she was essentially set up to fail. Asked about experiences of mentoring in her career, she responded: 'It's if you're lucky enough to have someone befriend you, you'll have a career on Wall Street. White males helped white males. White females helped white females. You'll even have a white male helping a white female, but then there was that . . . what I call the FQ: "Fuckability Quotient". The more fuckable you are in their eyes, the more they will help you.'[25]

In this way, the biggest bonuses, and the opportunities

to earn them, remained largely reserved for men. (All but 7 of the 76 interviewees were white.) Men's domination of the highest-paying jobs could not be entirely explained by women's lower inclination or ability to work very long hours and travel at the drop of a hat. For example, in order to access more manageable work hours, women would shift into support functions, equity research and asset management. Yet only very rarely were they able to move into sales and trading jobs that had similar hours but were much better paid. What's more, the less personally lucrative area of public finance had the largest proportion of women, even though this work also involved long hours and a high intensity of travel.[26]

Even after taking account of the area of finance – as well as background characteristics like marital and parental status, human capital and rank – men's compensation was higher. Women earned about 29 per cent less than comparable men with comparable jobs working in comparable firms. Weekly work hours did not explain the difference. Men working 40 hours a week earned about $100K more per annuum in 1997 than women working the same number of hours. At 100 hours a week, men earned close to $800K per annum, women $500K. What perhaps *does* explain the differences in compensation is the almost comically dubious practice of bonuses being allocated by managers based on subjective performance rankings.[27]

Indeed, there were two rather telling characteristics common to the women who, unusually, managed to carve out successful careers in the particularly well-remunerated fields of corporate finance and sales and trading. First, they typically had a powerful male mentor. Second, '[m]ost of these women deliberately chose or moved into areas where their success would not depend on subjective evaluations of performance among male managers and peers, or on buddy relationships with executives from male-dominated client companies'.[28] In other words, they had found loopholes that enabled them to slip through social closure mechanisms.

Lest you assume that the intervening decades have wrought a new era of diversity and inclusion in elite finance, consider the hedge fund industry. Hedge funds are private investment firms. They pool money from wealthy investors (including very rich individuals, pension funds, government funds and non-profit endowments) and invest it in financial assets such as shares, bonds and options. Between 2000 and 2024, the hedge fund industry grew from managing about $250 billion dollars per quarter to about $5 trillion.[29] Typical earnings are mind-boggling. Average portfolio manager pay in 2014 was about $2.4 million (that's base salary plus bonus).[30] In 2023, the top 25 earners made a combined total of $26.085 billion.[31]

Stanford sociologist Megan Tobias Neely's in-depth research underlines the extent to which inclusion and success in the industry depend on relationships with others. Hiring usually takes place through social networks and personal connections. Mentorship and success are contingent on becoming the protégé of a 'chief' or 'king' (as the hedge fund managers are known). Launching a new fund depends on access to people with very large pots of money. The industry runs on tracks of trust-based networks, and who better to trust in an uncertain, high-stakes environment than someone *just like you*.[32]

The upshot is that in 2021, white men were managing approximately 95 per cent of US hedge fund assets.[33]

As Neely points out, people don't necessarily realize what's going on:

> So [the fund managers] create these small firms that they think are more equal in many ways [than the big investment banks], that anybody can walk in. But what they don't realize is that when you're the leader, you may be comfortable in a setting that other people are not. When you're hand picking people who are exactly like you, who will behave and act and think like you, you just think, "Oh, it's a good fit."[34]

Cultural 'fit' is a critical and covert means by which dominant groups hoard opportunities for themselves. The French sociologist Pierre Bourdieu coined the term 'habitus' to describe and explain how people with similar backgrounds and life experiences come to share similar habits, unspoken knowledge about ways of interacting and behaving, and so on. When two such similarly 'mindshaped' people come together, it is like a perfectly executed waltz, thanks to 'the harmonization of agents' experiences and the continuous reinforcement that each of them receives from the expression . . . of similar or identical experiences'.[35] This creates problems for outsiders trying to join the dance.

One issue for members of non-dominant groups – women, racial minorities, the working class – is that they have the 'wrong' habitus. In the waltz of business, toes get trodden on, and people just tend to prefer colleagues with whom the steps of organizational life are more comfortable. The networks along which collegiality, influence, information and mentoring travel are smoother when they run between socially similar others. The motivation is comfort, not animus, but that offers relatively little solace to outsiders being overtaken by people no more talented or industrious than themselves.

The problem intensifies if and when a *feeling* ('these behaviours, appearances and ways of interacting make me feel comfortable') becomes an assessment of suitability ('these behaviours, appearances and ways of interacting are markers of merit'). One of Neely's interviewees, a seasoned white man with over 25 years of experience, quite openly explained his hiring process in these terms: 'There's a chemistry aspect to it. There's a connection between the interviewer and the interviewee, which goes something like, "I could work with that person everyday. I'm going to spend a lot of time – probably more time than I spend with my wife – so I need to be able to get along with that person."'[36]

Something similar has been seen in other elite professions. A compelling example of the importance of 'cultural fit' came from a five-year study of ten white working-class men who had been recruited as IT professionals to work in a regional office in the north of England of an upmarket professional services firm headquartered in the City of London (the UK's financial hub). In this elite setting, the men became acutely aware of what should have been job-irrelevant 'cultural capital' in drawing boundaries between those on the 'right' and 'wrong' side of it. Said one interviewee:

Where we come from . . . [working-class people] only wear a suit if you're in court or at wedding, but at work it's not that you'll wear a suit, it's that you'll wear the right suit in the right way with the right accessories . . . People in the professional world notice these things and they matter a lot . . . there are codes to it and working-class lads are not aware of it, it's like a secret code.[37]

Over time, the men started to assimilate to this code of corporate masculinity, even to the extent of developing skincare routines, getting dental work done and changing their accents to be 'less regional'. One man even wore fake spectacles to 'look the part'.[38] These changes, which to some extent alienated them from their family and friends, came at some personal cost. However, *failing* to take on the trappings of middle-class corporate masculinity would have marked them even more obviously as marginalized outsiders.

Studies of prestigious US law firms have revealed that recruiting practices seemed more like choosing a friend or a spouse than an employee. Researchers sent applications from fictitious students to US law firms, marking them with signs of social class as well as gender. They found that higher-class male applicants received roughly four times more invitations to interview than everyone else on average (that is, lower-class males, or women from either social class).[39] Follow-up studies, including interviews with lawyers, revealed that lower-class applicants of both sexes were perceived to not be a good 'fit' – perhaps better suited to lower-paying legal occupations.

But higher-class female candidates also tended to be rejected. Just as airlines in the previous century rationalized not hiring women as pilots on the grounds that they would only go off and have babies, so too did prestigious twenty-first-century law firms. As one interviewee explained: 'There's . . . a sense that these women don't really need this job. 'Cause they have enough money or they are married to somebody rich and they should be, you know, they're going to end up being a helicopter mom. They're eventually going to leave law.'[40]

The ideal worker norm marks another way in which women can be seen as a bad 'fit' for occupations that demand long hours and constant availability. Interviews with Norwegian women and men working in male-dominated areas of finance (asset management, markets, investment banking, corporate banking, and within large corporates) found that fathers did usually take their parental leave entitlements. However, as with the study of Swedish fathers mentioned in chapter 3, they did so in ways that enabled them to cling onto the clients on which career success and big bonuses are built. For example, they would take the leave on Friday afternoons, or in quiet periods like the summer holidays. Mothers, in contrast, took longer leaves in a block. As a result, they would have to hand over their clients to someone else, and rarely got them back.[41]

This is a classic example of a 'greedy job' for which there is a wage premium for constant and continuous availability. It is also a classic example of a job unnecessarily constructed around the expectation that workers will never take time off for family, or indeed for any other reason, ever. One male financial broker, recognizing these consequences of parental leave, suggested a more collectivist approach to client 'owner-ship': 'There should be a structure where the bank owns the client and not me. Therefore, if I'm away from my desk or get run over by a bus, it doesn't really matter because the client will be taken care of by the company. In addition, if anyone is on parental leave, it makes no difference because everyone knows all the clients, and there's a common pot – so everyone is equally happy.'[42] In other words, perhaps the problem is not so much that mothers are a bad fit with greedy jobs, but that greedy jobs are a bad fit with being human.

A further problem with dominant groups defining 'fit' is that non-dominant groups can be damned if they don't con-form to their codes, but also damned if they do. A classic illustration of the general principle was provided by fieldwork at three merchant banks in the City of London in 1992 and 1994, revealing the City as 'a gendered arena' that reveres 'a particular masculinized set of performances'. There were two models available: the youthful, supposedly testosterone-fuelled, greedy, sexualizing, risk-taking 'plebeian trader'; and a more senior, blue-blooded, patrician figure, 'stately and rational'.[43] Unsurprisingly, this proved to be a difficult fit for women, while also disadvantaging other potential ascenders to financial thrones on the basis of class, race and sexuality. Women were 'placed in "no win" situations in which their options are to become "one of the boys", a sort of ladette (which does not seem to work), or to be seen as aggressive and pushy, or to be seen as too sedate, too quiet', as one academic put it.[44]

The finance profession remains highly gendered. In hedge

fund management, the Goldilocks 'just right' appetite for risk is to be not too timid, but not too reckless. Or perhaps just to be a white man while taking risks. Performance metrics suggest that females working in the industry have it nailed: if anything, funds run by women outperform those run by men.[45] Nonetheless, Neely's interviewees often suggested that women's risk aversion was an obstacle to success. This perception was shared by women, despite showing little signs of risk aversion themselves. 'It's very non-intuitive to women to make leaps, but leaps are what this business is about,' said one. At the same time, a woman in the business who made evidently risky trades was dubbed too 'aggressive' and avoided, despite her 'great numbers'.[46] Neely also detected racial biases: a black male trader was described as 'arrogant' when he spoke in the highly abstract fashion common in his circle, and as 'threatening' when he responded to losses in the same physically expressive way as his white male counterparts.[47]

While the astronomical wealth of hedge fund management seems a world away to most of us, the industry nonetheless affects our lives. Like private equity firms, hedge funds that own company stocks can put pressure on management to make decisions that will maximize their short-term profits as an investor. The increasing influence of finance has had major effects on how corporations are run, including the rise of the ideology of shareholder primacy. The basic idea here is share price as oracle. Want to know the value being created by a firm? Look at its share price. Want to know how well the CEO is doing? Look at the share price. Want to make sure your CEO performs well? Tie his compensation to share price.

It is hard to overstate how profoundly the principle of shareholder primacy has affected work for all of us. Obviously, it would be rather simplistic to say that the financial system is responsible for all economic injustice, but it's not a bad lump of clay from which to commence moulding a more sophisticated thesis. One major effect of shareholder primacy ideology on corporate strategy has been that companies try to make themselves as tempting as possible to investors and analysts, by offering the highest profits while using the least assets – including human ones. As two business school academics neatly summarized the situation: 'Whereas the conglomerate firms of the 1960s and 1970s sought to straddle the Earth, the contemporary share-priced-oriented firm seeks to dance on the head of the pin.'[48] There not being much room for permanent workers on a pinhead, the rising number of off-pin 'precariat' make do as best they can with insecure employment and uncertain schedules, winningly spun as 'flexibilization'. (This 'pinhead' strategy has subsequently spread to not-for-profit organizations, like universities.)[49]

Corporate ethos has also changed a great deal for those left dancing on the pin to a tune set by share price. For instance, the rise of shareholder primacy, including the linking of CEO pay to short-term stock price changes, has been accompanied by an increase in pay-for-performance reward schemes, to incentivize results that disproportionately benefit upper management.

Is it sheer coincidence that the stalling of women's progress in corporate America coincided with these changes? Not according to legal scholar June Carbone and her colleagues, bringing us back to the gender story woven through the Wells Fargo scandal. In the business world of yore, the proto-typical 'organization man' was 'loyal, complacent, risk averse, and consensus oriented'. As Carbone drily points out, '"he" (and corporate executives in that era were almost all men) could have been a stereotypical woman'.[50] But today, an ethos of high-stakes competition, including pay-for-performance reward schemes that create large inequalities of compensation, select for, and cultivate, quite different qualities.

Readers might remember the shocking demise in 2001 of the once much-vaunted energy company Enron. The company adopted a highly competitive 'rank and yank' system, in which employees ranked in the bottom 20 per cent were fired, and the remainder were lavished with generous bonuses. It was designed as a way to enhance performance. But detailed analysis of Enron's undoing identified this evaluation system 'as a significant factor in its downfall'. The ranking systems were found to 'encourage greater emphasis on self-interest, higher levels of distrust that undermine teamwork, greater homogeneity in the selection of corporate management, less managerial accountability, and more politicized decision-making'.[51] As one journalist observed, the 'most visible consequence was the large amount of time people spent at the local Starbucks, buttering up superiors and bad mouthing peers'.[52]

Carbone links these changes in corporate culture to women's stalled advancement in corporate America by asking: who is likely to succeed in the amoral 'Hobbesian' environments these practices tend to cultivate? First, those who are willing and able to work long hours and behave in Machiavellian ways – both more common in males than females. This is the first part of the triple bind these corporate competitions pose for women.

The second part of the bind is that 'women become less likely to seek positions [in such environments] because they correctly perceive that they could not thrive and are more likely than men to decide they do not wish to do so on such terms'. The effect is to reinforce 'the male-identified character of such environments'.[53]

The third strand of the triple bind is that men have more licence to compete in the ruthless ways that get rewarded. Status norms and in-group biases mean that women 'are disproportionately disliked and punished for displaying the self-centered, rule-breaking behavior of men'.[54] Indeed, a 'gender punishment gap' means that the risks of rule-breaking are demonstrably greater for women in the finance sector. A detailed analysis of data collected by the US Financial Industry Regulatory Authority between 2005 and 2015 found that female financial advisers who engaged in misconduct were punished more harshly than male ones. They were 20 per cent more likely to be fired and 30 per cent less likely to find new work. This gap wasn't explained by differences between women and men in firm, branch, role, time period, costliness of misconduct, productivity, or being a repeat offender. Moreover, the gap was larger in companies with fewer female managers, pointing to straightforward in-group gender bias as the explanation. Reinforcing that explanation was a similar finding of an 'ethnicity punishment gap' for ethnic minority men, exacerbated in firms with lower representation of those men in management. (Among firms, Wells Fargo Advisors stood out as having the biggest gender punishment gap.)[55]

It seems that when looking around for a sacrificial lamb to show that misconduct is taken seriously, managers' eyes apparently tend to quickly skate past other same-ethnicity men who are equal or even bigger rule-breakers. This brings us back to in-group bias. If you are in a dog-eat-dog world, it is helpful if the most powerful dogs welcome you into their pack. When mostly male managers pick out favourites as allies in hyper-competitive environments, they naturally turn to other men 'like them' whom they feel they can trust.

Although Wells Fargo represents (we hope) an extreme case, plenty of organizations operate in a high-stakes, pressure-cooker environment. The scandal lifts the lid on flows of resources towards those at the top, at the expense of those lower down the chain. As Senator Elizabeth Warren put it to John Stumpf when, as Wells Fargo's CEO, he testified before Congress in 2016:

> [Y]ou squeezed your employees to the breaking point so they would cheat customers and you could drive up the value of your stock and put hundreds of millions of dollars in your own pocket. And when it all blew up, you kept your job, you kept your multi-million dollar bonuses and you went on television to blame thousands of $12-an-hour employees who were just trying to meet cross-sell quotas that made you rich.[56]

Highly competitive organizational environments with steep inequalities between 'winners' and 'losers' often give rise to so-called masculinity contest cultures, in which 'top performance' is confused with 'masculine gender performances'. These demonstrations of manhood entail a mix of 'swaggering confidence' and eschewal of any signs of vulnerability; exhausting displays of strength and stamina; a prioritizing of work above everything else, and a tendency to treat the workplace as a 'hypercompetitive or gladiatorial arena'.[57] As social scientist Jennifer Berdahl and colleagues explain, '[w]ork becomes a masculinity contest when organizations focus not on mission but on masculinity, enacted in endless "mine's bigger than yours" contests to display workloads and long schedules (as in law and medicine), cut corners to out-earn everyone else, or shoulder unreasonable risks (as in blue-collar jobs or finance)'.[58]

There are reasonable grounds to be suspicious that the well-paid winners of these corporate competitions may be much better at serving themselves, and others like them, than they are at serving the interests of their organization or its stakeholders. An analysis of co-ownership of global corporations (in 2007) identified 22 financial firms – including Credit Suisse, Lehman Brothers, Bear Stearns and Deutsche Bank AG – as 'the most central players in the global economy'.[59] The people at the top of those companies, predominantly men, were the very handsomely paid winners. Yet at the time of writing, the status of these firms is, respectively: dead and reincarnated; dead; dead; and back from a near-death experience.

Another time-honoured method of creating environments in which women do not feel welcome, and a common feature of masculinity contest cultures, is sexual harassment. An interesting twist in the previously mentioned analysis of the gender punishment gap in financial advisory firms is that it was about twice as big in firms with records of sexual harassment. This is no mere coincidence.

Sexual harassment is sometimes assumed to be an unfortunate side effect of men's prodigious and regrettably incontinent sexual appetites. News media reporting tends to feed that perception, with its focus on celebrity sexual assaults.[60] The allegations about Hollywood film producer Harvey Weinstein's sexually aggressive and predatory behaviour towards young female actors and models were widely reported. The media has been much less likely to cover 'the nonsexual, but still utterly sexist, forms of abuse Weinstein heaped upon less influential women who worked for him', as legal scholar Vicky Schultz points out, including the claims of his abuse by his assistant of 19 years, Zelda Perkins.[61] According to the findings of a four-month investigation by the New York State Attorney General, Weinstein 'regularly berated women using gender-based obscenities and stereotypes', such as 'cunt' and 'pussy'. (Men who displeased him got the same treatment, such as a male executive of whom Weinstein asked another employee, 'Can you smell [his] pussy?') Weinstein was charged with making derogatory enquiries about where female staff were in their menstrual cycles.[62] Some assistants were allegedly 'threatened with termination of employment if they did not serve in gendered roles such as providing childcare to his young children, obtaining prescriptions for medicine, and performing other domestic labor'.[63] According to the charges, he cursed at staff, and 'used his stature and threatening statements . . . to demean and frighten female employees'.[64]

It seemed as if women existed to help Weinstein fulfil his sexual desires and perform housewifely services. Although our attention is grabbed by the former, both abuses serve to mark women as inferior and unwelcome 'outsiders' – or welcome only in gendered or sexualized roles. Sexual harassment is an 'expression of workplace sexism, not of sexuality or sexual desire', argues Schultz. It is 'a way for dominant men to label women (and perceived "lesser" men) as inferior and shore up an idealized masculine work status and identity'.[65] Sex-segregated workplaces are both a cause and consequence of sexual harassment, of which the 'sexual' part is a bit of a red herring:

> From the perspective of the harassers, demanding sexual favors is no different from other sexist demands: regardless of whether a boss pressures female employees to tolerate sexual misconduct, to suffer his angry tirades, to serve food or clear up at work, to take notes or 'tone down' their behavior, to endure being ignored and interrupted, to sit in the back and avoid the limelight, or to attend to his personal needs, these are all patronizing, sex-based demands that preserve gender hierarchy and remind women of their proper place.[66]

In 2010, Julia Gillard became Australia's first (and so far only) female prime minister. The misogyny, sexism and double standards she experienced were astounding.[67] Consider a menu item at a fundraiser dinner for an opposition candidate in 2013: 'Julia Gillard Kentucky Fried Quail', featuring 'Small Breasts, Huge Thighs & A Big Red Box'. (For readers unfamiliar with Australian politicians: yes, the Honourable Julia Gillard is a redhead, and the 'joke' really was that disgusting.) It's hard to imagine a more demeaning, degrading and disrespectful way to refer to a woman holding the highest political office in the country. Yet apparently it was assumed that this grotesquely sexist comment would be well received in elite political fundraising circles. (It was not one of the high-status guests at the fundraiser who had the courage to make this misogyny public, but restaurant staff.)[68]

One historian has speculated that despite Gillard's considerable achievements while in office, 'What will mostly attract historians' attention . . . will be how she was treated, the rabid misogyny, the hysteria of men who could not abide the spectacle of a woman in power, who labelled her a bitch, a witch, a liar, a usurper, an illegitimate claimant who refused to bow down before her male rivals.'[69]

Along similar lines, in a recent study I was involved in, led by psychologist Morgan Weaving, we found that misogynistic online abuse against Hillary Clinton took a significant upward turn in 2015 when she made a bid for political power by announcing her presidential campaign.[70] The abuse rose steadily over the course of her campaign and only plateaued after the election, when the threat of a female president had subsided. In case you are wondering, it was not possible to investigate whether gendered online abuse against Donald

Trump also increased over the campaign period, because there are no male equivalents for 'Shut up and suck my dick', 'Get back in the kitchen' or 'Make me a sandwich'.

Of course, you don't have to be a powerful woman to experience sexual harassment. The most recent national survey of experiences of sexual harassment in Australian workplaces, conducted with more than 10,000 respondents, found that 41 per cent of women (and 26 per cent of men) had been sexually harassed in the last five years.[71] Experiences of low-intensity but high-frequency sexual harassment are consequential. They are linked to decreases in organizational performance and commitment among women, including workplace withdrawals and resignations.[72] And in keeping with the idea that sexual harassment operates as a form of social closure to keep women out of jobs where they don't 'belong', it is more common in workplaces in which men are 'numerically, structurally, or stereotypically dominant'.[73]

Schultz argues that sexual harassment thrives in environments in which those at the top of the hierarchy have relatively unconstrained power to allocate resources – jobs, training, opportunities, bonuses, and so on – and to define merit. This power is corrupting – *I have it, so I must deserve it.* This malignant influence doesn't come from testosterone-induced toxic masculinity or societal patriarchal conditions, but from the 'unchecked, subjective authority that is vested in many men's organizational positions by companies, industries, and the law'.[74] Schultz drolly observes that this point was nailed by Donald Trump, boasting of sexual assaults of women: 'When you're a star, they let you do it. You can do anything.'[75]

In 2024, members of the UK Treasury Select Committee investigating sexism in the City of London declared themselves 'appalled by testimonies we have received about the prevalence of sexual harassment in the financial services industry . . . It is worse in financial services than in many other sectors.' The report described the evidence taken as 'shocking'.[76] No doubt it was. But when considered through the lens of Relations-Thinking, given the riches and power up for grabs, it should hardly have been a surprise.

We've now seen several ways in which the boundaries around resource-rich opportunities are more permeable to (some) men than to women; how their associated identities (such as the 'chief' of a hedge fund, the 'geek' of a well-funded tech start-up, or the 'god' of surgery) are a better fit; and how their in-groups are more welcoming and supportive to them than to outsiders. But viewed from a distance, through rose-coloured spectacles, it can seem as though men just tend to be better suited for such roles. As we'll see in the next few chapters exploring the Different But Equal perspective, efforts to tie Patriarchy Inc.'s arrangements *du jour* to biological forces clumsily attempt to recruit science to support the status quo.

6

DIFFERENCES

'YOU'RE A MISOGYNIST AND A TERRIBLE HUMAN. I WILL keep hounding you until one of us is fired. Fuck you.'[1]

The recipient of this pithy missive, sent by a co-worker, was a junior software engineer at Google called James Damore. In 2017, Damore had written a ten-page memo challenging Google's diversity philosophy and policies, questioning their underlying assumptions about the sexes. In keeping with the tenets of the Different But Equal perspective, he was quite clear that women should enjoy equal opportunities to men in tech. But in accordance with another key plank of that viewpoint, he queried whether Google should expect equality of opportunity to lead to equality of outcome. He warned that in its attempts to create the latter, the company risked undermining equality of opportunity for *men*. A sketchy tour of scientific claims about sex differences in behaviour and their evolutionary and hormonal origins brought Damore to a controversial conclusion. He proposed that 'the distribution of preferences and abilities of men and women differ in part due to biological causes and that these differences may explain why we don't see equal representation of women in tech and leadership'.[2]

Damore sent his memo to the organizers of the company's diversity meetings. He got no response. (Possibly, given the launch the following month of a class-action lawsuit accusing Google of gender discrimination and pay disparities, the team was preoccupied with other matters.)[3] He then posted his memo to internal mailing lists and forums. There, it enjoyed a lively reaction. Some colleagues were supportive. Others, as we have seen, took great offence. Before long, the memo had been leaked to the tech website Gizmodo, and shortly afterwards, the internet exploded. Two days later, Damore was fired 'for advancing harmful gender stereotypes'. Google's chief executive officer, Sundar Pichai, swiftly pitched in with a message to all employees. The company was open to critical commentary about its diversity programmes, he said. However, '[t]o suggest a group of our colleagues have traits that make them less biologically suited to [the work of building Google's products] is offensive and not OK'.[4]

This much-discussed episode generated deeply polarized opinions. To some, it was obviously sexist and wrong-headed to try to trace links between evolved sexual biology and roles in twenty-first-century Silicon Valley. To others, it was no less obvious that evolved sex differences exist, and likely *do* continue to shape the gendered division of labour. Opinions rolled in at a furious pace. Contrasting the headline 'Silicon Valley's Weapon of Choice Against Women – Shoddy Science' with 'No, The Google Manifesto Isn't Sexist or Anti-Diversity.

It's Science' gives a sense of both the range and the passion.[5] Damore was an ill-informed sexist tech bro. No, he was a truth-telling hero. He got the science and its implications wrong. No, he got the science mostly right. He deserved to be fired. Wrong, the bad actor in the episode was Google's CEO, Pichai, who should resign.[6]

As this episode was unfolding, the same contradictions were playing out on the much smaller stage of my own life. While Damore was being publicly shamed on social media for expressing his views about the role of evolution and hormones in creating sex disparities in the workplace, I was being denigrated by a cadre of academics for *challenging* these kinds of claims in a book that had recently won a respected science writing prize. According to one of my critics, my scepticism was a symptom of my unscientific embarrassment about humans' biological heritage. He helpfully directed my attention towards Exhibit A – all other mammals – by way of prosecution of his case that evolution and hormones create psychological sex differences in humans.[7] After all, the reasoning goes, the evolutionary process of sexual selec-tion has given rise to sex role patterns – the most common being competitive males and caring females.[8] These aren't caused by gender stereotypes or patriarchy. Instead, they have been honed through genetic modification over millennia to ensure reproductive success. The male and female mammals that did best on this vital metric passed on their genes to the next generation, while those that behaved in sex-neutral ways that would meet the approval of 'sex-denialist' fem-inists produced far less in the way of progeny. And the primary tool for creating these sex differences in behaviour? Testosterone.

Of course, other animals don't write computer code. Moreover, the diverse and often arbitrary nature of gendered divisions of labour suggests cultural rather than biological inheritance as the important force. This includes the parenting roles we have in common with other animals, as we saw in earlier chapters. Scientifically speaking it should be considered a virtue, rather than the vice of special pleading, to liberate our minds from the assumption that when it comes to understanding human sex differences in behaviour, it is always best to modestly downplay our differences from rats and chimpanzees.

These points have not stopped some Evolutionary Psychologists from extrapolating from (varied) sex roles in other animals to gender roles in highly specialized divisions of labour in complex post-industrial economies. For example, Evolutionary Psychologist and writer Steve Stewart-Williams, together with co-author Lewis G. Halsey, suggest that evolved sex differences in values – men's greater commitment to paid work in the market versus unpaid work in the home – help to explain the persistent gender gap in time-greedy STEM jobs. Because women grow and feed babies with their own bodies, far outweighing men's minimum contribution, these researchers suggest an evolved 'inherited contribution' to sex differences in work versus family priorities.[9] Men can potentially do better than women, reproductively, from investing time pursuing status and resources (and therefore supposedly more opportunities to mate with many different women). In contrast, they argue, women invest more in existing offspring. Thus, it is therefore 'little surprise that more men than women prioritize the pursuit of status over family, whereas more women than men prioritize family and work-life balance'.[10]

To further explain men's greater representation in today's most valorized source of knowledge, science, Stewart-Williams and Halsey point to 'ancient, more primal differences' stemming from gendered divisions of labour among our ancestors: 'specifically the fact that women specialized in caring for the young, whereas men specialized in hunting and perhaps waging war with other groups . . . To fit them to these roles, women may have evolved a stronger attentiveness to the needs of the young, and to people in general, whereas men may have evolved a stronger interest in the tools used for hunting and warfare.'[11]

Linking spear-throwing prowess to interest and skill in microbiology, physics and software engineering is quite a stretch. There is also something of the feel of the Flintstones to the picture they paint of the daily life of our forebears, a throwback to the 1950s that jibes poorly both with the present and the past. Nowadays men, who are supposed to be work-prioritizing and resource-hungry, are less likely than women to invest in status-enhancing tertiary education,[12] and across the globe perform less work overall than women.[13] This fact is obscured by the distinction Stewart-Williams and Halsey draw between (unpaid) family work and work work, a separation that developed just a few centuries ago with industrialization. Their facile adoption of the ideal of motherhood as a devoted and exclusive calling, at odds with the many forms of hard work women throughout history have combined with childcare, hails from the same evolutionarily recent era.

Another example of applying evolutionary arguments to STEM representation comes from Evolutionary Psychologist David Schmitt's cautious commentary about the Damore episode. Schmitt judges some of Damore's claims to be fanciful. He also comes down in favour of Google's diversity practices, as an antidote to the gendered biases and barriers faced by women working in tech. However, he does agree with Damore that it 'seems likely' that 'culturally universal and biologically-linked sex differences' in personal values, some cognitive abilities, and occupational interests 'play some role in the gendered hiring patterns of Google employees'.[14]

But 'culturally universal' is a claim to be used with caution. Across cultures, 'expected' patterns can be remarkably small, non-existent, or even reversed. For example, Schmitt cites a cross-cultural study of sex differences in mental rotation (the ability to mentally rotate an object, or to imagine how it might look from a different perspective) that found a consistent male advantage across 53 nations, as well as consistent sex differences in occupational preferences.[15] While this might seem impressively diverse, participants were recruited via an internet survey run by the BBC. Much as I like to think of devotion to Britain's national broadcaster as an affection that unites the entire species, this participant pool is not exactly a wide sweep of humanity. As English-speaking internet users, they were presumably also well versed in the gender coding of the occupations (such as builder, car mechanic and carpenter versus costume designer, florist and social worker). And researchers who venture further culturally afield have found that sex differences in spatial abilities like navigational skills and mental rotation are not always found among non-industrialized, subsistence-based societies. Instead, they depend on local ecology and gender roles.[16] (To my knowledge, no one has asked hunter-gatherer foragers if they would rather be a car mechanic or a social worker.)

Sex differences in personal values can also surprise. For example, the value of universalism refers to the motivation to appreciate and promote the welfare of people and the environment, demonstrated by interest in social justice, equality, world peace and environmental protection. Western readers will think of this as a feminine value, and sure enough, it is more strongly held in women than men, on average, in many countries. Finnish female students, for example, on average express greater endorsement of the values of universalism than men (about two thirds of male students score below the average woman). Yet among Ethiopians, the pattern is roughly reversed, and in many other countries, no differences between the sexes are found.[17]

Moving beyond Schmitt's proposals, other examples of cross-cultural variation in sex differences in personality that see 'expected' patterns disappear or reverse include physical aggression in adolescents (effectively no differences are seen in Zambia, Tonga, Benin and Ghana),[18] agreeableness (sex similarity, or more agreeableness among men, were seen in Albania, Brunei, Cuba, the Dominican Republic, El Salvador, Finland, Ghana, Jamaica, Kenya, Kuwait, Mauritius, Morocco,

Myanmar, Nepal, Nigeria and Trinidad)[19] and self-reported economic risk-taking (with similar male and female risk-taking reported in a small proportion of the sampled countries).[20]

Or consider a recent study that separated out personality traits from the broad boughs of personality domains (like agreeableness), through to branches (like trust and tender-mindedness), to the little twigs of individual items (like 'I believe other people have good intentions').[21] Using machine learning techniques the researchers found that, contrary to what you would expect if there was a strong underlying coherence to personality differences between women and men, sex was better predicted across countries using little twigs distributed all over the 'tree' of personality, rather than with localised branches or boughs. Moreover, *which* combinations of individual items were most predictive of sex varied from country to country. In other words, 'many gender differences are specific to narrow traits and geographical contexts', and it is 'virtually impossible to predict someone's behaviour, thinking and feeling from their gender'.[22] It is striking that the largest sex differences were found for really arbitrary questions. It is easy to create plausible-sounding evolutionary stories about sex differences out of the rich cloth of concepts like agreeableness (*women have evolved to be less well suited to the competitive world of business*). It's harder to weave them out of idiosyncratic gossamer threads like 'I love flowers' and 'I believe in the importance of art' (to name the two largest sex differences), or 'I am often in a bad mood' and 'I like to begin new things' (to cite the items with the lowest cross-cultural variability).[23]

What about the common argument that occupational

sex-segregation can be traced back to testosterone? Canadian journalist Debra Soh offers a typical rendition of such arguments in her book *The End of Gender: Debunking the Myths About Sex and Identity in our Society*:

> Lower levels [of testosterone in utero] are associated with a preference for people-oriented activities and occupations, stemming from evolutionary roots. Women, who are tasked with the role of bearing children, evolved to be more sociable, empathic, and people-focused, while men, as hunter-gatherers, were rewarded for strong visuospatial skills and the ability to build and use tools. This explains why STEM (science, technology, engineering, and mathematics) fields tend to be dominated by men.[24]

In principle, this is a perfectly reasonable idea. Even a cultural evolutionary perspective, as we saw, points to a few different possibilities when it comes to whether and how gendered mindshaping might be helped along by sex-linked biology. To briefly recap, one option is that there is nothing special about gendered mindshaping. Every human society includes visibly different members of both sex categories. The wealth of information about gender roles in our culturally constructed niche, in combination with powerful social learning abilities, is what leads infants to pay attention to sex categories, soak up gender norms, develop a gender identity, imitate others of the same sex, and so on. An alternative view is that we evolved a biologically inherited propensity to pay attention to, and learn from, people of the same sex. An extension of this idea is that through gene–culture coevolution, we became genetically endowed with sex-differentiated learning biases that facilitated the ancestral gendered division of labour, such as an interest in infants (for females) versus propulsive motion (for males). But as I mentioned in chapter 1, there is currently little evidence to support this interesting proposal. So where do these confident claims linking testosterone and twenty-first-century post-industrial jobs come from?

These assertions lean heavily on studies of groups of children and adults who experienced atypical hormonal environments *in utero* and were reared as members of their genetic sex. The idea is that these 'experiments of nature' enable scientists to tease apart what normally goes together: female-typical hormone exposure and gender socialization as a girl; or male-typical hormone exposure and gender sociali-zation as a boy.[25]

The most extensive research of this kind comes from studies of girls and women with a genetic condition called congenital adrenal hyperplasia (CAH) that affects the adrenal glands. One consequence of the condition is the production of excess androgens (including testosterone) during foetal devel-opment.[26] Supposedly, by comparing the gendered behaviour of girls with and without the condition, researchers roughly isolate the effects of androgens on the brain, over and above the effects of gender socialization as a girl.

Interesting but often overlooked are the many ways in which girls with CAH are similar to other girls. Some might expect the extra testosterone they experienced prenatally to

154

create differences in spatial abilities, verbal abilities, aggression, competitiveness, assertiveness, dominance and (if you subscribe to a belief in female intellectual inferiority) general intelligence. But sadly for the quest for a biological explanation to explain gender representation at Google, research has failed to find consistent support for differences in these traits between girls with and without CAH.[27]

However, studies *do* consistently find that girls with CAH are more interested in 'boy toys' and less interested in 'girl toys' than are girls without the condition.[28] As we've seen, this is commonly taken as a decisive blow against the idea that these gendered interests are created purely by social expectations. Instead, the argument goes, male-typical hormones drive a greater interest in masculine objects and activities, while female-typical hormones contribute to a greater interest in feminine ones. That's why girls with CAH, whose prenatal hormonal profile includes more androgens than is typical for their sex, have more boyish preferences.

As an important critic of these arguments, Rebecca Jordan-Young, explains, the theory underpinning it

> rests on a very simple idea: the brain is a sort of accessory reproductive organ. Males and females don't just need different genitals in order to have sex, or different gonads that make the egg and sperm necessary for conception. Males and females also need different brains so they are predisposed to complementary sexual desires and behaviors that lead to reproduction. This theory suggests that the same mechanism is responsible

for both kinds of development – that is, for sexual differentiation of 'both sets' of reproductive organs: the genitals and the brain.[29]

That mechanism is the hormones produced by the gonads (testes and ovaries), with testosterone enjoying a starring role. The idea is that these hormones, acting very early in development, 'organize' the brain with male or female circuitry. (These circuits can then sometimes be 'activated' later in life, such as during the mating season or in pregnancy.) Support for the theory comes from experimental animal research. For example, when scientists tinker with early hormone exposure by exposing females to high levels of androgens, the animals show more male-typical reproductive behaviour, and fewer female-typical varieties, later in life.

But the kinds of behaviour studied in animals are very different to the gendered division of behaviour in complex human societies.[30] Testosterone-linked behaviours in animals – like one rat mounting another – are relatively simple and reflexive. The rat does not pause to consider long-term consequences: how he will feel about the relationship in the morning, or whether the act will increase or decrease his social standing as a result of office gossip. In contrast, the kinds of behaviours observed or measured in studies of girls and women with CAH are far more intentional. They involve activities like pretending to bottle-feed a baby doll, play-fighting with action figures or a toy car, or considering what jobs one might enjoy. To a greater or lesser degree, they involve people representing their actions – their goals, purpose, motives – to themselves. To return to the idea of the self-constituting narrative, these actions are part of the person's unfolding story of 'who I am'. They recruit parts of the brain that barely exist in rats, and features of the self-conscious mind that are probably uniquely human.

In her interviews of key scientists studying females with CAH, Jordan-Young found that many thought the more boyish behaviour in this group could be explained in terms of 'developmental cascades'. To take the metaphor of a marble rolling down a landscape of hills and valleys, the idea here is that a prenatal hormonally induced 'spin' on the marble inclines it in a particular developmental direction. That trajectory is then maintained by a deepening of the valley of that pathway – nature recruits nurture. Young girls tend to gravitate towards feminine activities and objects, boys towards masculine ones, and these tendencies are then noticed and responded to by their caregivers. Over time, typical boys and girls roll further apart.

But as Jordan-Young observes, 'this is only half the story – one in which the small initial differences almost inevitably grow larger as additional effects accumulate. But an early push in a certain direction can be either enhanced or entirely eliminated by subsequent experience, such that development from that point forward would proceed as though the early hormone exposure had never happened.'[31] This is not mere hopeful theorizing. Even when it comes to animal mating behaviour, some 'organizing' effects of hormones, rather than being permanent, are readily modified by experience.[32] To be clear, Jordan-Young's point isn't that early hormones don't really do anything. It's rather that the effects of these hormones on behaviour should be seen as an '*interim state* in the organism's development'.[33] And while the time between birth and adult-hood is counted in weeks and months if you are a rat, for humans it is counted in years and decades, and is saturated in mindshaping. 'The widest canyon', writes philosopher John Dupré, 'leads to the "normal", i.e., most typical, outcome.' But the topology of the landscape itself can change, as alterations to the many factors that normally hold it in place – and here, the culturally constructed niche joins genes and hormones – flatten hills, create new valleys or divert the marble to side canyons.[34] As the evidence for cross-cultural diversity in sex differences nicely demonstrates, even from a sex-tilted initial starting point, many and varied developmental outcomes are possible.

So, what is going on with girls with CAH?

This is a useful moment to return to the concept of gender identity as a story, if you will, of oneself as a woman, man, boy, girl or some other gender category, that helps us to chart our marble-like journey down the landscape of life. Gender identity is shaped throughout the life course by continuous interactions between personal factors that include biological proclivities, but also self-conceptions, goals, personal stand-ards about how to behave, social influences from caregivers, peers, teachers and media, and the experiences gained from one's own actions in the world.[35] Girls with CAH often end up 'off cascade' when it comes to gender role interests. But it is hasty to attribute this to the effect of prenatal testosterone on biological proclivities. Many factors swirling in and out of ongoing gender identity development are very different for females with CAH, compared with their non-clinical counterparts, as Jordan-Young has pointed out.[36] For example, depending on the level of androgens they experience *in utero,* girls with CAH may be born with an enlarged clitoris, sometimes so much so that it resembles a penis. CAH also has significant effects on height, weight, skin and hair, resulting in a more masculine appearance in girls that breaches conventional feminine standards of appearance. Jordan-Young suggests that these physical consequences of the condition might contribute to the slightly higher rates of a male gender identity observed in this clinical population, as well as the observed rates of higher unhappiness and dissatisfaction with a female gender identity.

The girls with CAH participating in these studies have also commonly experienced intense, protracted medical management, potentially involving multiple genital surgeries, including in infancy. They may face fertility problems. They are likely to have experienced 'invasive physical procedures and persistent scrutiny and heightened concern about gender and sexuality'.[37] Jordan-Young also suggests that the diagnosis of CAH itself – not to mention the experience of being born with masculinized or otherwise atypical genitalia – quite possibly 'activates expectations of masculinization'. There is, she argues, likely to be a 'looping' effect, whereby these girls are, as she puts it, 'seen as having a "diminished" femininity, or rather, are *suspected of being masculine'.*[38] This, in turn, may shape their behaviour and sense of self.

Further evidence that the hills and valleys of gender

identity development are unusual in this population comes from findings that girls with CAH aren't as responsive to cues saying 'this toy is for girls and this toy is for boys'. In one study, researchers showed various paired gender-neutral items to girls and boys between four and eleven years of age.[39] They were told that the green balloon was 'for girls' and the silver balloon was 'for boys' (or vice versa). Other objects, like a toy cow paired with a toy horse, were shown being chosen by either a man or woman, a form of gender modelling. The researchers then looked at whether children chose the items culturally cued as being 'for them'. Boys, and girls without CAH, reliably conformed to these brief, fictional gender cues. Simply seeing a man select a toy cow and a woman choose a toy horse or being told that the green balloon is for girls while silver ones are for boys increases the chances that a boy will want the cow and the silver balloon. In contrast, girls with CAH seemed to be impervious to these gender cues. A later study along somewhat similar lines found that while two thirds of control girls preferred stereotypical pink over stereo-typical blue, the ratio was flipped for girls with CAH.[40]

In other words, for reasons that have yet to be worked out, gender self-socialization is atypical in this group. And, of course, without gender self-socializing, mindshaping will be less effective.

Why don't girls with CAH show the same propensity to gender-self-socialize, compared with many other girls? Perhaps there is a direct effect of prenatal androgen exposure on sensitivity to same-sex cues. Maybe there is a direct effect of hormones on gender identity. It could be that as these girls come to realize that they don't especially like 'girl stuff', this dampens the motivation to conform to gender norms.[41] Or perhaps there are *indirect* effects of the kind Jordan-Young suggests — that they and others don't have the same expectations about what they are 'meant' to be like. This is an intriguing idea — perhaps these girls represent what happens when girls are no longer expected to conform to gender norms.

We can't make any confident claims about *why* girls with CAH show more boyish play preferences. But it seems plausible that the effects of atypical hormones on the boyish play behaviour of girls with CAH is influenced by differences in their mindshaping experiences. In fact, it is arguably *more* plausible than a story in which testosterone directly affects the brain in ways that makes 'boy toys' such as toy cars, construction tools, toy guns and blocks more appealing. This is because it is very difficult to explain what these 'boy toys' have in common, other than that they are culturally designated as 'for boys' in a particular time and place. What features distinguish them from the balls, board games, books and puzzles that are dubbed gender-neutral? We can ask the same question about 'girl toys'. What do dolls, toy telephones, irons, play kitchens and comb-and-brush sets have in common that could be linked to female-typical prenatal hormones?

The challenge deepens when we look further afield. For example, the study of children's play in Hadza and BaYaka hunter-gatherer societies, mentioned in chapter 1, found that boys and girls were quite similar in their likelihood of participating in what in the Global North would be coded as masculine play, such as playing at making tools, or in 'object play', including 'playing with balls . . . throwing rocks, chopping down trees for the purpose of fun, building toys, such as making balls out of rubber or leaves, fixing dolls, fixing play spears, and making toys'.[42]

There is a similar problem with studies showing that girls with CAH have more masculine career interests than girls without the condition. The most rigorous of these used a measure called the Occupational Interests Inventory, which solicits the appeal of six well-known dimensions of occupations, informally known as Doers, Thinkers, Creators, Helpers, Persuaders and Organizers (of stuff, such as data, not people).[43] These six dimensions are also often boiled down into a single 'things versus people' dimension. The Doers, Thinkers and Organizers components contribute to the 'things' dimension, while the Helpers, Creators and Persuaders components contribute to the 'people' dimension.[44]

Among the control children, the researchers found substantial sex differences in four of five dimensions. Boys were a lot more interested than girls in Doer occupations, and they were also significantly *less* interested in Helper, Creator and Persuader jobs.[45] As a result, on the 'things versus people' measure, boys were significantly shifted towards the 'things' end, compared with unaffected girls. So far, so unsurprising, since sex differences on the 'things versus people' dimension are well established.[46] The big question is whether there is a biological contribution to those differences – supposedly revealed by comparing girls with and without CAH. The researchers found that girls with CAH were significantly more interested than control girls in both Doer and Thinker occupations (but with no statistically significant difference for the Helper, Creator and Persuader jobs), pushing them further towards 'things' preferences (though not to the same degree as boys). Moreover, the extent of the shift was related to prenatal androgen exposure. The researchers therefore concluded that their results 'support the hypothesis that sex differences in occupational interests are due, in part, to prenatal androgen influences on differential orientation to objects versus people'.[47]

But were researchers really comparing 'things–people' rather than 'men's jobs–women's jobs'? As psychologist Virginia Valian has argued, simply labelling a dimension 'things versus people' doesn't make it so. Consider the Doer subscale, which is the one that most strongly contributes to the sex difference in interest in 'things'. (It includes items like 'repair and test locks', 'drive a truck to deliver packages to offices and homes', and 'put out forest fires'.)[48] Valian suggests that unexamined preconceptions about which sex *does stuff with things* have influenced the very creation of the items for the subscale. Why, for example, do items tapping interest in 'things' not include activities like 'Take apart and try to reassemble a dress' or 'Try to recreate a dish tasted in a restaurant'?[49]

Taking together all three subscales that make up the 'things' dimension entails conceptualizing 'things' so broadly – including the 'global economy, string theory, mental representations, or tennis' – that the term 'is vacuous'.[50] Although the items of this scale do cluster together statistically, as Valian notices, there is no obvious feature that links them. Instead, she suggests, 'there is an underlying concept that indirectly ties those items together. Radically different items that exemplify the underlying concept can cluster together if they are different aspects of an underlying theme. In this case, the underlying theme is "activities that men have tended to spend more time at than women have".[51]

Valian's point is well illustrated by the occupations used to represent Doer occupations in the study of girls with CAH, such as auto mechanic, auto racer, farmer, building contractor, carpenter and electronics technician. The male-typing wasn't inevitable. There are other occupations, surely equally worthy of 'things' classification, that are gender-balanced, or even female-dominated: bakers, bookbinders, compositors and typesetters, decorators and window-dressers, furriers, jewellers, tailors, textile and garment crafts and food assembly.[52] If the study were run without conflating 'things' jobs with masculine jobs, would we find that girls with CAH are more interested in window-dressing, jewellery and dressmaking than other girls? It is at least as plausible that we see exactly the opposite, because perhaps the reason girls with CAH are less likely to conform to local cultural meanings of femininity is because they are less sensitive to gender norms.

The scientists who do this research typically reject the suggestion that unusual gender socializing experienced by girls with CAH might account for their greater interest in masculine activities. They point out that they have done studies in which they observe parents with their children in the lab, to see if, for instance, girls with CAH get more latitude to play with 'boy toys'. The findings are a bit mixed in this respect.[53] But regardless, the bigger problem is that gender socialization is being conceived in a simplistic 'blank slate' view: Step 1 is for caregivers to categorize the child as a boy or girl; step 2 is to enforce gender conformity. But as should by now be clear, this is a very impoverished understanding of how we are shaped into gender roles.

The same problem stalks recent research with another clinical group – men with a rare hormonal condition called isolated gonadotropin-releasing hormone deficiency, in which the testes don't produce androgens as they normally would. Males with this condition experience 'low or absent gonadal hormone production after the first trimester of gestation' and beyond, until hormone replacement therapy begins.[54] Nonetheless, due to typical androgen production in the first trimester, the external genitalia develop as unambiguously male. So the boys are recorded as male at birth, and raised as boys. Usually, the condition isn't even diagnosed until puberty doesn't begin at the expected time.

From a perspective that sees gendered behaviour as the combined product of hormonal effects on the brain and 'blank slate' style socialization, this clinical group seems to offer a clean way of testing for hormonal influences. The researchers therefore asked the men to recall how gender-conforming they were as children, using a measure so quaint it reads as though its creators drew on a close study of Enid Blyton books for inspiration. According to the questionnaire, to be masculine is to like outside chores like house painting, to be drawn to racing cars and adventure stories, to dream of being a pilot, a courageous leader or a hunter of big game, and to play base-ball and football. To be feminine is to play with dolls and marbles, to experiment with cosmetics and jewellery, to aspire to being a dancer or a dressmaker, to prefer cleaning houses to painting them, and to immerse oneself in romance.[55]

Once again, we have the familiar problem of late-twentieth-century Western gender norms being implicitly treated as timeless, universal markers of biologically driven masculinity and femininity. Feminist scientists have been pointing this out since the 1980s.[56] But there is another issue. With a more sophisticated understanding of gender develop-ment in mind than the 'blank slate' model, other information becomes relevant. For example, depending on the underlying cause of isolated gonadotropin-releasing hormone deficiency, boys may experience a lack of smell, cleft lip and palate, hear-ing problems, a missing kidney, or eye movement issues. There are also potentially a range of issues that make it harder to live up to masculine gender norms of physical prowess – such as 'mirror hand movement' (this is where, when one arm is inten-tionally moved, especially the hands and fingers, the limbs, hands or fingers on the other side move too) and cerebellar ataxia (linked to a wide range of issues, including unsteady gait, poor hand–eye coordination and double vision).[57] Mean-while, the hormonal disruption can result in undescended testes or microphallus in roughly 20 to 40 per cent of men.[58] (The condition also requires medical intervention in the form of hormonal treatment to stimulate pubertal changes, fertility and testosterone secretion.)[59]

It is surely not that much of a stretch to suggest that such physical limitations and experiences could shape gender identity processes.[60] A child with cerebellar ataxia may well struggle with activities like playing soccer in the playground, and is likely to know that being a pilot or racing driver or standing on tall ladders to paint houses are unwise career options. Nor is it unreasonable to suggest that for a man looking back on his boyhood, the knowledge that his testes don't produce androgens might shape recollections and responses to questions such as how masculine he felt compared with other boys. It was suggested that the clinical group might remember being *more* masculine than they actually were.[61] In my view, the reverse seems more plausible. (And interestingly, on a measure of masculine behaviour *not* susceptible to memory bias – namely, exclusive sexual attraction to women – there was no difference between the clinical group and controls.)[62] The point is, we just don't know.

All of this makes it especially difficult to know what to make of the fact that men with atypically low prenatal testosterone exposure reported non-trivially less childhood gender conformity. But importantly, their scores were much more like those of other men than like women's.[63] In other words, a male gender identity, and being in the social world as a boy, is enough to ensure masculine gender role conformity. If, as the Patriarchy Inc. account proposes, gender roles are primarily culturally inherited, this is just what we would expect.

The debate rolls on. Evolutionary Psychologist David Geary recently drew on evolutionary claims about neurobiological differences between the sexes to argue that

> sex differences in occupational segregation in STEM and in other areas of life are not surprising and not likely to change even with continent-wide interventions.

Pushing the equal-outcomes agenda in STEM and in other socially valuable areas provides feel-good experiences for gender activists, a self-serving diversion of the public's money, and lots of bureaucratic jobs. But in many cases, it will not have the intended effects and it is therefore not a good use of these resources.[64]

I don't think that subscribing to Evolutionary Psychologists' views on sex differences in personality makes someone a misogynist or a terrible human – the charge levied at James Damore. But it *does* seem to be rather strongly correlated with overconfidence and casualness when it comes to the standards of evidence acceptable for inferring that the divisions of labour that maintain men's higher status and power have biological roots. The cavalier spirit continues in the next chapter, as conclusions that sex differences persist or are even enhanced in gender-egalitarian countries are marshalled as evidence that contemporary gender arrangements represent a 'natural state' of happily 'different but equal' gender relations.

7

GIRL, UNINTERRUPTED?

IN 1957, A PROGRAMMER CALLED ELSIE SHUTT founded a freelance programming business, Computations, Inc., based in Harvard, Massachusetts. It was a pioneering entrepreneurial move on Shutt's part, given the fledgling nature of the software services industry at that time. But her enterprise would be considered extraordinary even today. By design, her workforce comprised new mothers, working part-time from home.

The business came about because state law forced Shutt to leave her programming job at a company called Raytheon Computing when she became pregnant (as Janet Abbate describes in *Recoding Gender: Women's Changing Participation in Computing*).[1] Keen to continue working, she took on freelance work to do at home while waiting for her baby to arrive. With more work available than she could handle on her own, she recruited two new mothers to join her. As the business grew, she continued to deliberately hire mothers of young children. Indeed, the business 'soon developed an explicit social mission of providing rewarding technical work for at-home mothers; profit was secondary', Abbate explains.[2]

The business model was a success – arguably not despite its unusual workforce, but *because* of it. Motherhood created necessities that in turn birthed invention. Shutt had to coordinate physically dispersed part-time workers, in the days before email and Zoom. The women stayed in touch with weekly meetings and phone calls. But overcoming the remaining communication gap spurred her to implement practices and habits – collaboration, meticulous programming, painstaking double-checking of code and careful documentation of each coding step – to keep things running smoothly and efficiently. This collective, thorough approach went against the grain of the prevailing programming culture. From the 1960s, employers were complaining about competitive, macho programmers who refused to share their code (and the glory).[3] Clients clearly appreciated the results produced from within the quite different ethos of Computations, Inc. Forty-five years later, it was still in business.

Shutt established her career at a time when women enjoyed 'a significant presence' in computing's early history – as code-breaking programmers during World War II, and in the early post-war computer industry.[4] Numerically, the industry was still male-dominated and women tended to be clustered in lower-paid, less prestigious jobs within computer specialities.[5] But being a woman was not necessarily in conflict with being a programmer – it was not yet a clearly masculine pursuit. As this newly minted occupation sought to define and establish itself, programming was variously framed as 'high or low status, abstract or concrete, creative or routine', in ways that shaped women's prospects and 'fit' quite independently of the actual work.[6] Experts who thought women well suited to programming often drew comparisons between programming work and feminine pursuits. Programming required fastidiousness, perseverance and attention to detail – like embroidery and dressmaking. Programming was a kind of puzzle-solving – like crosswords. Programming was like teaching maths – just with a computer, rather than a child, as pupil. Programming was like writing a humanities essay – no need for a degree in mathematics, engineering or the sciences. Programming was like cooking dinner – just with data, rather than ingredients, being prepared and combined in a time-sensitive order. Programming was a labour of love, much like mothering – requiring endlessly patient coaxing and effort. As Elsie Shutt reflected in 2001: 'It really amazed me that these *men* were programmers, because I thought it was women's work!'[7]

In many parts of the world, computer science remains relatively ungendered. For example, in Qatar and the United Arab Emirates – countries not exactly famed for female emancipation – nearly equal or greater numbers of women compared with men graduate from computer science bachelor degree programmes.[8] Why? One broad-brush answer is that the cultural journey of gender roles in these countries is currently paused on shared beliefs that computer science is an appropriate occupation for women.

The advocates of the Different But Equal perspective offer a quite different explanation: women from the Middle East have less freedom to pursue occupations that match what women are *really* like (on average).

The argument is inspired by a phenomenon often described as the 'gender equality paradox'. The paradox is that gender gaps in some personality traits and occupational roles (like being a coder) are *larger* in countries in which women enjoy greater equality with men. This, say Different But Equal-ers, poses a serious threat for claims that the social forces of patriarchy offer the most powerful explanation of gender roles in those more egalitarian countries.

To help understand the underlying logic, consider the problem identified by John Stuart Mill that, so long as women are subordinate to men, 'no one can safely pronounce that if women's nature were left to choose its direction as freely as men's, and if no artificial bent were attempted to be given to it except that required by the conditions of human society, and given to both sexes alike, there would be any material difference, or perhaps any difference at all, in the character and capacities which would unfold themselves'.[9]

According to the Different But Equal-ers, we now have the necessary data in hand. The method of gender equality paradox research is to rank countries according to how far they have progressed in straightening that 'artificial bent' due to women's subordination. This is usually done using global gender equality indices, which track women's position vis-à-vis markers of emancipation, such as political power, education, health and economic participation. (I'll refer to higher-ranked countries as more gender-egalitarian.) Scores correlate strongly with economic development – more gender-egalitarian countries are also wealthier, offering even more freedom to their residents.[10] The next step of the approach is to look at gender gaps in personality – how different are women and men in each country? Do those gaps get bigger or smaller as the 'artificial bent' of women's oppression decreases?

A variety of gender gaps have now been run through the gender equality paradox research mill. A recent review of this growing body of research found little evidence of any of these gaps being *smaller* in more gender-egalitarian countries. It did, however, find studies reporting larger gender gaps in more gender-egalitarian countries when it came to reading, mathematics attitudes and personality.[11] Different But Equal-ers argue that these findings are fatally paradoxical for 'blank slate' social science and feminist explanations of those sex differences. If it is the gender system that pushes the sexes apart, how can sex differences stay the same or even get *bigger* as the force of gender gets *weaker*?

Different But Equal-ers offer a solution to the apparent paradox: rich, gender-egalitarian countries allow 'the character and capacities' of both sexes to 'unfold' freely. Or, as Evolutionary Psychologists put it in an article published in 2008: 'personality traits of men and women . . . [are] less constrained and more able to naturally diverge in developed nations. In less fortunate social and economic conditions, innate personality differences between men and women may be attenuated.'[12]

In his infamous Google memo arguing for biological and evolutionary explanations for the low representation of women in tech, James Damore drew on this same article, quoting the researchers' suggestion that 'as a society becomes more prosperous and more egalitarian, innate dispositional differences between men and women have more space to develop'.[13]

Although there was a rush for the exits by a number of scientists on whose work Damore had drawn, some academics have made similar arguments. Like Damore, some even issue warnings to policymakers not to ignore what this evidence is telling us. Evolutionary Psychologists are fond of patronizingly telling feminist critics that they don't need to 'deny' biology in order to improve society: we shouldn't equate what is natural with what is right.[14] But when it comes to the gendered division of labour, it seems some think the two *do* go hand-in-hand. For example, Stewart-Williams and Halsey draw on gender equality paradox findings to suggest that sex differences in STEM participation are a 'sign of social health'. They propose that 'in an enriched and relatively unconstrained environment, nascent differences between individuals – and average differences between the sexes – have more opportunity to emerge and grow'. This includes 'greater freedom to pursue what interests them and to nurture their own individuality'.[15] The authors therefore warn against policies that could potentially 'exact a toll' by encouraging occupational outcomes that 'override people's preferences'.[16]

A recent contribution to a themed economics journal issue on sex differences ran a similar line of argument. The authors claimed that 'understanding men and women's differing occupational choices in the light of knowledge about variance in traits that are predominantly biologically informed resolves the [gender equality] paradox'.[17] Translation: when they have the freedom, women and men choose different jobs, mainly for biological reasons.

The authors summarily dismiss decades of careful criticism of simplistic hormonal, neural and evolutionary explanations of sex differences in personality. Even scholarly books published by prestigious academic presses are disregarded as ideologically skewed popular science.[18] For example, the authors assert that testosterone mediates sex differences in risk-taking, despite extensive challenges to such claims.[19] They draw an even longer bow by then linking this idea to the fact that most 'Fortune 500 CEOs, Wall street [sic] yuppies, inventors, and other successful entrepreneurs' are male, but also so are most 'business failures, destitutes, drop-outs and fatalities'. Predictably, they follow-up with the smooth Different But Equal reassurance that '[d]ifferences between groups do not imply that one group is better or worth more than the other overall'.[20] The implication is merely that it is biologically natural for elite men to hold the majority of positions of authority and oversized shares of resources, for women to be mediocre, and for less fortunate men to be economically left far behind or meet untimely death.

Having explained the biological basis of the occupational status quo, the researchers then issue a warning to policymakers that '[t]o include biologically-based differences between women and men as inputs into scholarly theorizing of occupational segregation is an important path towards improving political decision making.'[21] For those of us prophesied to be biologically inclined to less glamorous roles in the division of labour, it may be comforting to know that those who draw on gender equality paradox patterns as support for such ideas rest their case on shaky empirical and conceptual grounds.

On the empirical side, the evidence for the gender equality paradox is complex, and doesn't yet lend itself to confident claims. STEM is one of the most intensively researched domains, with many studies reporting relationships between global gender equality index rank and STEM-related achievement, attitudes, aspirations and choices. According to the gender equality paradox, more egalitarian countries should have lower female participation in STEM. But relentless scientific scrutiny and refinement of how this research is done has led one recent team of researchers to conclude that the evidence for the gender equality paradox 'is generally inconsistent and weak'.[22] For instance, statistical patterns seen in some datasets aren't seen in others. Gender equality paradox results can be contingent on which index is used, or fail to replicate when researchers use the most sensible subscales of those indices. Moreover, statistical modelling suggests that the gender gap in strength in science (relative to maths and reading) doesn't neatly increase in a linear fashion as global gender equality index score increases. Rather, results are driven by outliers at either end: namely, Nordic countries with larger gender gaps because girls have pulled ahead in reading (not because they are weak in science or maths); and Arabic countries with smaller gender gaps because hard-working girls are outperforming boys across the board. This deflationary conclusion should make us very cautious about scattered reports of 'gender equality paradox' patterns for other less heavily studied personality variables.

Another issue with the very idea of the gender equality paradox is the tacit assumption that the gender equality index captures a single dimension of gender equality that runs from (very unequal) Iraq to (almost equal) Iceland. The problem is well illustrated by a feature of the indices themselves: the different subscales that are put together to calculate the overall score don't necessary intercorrelate much with each other.[23] The gender system is multidimensional, and the various facets of gender equality don't neatly rise and fall in synchrony. This isn't so surprising when we understand the gender system as gender roles *evolving* rather than simply withering away. Ironically, Different But Equal ideology itself offers a good example. As political, economic and social factors pushed towards greater female emancipation,[24] Different But Equal attitudes partly replaced the gender traditionalism of fixed gender roles and male supremacy that offered a pleasing ideological pairing for last century's division of labour.[25]

Also, while rich gender-egalitarian countries surely have 'less' gender in some respects, they have 'more' gender in others. Children are absolutely saturated in gendered culture from birth, and caregivers in post-industrial countries appear to spend more time engaged in the kinds of direct and active teaching that transmits culture,[26] compared with caregivers in developing countries. One team of cultural evolutionists suggest that advanced, wealthy economies offer an especially wide and rich range of sources of cultural transmission of gender norms, via toys, mass media and educational systems, that 'likely magnify the effects of social learning'. Personality also has more scope to vary in complex industrialized settings, and '[w]here there is more variability in personality traits, there is more scope for men and women to differ in a manner which has been shaped by cultural learning'.[27]

Finally, Different But Equal-ers' explanation of gender equality patterns depends on highly contestable gender essentialism. An 'essence' can be understood as a causal mechanism, shared by virtually all (and only) members of a category, that makes them what they are. Philosophers' standard example of an essence comes from the periodic table of the elements (such as hydrogen, oxygen and titanium) that you might dimly remember from school chemistry lessons. Each element has – is defined by – its unique atomic number, and this number explains important characteristics of the element. So, the essence of gold is that it has the atomic number of 79. All and only things made of gold have that atomic number, and it is this property that explains other enduring features of those gold objects, like their distinctive colour, resistance to tarnishing, and soft but solid state at room temperature.

Similarly, Evolutionary Psychologists propose sex-specific psychological adaptations. Male psychological adaptations are causal mechanisms, shared by virtually all members of the male sex, that explain why men are the way they are (and why they are different to women). Female-specific adaptations are causal mechanisms, shared by virtually all members of the female sex, that explain why women are the way they are (and why they are different to men). To put it another way, Evolutionary Psychologists are gender essentialists.

Evolutionary Psychologists, it must be said, do not necessarily identify with this label. Schmitt calls the description of Evolutionary Psychology as essentialist as 'one of many poisonous misrepresentations of evolutionary psychology'.[28] He is quite right when he says that Evolutionary Psychologists don't think that all men are like *this*, all women are like *that*, that no men ever express feminine traits, nor women masculine ones, or that gendered behaviour is completely impervious to outside influences. These would be patently absurd positions to take. (Although nor is anyone serious accusing Evolutionary Psychologists of holding them.)[29]

But a gender essentialist conception of the sexes doesn't preclude the existence of plenty of differences among men, and women. It doesn't exclude the possibility of extensive overlap between male and female populations. Nor does it reject the possibility of environmental influences – meaning that sex differences in one population may be different to the sex differences that arise in a population with another kind of environment.

To help us understand why Evolutionary Psychologists are gender essentialists, despite their recognition of the diversity within men and women, the overlap between them, and the sensitivity of both to external influences, we need to turn to a very old scientific idea, which has been dubbed the Natural State Model, first laid out by the famously essentialist philosopher Aristotle.[30]

Aristotle is a touch notorious when it comes to matters of sex and gender, as some readers may be aware. According to his theory of sexual reproduction, female offspring are a bit like the cut-price bags of misshapen vegetables you can buy at the supermarket. Just as a carrot bent double does not embody the true and proper nature of a carrot, females, according to Aristotle, represent development gone awry – a deviation from the natural state for the species. In Aristotle's account of sexual reproduction, the semen provides instructions for how the receiving female matter will be moulded. All being well, the result will be its natural state, a male. (In fact, in the perfect process, the offspring would exactly resemble the father.) However, if implementation of the instructions is derailed by interfering forces, the outcome is a female. Girls and women, in other words, are really deficient males.

Aristotle's Natural State Model explanation of diversity in the wider natural world followed similar lines. Variation is 'the joint product of natural regularities and interfering forces', as a contemporary philosopher of biology paraphrases the view.[31] From here, we get to the idea that the developmental conditions of rich, free countries 'accentuate evolved sex differences'.[32] Under good conditions (twenty-first-century Norway, for example), the individual approaches his or her natural state. But to the extent that interfering forces come into play (as in less well-developed countries), individuals' natural tendencies are thwarted (and the Jordanian woman becomes a computer programmer).

Consider, for example, the interpretation of cross-cultural variation in sex differences in so-called basic values, like benevolence (being caring, helpful, supportive and loyal) and power (desiring authority, control over wealth and social power). Researchers have reported that sex differences in these values are *larger* in countries in which women have greater equality.[33] (As a reminder, we should take claims of such patterns with a substantial grain of salt, but set that aside.) They therefore suggest that '[i]ncreased independence and equality of women in the labor force may encourage them to express distinctive values rather than to accommodate their values to those of their husbands'.[34] (The incongruency of patriarchal societies giving rise to subordinately power-seeking, unsupportive and disloyal wives is a puzzle left for the reader to solve for themselves.) More generally, the researchers suggest, the lessening of externally imposed gender norms might 'permit both sexes to pursue more freely the values they inherently care about more'.[35] Or to put it another way, gender-egalitarian environments are relatively free of interfering forces, allowing both women and men to achieve their natural state when it comes to the moral values they express.[36]

To recap, the Different But Equal perspective proposes that the sex differences in personality we see in the rich, gender-egalitarian countries of the Global North are a better reflection of the 'natural state' for men and women than the smaller gaps seen in other countries.

But returning to our marble metaphor, it is one thing to claim that a developmental outcome represents a 'natural state' when we are talking about the development of the eye or the genitals. It is quite another to make the same claim about complex behaviour in evolutionarily novel social, political, technological and economic conditions. The lesson both of cross-cultural diversity and of cultural evolutionary perspectives is that

[O]ur capacity for cultural learning may be adaptive precisely because its biases are broad and largely content independent, because genes cannot predict which behaviour patterns will be adaptive in changing environments. Consequently, an understanding of why a cultural trait has been acquired as opposed to its alternatives may be better framed in terms of the question 'what is the local culture?' or 'who is the transmitter?', rather than 'what is the genetic predisposition?'[37]

Even if we *do* accept the tenets of Evolutionary Psychology, the idea that twenty-first-century Sweden currently furnishes the best conditions to achieve our natural state is somewhat startling. In the grand sweep of human history, the inhabitants of rich post-industrial countries are far from representative. Indeed, they have been aptly dubbed with the acronym WEIRD: Western, Educated, Industrialized, Rich and Democratic. Joseph Henrich and colleagues have marshalled considerable evidence that the 'WEIRD' subjects of so much behavioural science research 'are particularly unusual compared with the rest of the species' and 'among the least representative populations one could find for generalizing about humans'. Henrich and colleagues warn that these populations are 'frequent outliers' and a 'particularly thin, and rather unusual, slice of humanity'.[38] Why would we think they show us as we *really* are?

While it is a lot more work than drawing tenuous links between speculative ancestral pasts, hormones and twenty-first-century jobs, old-fashioned humanities and social science scholarship promises better understanding of occupations' gender coding. Computing offers a good example. There's no definitive answer to the question of why the early, promising representation of women in programming declined, after reaching its peak in the mid 1980s. (In the US, the highest percentage of women earning computer science bachelor's degrees, 37.2 per cent, was in 1984.)[39] But it is surely not irrelevant that during the post-war period, computing technology really started to take off. When the pay and prestige of computer programming rose with growing demand, the field began to attract an increasing number of men. What 'began as women's work . . . had to be made masculine', as Nathan Ensmenger, a social and cultural historian of computing, has put it. 'An activity originally intended to be performed by low-status clerical staff – and more often than not female – computer programming was gradually and deliberately transformed into a high-status, scientific, and masculine discipline.'[40]

Ensmenger explains how in the 1950s, 'computer programming was beginning to acquire new status and a new gender identity'. One significant shift was that coaxing programs into the primitive hardware of the time and ensuring that they could run at an acceptable speed required learning what was, in effect, a kind of craft technique, but one developed through tinkering and idiosyncratic skills and knowledge. The work, which involved working alone with very little in the way of apprenticeship-style education, never mind formal education, attracted 'a certain kind of male'.[41]

Another critical moment in the masculinization of computer science was a professionalizing move, made at a major conference in Germany in 1968, to reconceptualize programming as 'software engineering'. The new term was 'not a simple description', as Abbate notes.[42] It was a strategic branding move. There were several other plausible metaphors for programming available, many of which would have been more woman-friendly than 'engineering'. As one important analyst of the industry wrote in the 1968 Proceedings of the Association for Computing Machinery National Conference: 'To many people computer programming is an art, or even a science, although its functions, characteristics, and the lack of research are more suggestive of a trade.'[43]

This was also roughly the period in which convenient but dubious and gender-biased aptitude tests and personality profiles were developed, to help employers sift through and find people to fill a growing number of roles in the industry. For example, some screening tests required formal training in mathematics. This put women of that era at a disadvantage, despite 'growing consensus within the industry' that training in mathematics was not a relevant prerequisite for successful commercial programming.[44] Similarly, despite any real evidence that this would help select the best programmers, there was increased interest in using personality profiling. These tests were necessarily based on existing computer programmers, who were mostly male. They entrenched the stereotype of a lack of social skills and a distinct lack of interest in personal interaction as the mark of a good computer programmer.

This persistent 'computer nerd' typecasting may have had little to do with genuine correlations with programming ability. (The data tell us that being interested in 'things' doesn't preclude being interested in 'people.')[45] Ensmenger argues that a key detail in the history of computing is that computers used to be very big and very expensive, with students only able to access them outside business hours. Moreover, some of the earliest universities to develop computer centres were rather slow to admit women as students. The result was a distinctively masculine 'nocturnal' computing culture. This historical twist, a contingency of fate that might have been otherwise, together with the widespread use of aptitude and personality tests, set up a 'feedback cycle'. 'The primary selection mechanism used by the industry selected for antisocial, mathematically inclined males, and therefore antisocial, mathematically inclined males were overrepresented in the programmer population; this in turn reinforced the popular perception that programmers ought to be antisocial and mathematically inclined (and male), and so on ad infinitum.'[46] As a result, companies focused on hiring programmers with unnecessary maths skills and paid far less attention to ensuring that they were proficient at understanding and communicating with clients and users, despite failings in this area leading to catastrophically expensive problems. The neglect of these so-called 'soft skills', so critical to project success, indicated 'an underlying resistance to investing resources and reputation in these lower-status "feminine" areas', Abbate suggests.[47]

This resistance is unsurprising. We saw in chapter 5 the various means by which dominant groups hoard valuable opportunities for themselves. Fashioning computing as well suited to individuals who are decisively 'non-feminine' is a good start to achieving social closure. (Prolific sexual harassment provides a helpful backup in case of failure.)[48] As Abbate puts it: 'Since technical skill conveys power — including prestige, access to well-paid employment, and the opportunity to shape the tools used by a whole society – the dominant groups in society tend to assert their "natural" superiority in these fields.'[49]

If this is so, we should expect a 'tech identity' to feel like a better 'fit' for dominant males than for marginalized ones. Consider, then, a recent comparison of Jewish and Arab/Palestinian high school students in Israel.[50] Israel is one of the world's major tech hubs, brimming with economic opportunity.[51] This makes it a good location for investigating potential social closure. Within the Israeli national educational system, there is a distinct split between the more affluent Jewish majority, and Arab/Palestinian minority schools. In a 'within-country' echo of gender equality paradox findings, researchers have found that the gender gap in interest in tech jobs among ninth-graders is larger in high schools serving the Jewish community than in those serving disadvantaged Arab/Palestinian families. A 'tech identity' – whether a teenager perceived themselves as having qualities like those of computer programmers – was the strongest predictor of a young person aspiring to a computing career. This demonstrated the importance of identifying with the incumbents of a particular job for being interested in doing it oneself.

But this didn't explain why the gender gap was larger among Jewish students than among Arab/Palestinian ones. (Nor could two other ostensibly promising social-psychological variables: affinity to mathematics, and an instrumental, 'what will this do for my career prospects?' mindset towards subject choices.) Students from both groups stereotyped tech as masculine. But it was only among *Jewish* boys that endorsement of this stereotype increased their interest in a tech career (thus widening the gender gap).

According to the Different But Equal interpretation of gender equality paradox patterns, the Arab/Palestinian boys should have been *more* interested in tech than the Jewish boys. Arab/Palestinian boys are both male *and* part of a socioeconomically precarious minority – two factors that according to the Different But Equal interpretation of gender equality paradox patterns should push them towards interest in tech careers. Instead, a social closure dynamic better explained the data, according to which desirable fields are construed as best suited to high-status individuals – in this case Jewish males.

Every occupation has its own gender-coding history. As sociologist Maria Charles (a co-author on the Israeli study) explains in an interview for Harvard University's GenderSci Lab, after World War II, advancing economies did not incorporate women into the labour force as equals to men, but '*as women*':

[P]olicies promoting expansion and democratization of higher education in the US and Europe were infused with stereotypes about gendered abilities and career paths. In the ensuing decades, presumed feminine aptitudes and affinities were accommodated through establishment and expansion of female-labeled programs in home economics, healthcare, business administration, and hospitality. Expansion of service industries was made possible in large part by the growing availability of these educated women to fill new sales, service, and clerical jobs.[52]

Thus occupational sex-segregation is neither an accident nor a biologically decreed final destination, but rather a series of policy decisions that resulted in a new gendered division of labour becoming 'an organic feature of modern economies', as Charles and her co-author David Grusky have put it.[53]

So, the role of women in the post-industrialized workforce continues to represent an uneasy compromise. On the one hand, post-industrial societies helped integrate women into the labour market, thanks to the kinds of social transformations mentioned in chapter 3. The sexual revolution gave them more control over their fertility. The civil rights movements gave them greater access to education and employment. A rising liberal agenda promoted choice over tradition. Women began to enjoy experiences and choices that were previously reserved for men.

On the other hand, these same economies simultaneously experienced sex-*segregating* forces. They grew, in part, by drawing women into the 'pink ghetto' of service work. Of necessity, these lower-status non-manual occupations became family-friendly, and therefore coded even more strongly as female, while traditional masculine occupations continued to assume a male ideal worker – better paid but with long hours that required someone available at home to take care of family life. This is a point that always reminds me of an exchange I witnessed at a gender diversity workshop, in which a senior police leader explained that uniformed police work wasn't suitable for part-time workers because of the 24/7 demand for policing. 'Oh, like nursing,' another participant drily observed.

Other features of post-industrial countries, including government policies to support women in combining work and family, childcare provision and parental leave, may also have contradictory push-pull effects. For example, although the evidence has yet to yield a clear consensus, the long, generous parental leave offered by some Scandinavian countries, particularly combined with employment regulation that makes it hard to hire temporary replacement staff, may promote women's integration into the labour force, helping push those countries up global gender equality indices. But at the same time, these factors may increase inequality *within* the labour market: for example, by making women particularly unappealing as employees to profit-focused private firms.[54]

Even the cultural values characteristic of rich post-industrial economies – that emphasize autonomy, self-expression and choice – may push towards gendered outcomes. When people are younger and laying down the train tracks of their future lives, it is easy for them to be influenced by gender stereotypes when anticipating what they will be good at and what they will enjoy.[55]

The gender equality paradox pattern may ultimately be found to apply to some gender gaps. One recent large study suggests it does indeed apply for care sector jobs, with greater gender gaps in wealthier countries. However, the authors speculate that this may be because men are especially likely to disidentify with communal values in cultures that prize individualism.[56]

But it is time to stop referring to the gender equality paradox as paradoxical. As Charles explained:

> The so-called paradox is more evidence of what feminist scholars have been saying for decades: that gender is a multidimensional structure. The observed negative correlation seems paradoxical because gender equality is so often conceptualized as if it varied on a unidimensional continuum. Even among social scientists, 'the status of women' is frequently represented as a single quantity that rises or falls depending upon a society's level of patriarchy or modernity.[57]

None of this is to say that there is *no* sex-linked biological 'spin' on those pink and blue marbles that career down the hill of development towards fulfilling lives as nurses, librarians, aircraft mechanics and CEOs. But that starting point isn't an essence, it is potential.[58] By the same token, occupations are not simply 'empty slots' that get filled by workers with the best-suited human capital.[59] They are gender coded, in ways that wind up shaping both occupations and workers. More generally, the variation across time and place that we see in occupational sex-segregation is, as Charles neatly puts it, 'difficult to reconcile with simple biological interpretations of gender segregation'.[60]

Towards the end of the nineteenth century, a writer and women's rights campaigner called Mona Caird drew on Darwin's anti-essentialist theory of evolution to challenge prevailing views of women.[61] As she sardonically observed:

Now, it is popularly understood that the whole race of women has been specially created in order to occupy precisely the position which they occupy at this era, with precisely the amount of freedom now accorded, neither more nor less – for the happy moment has apparently arrived when matters have reached perfection. And that precise position, we are also given to understand, is indicated by the qualities and instincts that women manifest or are said to manifest.[62]

Current popular understanding that Sweden today is in that 'happy moment' will perhaps seem no less laughable in another 150 years.

Tech and e-commerce firms are now giving rise to some of the richest people – *men* – on the planet (think Bill Gates, Jeff Bezos, Mark Zuckerberg, Sergey Brin, Larry Page and Steve Jobs).[63] In contrast, the typical nursing salary in England's NHS is between £33K and £35K per annum.[64] One well-known Different But Equal-er, Canadian psychologist and bestselling author Jordan Peterson, has argued that the reason we see particularly low numbers of male nurses (and female engineers) in countries like Sweden is because 'ineradicable differences' mean that 'if you leave men and women to make their own choices [about occupations] you will not get equal outcomes'.[65] By way of justifying the gender pay gap to which these gendered divisions of labour contribute, he has astutely pointed out: 'The thing about working with people, it's not easily scalable, right. Whereas working with things, man, that's scalable, right. I mean, if you write a computer program, if you write a piece of software, like, a billion people can use it. That's scalable. You're not going to have a billion human interactions in a day.'[66] But, unlike Peterson, we have probed a little deeper into the reasons women are seen as 'naturally' people-focused, while computing is no longer cast as a feminine pursuit like embroidery.

Rumours of the demise of gendered forces in twenty-first-century countries of the Global North are greatly exaggerated. The gender system of Patriarchy Inc. 'is deeply embedded as a basis for stratification', as one sociologist puts it, 'not just in our personalities, our cultural rules, or institutions but in all these, and in complicated ways'.[67] The gender system is built into the very economic structure of our post-industrial economies. It is built into the ideal worker norm, which in turn is built into wages, interactions and workplace infrastructure. It is built into evolving norms of what it means to be a good mother (and wife) or a good father (and husband). It is built into the gender coding of occupations, like the computer geek, the supposedly testosterone-fuelled trader and the 'angelic' nurse. It is built into the 'Hobbesian' masculinity contests turbo-charged by a winner-takes-all economy. It is built into the sexual harassment that polices the 'idealized masculine image' of male-dominated work, and the networks of information and opportunities that flow towards similar others.[68] It is built into the earliest infant–caregiver interactions, into 'girl toys' and 'boy toys', and into overconfident claims that gendered play and occupational outcomes have been neatly tied to hormones, or reflect our natural state. It is in the background as we 'navigate life in relationships with family, neighbors, suppliers, customers, employers, and co-workers', tussling over *who does what* and *who gets what*.[69]

Digging Patriarchy Inc. out of the division of labour requires careful thought and deep reform.

Instead, we have DEI.

8

FROM EQUALITY TO DEI

IN MARCH 2016, AT THE REQUEST OF THE UK GOVERN-
ment's Treasury, the chief executive officer of Virgin Money
UK, Jayne-Anne Gadhia CBE, led a review on women in senior
management in the financial services sector. In her foreword,
Gadhia wrote that '[t]his Report and its recommendations are
about fairness, equality and inclusion for men and women'.[1]
An admirable goal. However, the report's title, *Empowering
Productivity: Harnessing the Talents of Women in Financial Services*,
furnished a giant clue that its contents might be a bit off-beam
with respect to this noble aim.

Another such signal appeared in its epigraph, penned by
the then governor of the Bank of England, Mark Carney.
This encouraged readers to ask not what the financial services
sector can do for women, but what women can do for the
sector: 'The business case for fairness, equality and inclusion
is clearer than ever, and financial institutions must embrace
diversity in their organisation in order to reap the benefits.'[2]

One of the recommendations of the *Empowering Productivity*

report was a voluntary Women in Finance Charter. This was launched by the Treasury to reflect 'the government's aspiration to see gender balance at all levels across financial services firms. A balanced workforce is good for business – it is good for customers, for profitability and workplace culture, and is increasingly attractive for investors.'[3] (Notice anything *missing* in this aspiration?) Charter-related activities and communications have continued to unabashedly see things from the point of view that business must help women to help itself. For example, in her foreword to an annual review of the progress made in 2022 by signatories to the Charter, Baroness Penn, then the Treasury Lords Minister, expressed her commitment 'that the Charter continues to be a tool for keeping the sector competitive, innovative, and productive'.[4] What more compelling reasons could there be to include more women in senior roles?

The following year's annual review revealed an average 1 percentage point increase in female representation in senior management, from 34 to 35 per cent.[5] (Companies chose how to define who counted as a senior manager, a category that in practice included anything from less than 1 per cent to more than two thirds of the workforce, and set their own voluntary target.) A wide spread lay behind these average statistics. Consistent with the concept of social closure, the numbers ranged from a high of 46 per cent female representation in the relatively poorly paid government, regulation and trade body sectors; to a low of 29 per cent in the lucrative global and investment banking sectors. As to how these modest gains were being achieved, common tactics reported by signatories included creating diverse shortlists and longlists, female development programmes, and diversity training. Flexible work policies also got a look-in, particularly post-COVID.

As for *why* companies made these efforts, the then president and CEO of Women in Banking & Finance, a UK not-for-profit, volunteer-run organization, commented in a panel discussion about the Charter that '[o]ne of the things I've found is that there is very little traction in talking about equality, but there is an awful lot of traction in talking about the business case. And if you can't win their hearts, you can certainly win their minds when you start to discuss the business case.'[6]

The Women in Finance Charter is classic business DEI. (As a reminder, I am using the acronym to refer to a particular approach to diversity, equality and inclusion – not the concepts themselves.) DEI has a contradictory heritage, as if a social justice activist had mated with a business tycoon. One half of its parentage is the civil rights movement, which, in the second half of the last century, took the form of successful campaigns for equal rights and opportunities, along with affirmative action to promote genuinely equal opportunities. Back then, 'inclusion' meant 'a reversal of the exclusions of the past so that everyone is now free to participate in the workforce, education, and all other areas of social life', as Australian philosopher Russell Blackford explains.[7]

Today, he argues, concepts such as diversity and inclusion have taken on more demanding meanings, including a tendency to treat members of marginalized groups 'as if they are sacred'.[8] This includes imperatives to prevent speech that, according to cultural elites, is harmful, hurtful and offensive to disadvantaged groups, even as those concepts have expanded to include a broader (and milder) range of phenomena.[9] Blackford mentions the James Damore episode as an example of these dynamics. A case in point is the comment one manager made about Damore's memo on an internal Google message board: 'I intend to silence these views. They are violently offensive.'[10]

Like others, Blackford detects an intensification in these political dynamics from around 2010. He attributes this to the rise of social media, in combination with a pre-existing predilection among employers to surveil and control employees, both to enhance productivity and to protect their brand. (Indeed, this censoring of employee speech offers employers a relatively cheap way of signalling commitment to diversity, equality and inclusion, potentially in lieu of the much harder work of meaningful change.) Blackford argues that the shaming and punishment of individuals for expressing the 'wrong' views 'has become so ubiquitous that its existence can no longer be doubted in good faith'.[11]

The other half of DEI's heritage hails from the rise of the relentless prioritizing of economic goals. The topic is now absolutely saturated with 'business case' arguments. An analysis of 20 years of professional management literature, from 1975 to 1996, charted DEI's ascension.[12] Articles with a pure civil rights rhetoric – references to equal employment opportunity and affirmative action – peaked in 1980, then steadily dropped off into obscurity. Meanwhile, a new 'diversity' rhetoric made its entrance in 1987. That same year saw the publication of a highly influential report, *Workforce 2000*, that misleadingly indicated an imminent shortage of white men as new entrants to the United States workforce. This meant that welcoming previously excluded groups was a matter of competitive advantage, perhaps even survival. The new 'diversity' concept shot ahead in popularity within the professional management literature, overtaking 'civil rights' rhetoric in the early 1990s.[13]

Its triumphant rise continues. The most visible example of the DEI approach to gender is the 'Lean In' phenomenon. Following a highly successful TEDWomen talk about women and leadership,[14] the then Facebook chief operating officer, Sheryl Sandberg, wrote what would become a bestselling book, *Lean In: Women, Work and the Will to Lead*, published in 2013. As the title suggests, it encourages ambitious women to 'lean in' to their careers: to not hold themselves back, to overcome their fears, to cast aside negative mindsets and to seek support to help them succeed.[15] Around the same time, the Lean In foundation was set up, with messaging and resources for women and companies.[16]

These resources perfectly illustrate the DEI approach. The centrepiece is materials and information about running 'Lean In Circles' – social gatherings where 'women get and give peer mentorship, sharpen their skills, and have a place to be unapologetically ambitious'.[17] The foundation also promotes programmes for companies to help them to create more equal opportunities. For instance, on what is called the Allyship at Work programme, once participants have duly performed a moral accounting of their privilege, they receive practical suggestions for assisting less fortunate co-workers, such as tips on how to reduce interruptions in meetings, and be sure that everyone gets heard.[18] Another programme on offer, 50 Ways to Fight Bias, arms employees with tactics with which to disarm sexists and mansplainers. Workshop attendees are taught how to raise awareness of unconscious biases with diplomatic interjections such as 'You may not know this, Jim, but Gloria is our resident expert on corporate tax structure.'[19] The Lean In foundation also promotes International Women's Day resources every year, with somewhat milquetoast themes like #EmbraceEquity, #BreakTheBias and #InspireInclusion.[20] And in line with the core tenet of the DEI approach, managers and employees are not expected to be allies and bias busters simply out of the goodness of their hearts. Sandberg, for example, argues that '[t]he laws of economics and many studies of diversity tell us that if we tapped the entire pool of human resources and talent, our performance would improve'.[21]

DEI is now thoroughly infused with what journalist Anand Giridharadas has dubbed 'MarketWorld' values. MarketWorld, he says, 'is defined by the concurrent drives to do well and do good, to change the world while also profiting from the status quo'.[22] This is accompanied by a faith in free markets, in combination with the good intentions of the winners within those markets, to effect positive social change. Governments cite gender equality as a route to a more competitive economy.[23] Consultants churn out statistics linking the share of women on boards and top management teams with financial indicators.[24] Academics have followed suit (some sounding a more cautious note about the dubiously extravagant claims of consultancy groups).[25] When my colleagues and I analysed five years of mainstream Australian print media about workplace gender diversity, we found that journalists elaborated specific 'business case' arguments (like enhancing company performance and growing the talent pool), but became vague when it came to matters of justice and fairness.[26] Companies' diversity communications, including organizations 'top-ranked' for diversity, lead with business framings.[27]

Diversity consultants are securely strapped into the bandwagon. For example, an interview study of DEI practitioners working in large private companies in the UK found that they 'strategically drew on the business case discourse in order to increase the resources and support available to diversity management activities'. As one interviewee from the retail sector put it:

> You know, giving people a reason to change . . . OK you might know that you're excluding a couple of people, equally, if you've got enough talented people, there's no sort of burning platform, there's no reason to do things differently. Why would we then do something differently? . . . If you know the increased customer and staff satisfaction or if you can say that the average number of companies who do this will see a reduction in their recruitment costs of x per cent and then there are real tangible benefits.

'[D]iversity', the researcher observed, 'was treated as a "product" to be "marketed" and "sold" to different stakeholders in the company.'[28]

It turns out that women, racial minorities and gender and sexual minorities don't much like being treated as products to boost profits or reputation. One series of experiments found that members of these groups were put off by companies that promote diversity because it's good for the bottom line (as opposed to just the right thing to do). For example, these kinds of statements triggered suspicions in women looking for STEM jobs that they would be stereotyped, regarded as interchangeable with other women and exploited to make the company look good.[29]

But the biggest problem with DEI is that, because it is underpinned by MarketWorld values, the headline goal is to profit more from female labour, not to change the status quo. Despite the feel-good rhetoric, in DEI the issue is framed as an under-utilization of female human capital.

The first problem, as DEI diagnoses it, is that women are backward about 'leaning in' to opportunities to grow their human capital, and are less likely to self-promote their existing assets. DEI's remedy for these deficiencies is to Fix the Women (as Robin J. Ely and Debra Meyerson have dubbed it).[30] One popular cure of this ilk is women's leadership and development programmes. As an indication of demand in the last few decades, a third of top-ranked US business schools, and a third of UK and Australian universities, were found to run development programmes just for women.[31]

Women who consider themselves in need of fixing can also turn to the many materials for female self-improvement available at the Lean In foundation webpages. As well as resources for the setting-up and running of Lean In Circles, these include videos with titles like 'How to Use Body Language for Power and Influence', 'How Women Can Be Powerful Speakers and Own Any Room', and 'Dealing with Challenges as a Female Leader: Frame and Overcome Them'.[32]

Fix the Women initiatives are not unremittingly bad. They credit women with agency, rather than depicting them as passive victims of the patriarchy, as two contributors to a symposium on the *Lean In* phenomenon observed. Sandberg's materials offer women career advice that unlike, say, bringing about childcare reform or dismantling capitalism is 'within the individual's control'.[33] There *are* some things that some women can do to advance in their careers, and it's quite useful to have them set down in a book. (Whether you should call that book a 'sort of a feminist manifesto', as Sandberg did, is another matter.)[34]

So, to any woman who likes the idea of leaning in, owning the room, reframing their challenges or deploying knock-out body language, be my guest. I freely admit that there are aspects of my own professional deportment that would benefit from a spit and a polish. In an interview for the *Financial Times*'s Women at Business School series – the perfect opportunity for self-promotion – I reminisced about falling off a podium while drawing attention to the extremities of a PowerPoint slide, and revealed that my motto for handling pressure is to panic first, think later. As for being a Powerful Speaker, as a notorious hand-wringer, I don't so much Own Any Room as infuse it with the stress hormone cortisol. What I am trying to say is that there are no doubt resources I could usefully study closely myself, and I lay no blame on others for utilizing them.

And although some feminists have described 'Lean In feminism' as 'equal opportunity domination' by the 1 per cent over the oppressed majority,[35] female leadership is important. Workplaces are the main venues for positions of status and power, and research suggests that organizations and industries led by men tend to treat members of their own sex as the default stakeholder. In *Invisible Women: Exposing Data Bias in a World Designed for Men*, feminist campaigner Caroline Criado-Perez detailed the many impacts on girls and women of policies, workplaces, design, medical research, buildings, and more, unthinkingly based on men's bodies, needs and typical life patterns. Pointing to examples such as studies showing that female medical researchers are more likely to concentrate on sex- and gender-related medical issues, she plausibly suggests that 'women simply don't forget that women exist as easily as men often seem to'.[36]

DEI's focus on women's leadership also offers a useful counterpoint to the censure women sometimes face when any but the least advantaged among them attempt to advance their own cause. Sandberg was slammed by many feminists for writing a book most useful for women already doing quite well.[37] Bizarrely enough, contemporary gender politics can bear striking similarities to anti-feminist commentary in the early twentieth century, like the 1915 *New York Times* opinion piece that likened women campaigners' demands for the vote to children wailing for doughnuts.[38] There were, after all, so many more important matters – poverty, crime, war – to be dealt with first. Julia Gillard (former prime minister of Australia) and Ngozi Okonjo-Iweala (who served as Nigeria's first female finance minister and foreign minister) pinpoint the absurdity of these criticisms in their book *Women and Leadership*: 'Can you think of a time when a white, male political leader was told he should never complain about anything – name-calling by his opponents, inaccurate reporting by the media, lack of assistance from important stakeholders – until the most disadvantaged men on the planet are lifted out of poverty? No, this kind of guilt trip is only laid on women leaders calling out sexism. Let's see it for what it is.'[39]

Certainly, in some academic circles I occasionally enter, some women scholars seem to be on a guilt trip with a one-way ticket. At one workplace gender equality conference I attended, a white female researcher began her short presentation by apologizing for having done research that didn't focus on the experiences of women of colour. This was swiftly followed by a further apology for subsequently doing research that *did* focus on women of colour even though, being white herself, she lacked the requisite authority of 'lived experience'.

When I got home, I relayed the episode to my partner, a finance academic, and asked if his colleagues ever publicly flagellated themselves for studying, say, asset prices. 'Are you asking,' he cautiously responded, as if speaking to someone in a potentially highly fragile mental state following a long day amongst gender studies scholars, 'if my colleagues apologize because they don't themselves have first-hand experience of being bought and sold in the stock market?' When I explained that no, I meant do affluent, mostly white and male economists prostrate themselves to their audience for studying topics that help make other wealthy white men even wealthier, he answered without hesitation that they do not. No doubt there is a happy medium to be found, but my intuitive response to the entire episode was: *Come back, Sheryl Sandberg. All is forgiven.*

However, there is very little evidence that women's leadership programmes actually work.[40] Moreover, the positive framing of empowering women may allow subtle victim-blaming to fly under the radar. People exposed to text from Sandberg's *Lean In* – specifically, passages claiming that women can address gender inequality by working on puffing up their confidence and ambition to man-size proportions – were slightly more likely to hold women responsible both for solving the problem of gender inequality and for creating it in the first place.[41]

The Fix the Women approach also neglects the possibility that it might be women's jobs and workplaces that need fixing, not women themselves. An analysis of pre-COVID data, from the nationally representative UK Household Longitudinal survey, looked at the associations between gender and parenthood, and 12 dimensions of job quality. This found that mothers working part-time were more likely than their childless female counterparts to have poor-quality jobs, and less likely to have high-quality ones.[42]

Or consider a detailed analysis of a large, statistically representative survey of Australian workers, which found that women were less likely than men to ask for a pay rise or a promotion. While on first inspection this looked like a female reluctance to Lean In, it was largely due to low rates of asking by *part-time* workers of either sex, most of whom were women. Making it even more plain that the problem wasn't within the women themselves, the clearest difference between the sexes lay not in who asked, but who received: women's requests for a pay rise were about a quarter less likely to be success-ful.[43] Similarly, a study of German wage negotiations found that women are less likely than men to be in jobs where it is even possible to negotiate. (So too for immigrants, fixed-term employees, part-time employees and low-skilled workers.) This was the case even after taking account of levels of education and experience. Women who *were* in a position to negotiate were less likely to take up this option than were men. But then again, men were more likely to secure better wages when they asked for them. (The analysis revealed that the same disadvan-taging processes were at play for people in lower-class jobs and for immigrants.) '[T]he advice to "lean-in"', the researchers concluded, 'will not substantially lower wage inequalities for everyone, although men who lean in do benefit relative to men who do not.'[44]

The second gender problem, according to DEI, is that decision-makers sometimes fail to appreciate *feminine* forms of human capital. The associated remedy is to encourage everyone to Value the Feminine. It probably goes without saying that this does not involve finding better jobs for women in part-time work. Instead, it has licensed egregious gender stereotyping. While James Damore was publicly shamed and fired for referencing carefully described average sex differ-ences in behaviour, self-anointed diversity experts are paid by companies for their extravagant over-egging of these modest differences.[45]

A typical offering of this kind is *Work with Me: The 8 Blind*

Spots Between Men and Women in Business. The authors, Barbara Annis and John Gray (author of *Men are from Mars, Women are from Venus*), recommend that leaders acquire 'gender intelligence', such as a fulsome appreciation of innate female talents for communality, collaboration, intuition and empathy that complement men's intrinsically competitive, goal-oriented and less socially skilled modes of behaviour. The authors of *All the Brains in the Business*, published by an academic press, declare a powerful link from gonads to mind, asserting that '[t]he way men and women see their worlds is fundamentally different; and that difference comes from their basic reproductive biology'. Women's and men's brains have 'very different operating modes', they claim, namely the 'Problem-Solving Male Brain' and the 'Collaborative Female Brain'.[46]

I do sympathize with perceptions that it is less objectionable to draw on gender stereotypes to challenge inequalities than to justify them. A small part of me enjoys the idea of women in finance having the pleasure of hearing Mark Carney – a man celebrated as the George Clooney of central banking – sing their praises.[47] Carney, in observance with the sacred state in which disadvantaged groups are now ostensibly held, stated in his opening remarks to the launch of the 'Empowering Productivity' report that 'women are found to excel at people development, participative decision making, presenting a compelling vision and acting as role models – all drivers of financial performance'.[48]

But these compliments reinforce crude stereotypes. (The difference between women and men in democratic versus autocratic leadership style is so small that there is about 90 per cent overlap in the male and female distributions.)[49] In addition, the implication that simply air-dropping in some women will see both profits and diversity rise obscures deeper issues. For example, role models are only effective when the more junior workers who look up to them perceive that similar successes are achievable for them too. Aspirants will not regard even a star performer as a role model if their achievements were gained in ways they find distasteful.[50] Wells Fargo, you'll recall, had a woman, Carrie Tolstedt, installed as the head of community banking. But as a practitioner of the 'flogging' school of management, she could only have been a role model for women willing and able to operate within a business model that relied on threatening, pressuring and intimidating employees.[51]

If a lack of women at the top of financial services organizations is in part a symptom of a Hobbesian masculinity contest culture, fuelled by pay-for-performance reward systems and executive pay tied to stock option schemes, then paeans to women as the exotic mistresses of the feminine arts of people development and participative decision-making won't much help.

As Ely and Meyerson point out, merely entreating people to value stereotypically feminine traits – and reinforcing their cultural association with females – does not, on its own, mean that those traits *will* be valued. Arguably, they say, this approach 'does little more than reinforce women's appropriateness for performing what are essentially the "housekeeping" duties of management, tending the corporate fires on the home front, while men are out conquering the global frontiers and exercising the real power in today's multinational corporations'.[52] Their point is that even if women dutifully perform acts of people development and participative decision-making, they are unlikely to be adequately rewarded for it. Many white-collar occupations are steeped in the assumption that the epitome of competence and merit is self-aggrandizing individualism. Rewards accrue to the self-promoting 'stars', who may 'define problems that fit solutions they can heroically provide' (perhaps leaving a trail of devastation behind them as they ascend to their next position). Overlooked and underappreciated are the 'behind-the-scenes builders and planners', who engage in the female-typed and 'often invisible work' of 'collaboration, team-work, capacity-building, smoothing difficulties, and developing others'.[53] It takes more than a bit of woman-friendly lip-service to counteract masculine norms about how to get ahead.

The third problem diagnosed by DEI, directly inherited from the civil rights movement, is that women lack the same chances that men do to grow, invest and trade on their human capital, particularly in male-dominated environments. The DEI remedy for this has been dubbed Create Equal Opportunities: to provide a level playing field for women to use and develop their human capital by removing external barriers and eliminating biases.

Obviously, this is admirable in principle. But in practice, many common diversity practices intended to bring about equal opportunities don't work. Or so conclude sociologists Frank Dobbin and Alexandra Kalev, based on their analyses of data from more than 800 US companies and eight million workers over roughly four decades. By cross-linking demographic data with the diversity practices in use at each company, they have identified which diversity practices are statistically associated with increases in the proportion of women and racial minorities in management positions. Conversely, they can also report which practices are associated with no change, or even *decreases* in already underrepresented groups.[54]

One disappointing example of the latter is anti-bias training, such as Lean In's 50 Ways to Fight Bias programme. As Dobbin and Kalev point out, 'hundreds of studies dating back to the 1930s suggest that antibias training does not reduce bias, alter behavior, or change the workplace'.[55] They cite several reasons why this is so, including that people naturally resist 'education' that tars them as prejudiced or that is perceived as targeting wrong-think, that the training has the ironic effect of *activating* stereotypes, and that short interventions don't change long-standing attitudes and behaviour.

Popular sexual harassment policies also fail to deliver. For example, educating workers on its legal definition does not seem to reduce how often sexual harassment takes place.[56] This might be surprising to the Evolutionary Psychologists who think sexual harassment is a symptom of an evolved male bias to overperceive sexual interest, and therefore misjudge what women will consider to be harassment.[57] But for those who understand sexual harassment as a way of marking out masculine territory, it is not surprising at all.

A more promising form of Create Equal Opportunities initiatives is flexible work policies that give workers more control over when and where they do their work. But as we saw with the case study of the professional consultancy firm discussed in chapter 3, policies on their own are not enough. There, taking up flexible work accommodations was a signal to not be taken seriously. As Vicky Schultz warned over a decade ago, merely offering people opportunities to 'opt out' of organizational norms – which is often what flexible work policies do – does nothing to change those norms. For lower-waged or casual workers, or those in highly competitive jobs, opting out of the norm of making oneself constantly available is to invite being passed over or laid off. In less pressured managerial and professional occupations, flexible work policies do expand choice but, as Schultz observes, 'the social meaning and the value of those choices is always constrained by what other people are doing'.[58]

A perfect example was the implementation of a flexible work initiative at one of the Big Four accounting firms. Interviews with employees revealed that the '"untold truth" was that the road to partnership required undivided commitment'. It was understood – part of tacit institutional knowledge – that anyone working flexible hours wouldn't work with the important, career-making clients. The use of flexible work therefore functioned as 'a stigma . . . that rendered visible and differentiated the ostensibly committed from the not so committed'.[59] Seven years into the programme, the number of female directors at the firm had slightly *fallen* (from 26 per cent to 21 per cent), suggesting that rather than helping to redress gender inequality, the initiative entrenched it. Naturally, the firm then won a national award for their initiative, as a 'Leading Organization for the Advancement of Women'.

I should emphasize that all organizations are different. When it comes to diversity, equality and inclusion, there are huge variations across, and even within, organizations when it comes to how, and how well, they tackle these issues. Many organizations have made, or are pursuing, substantial and beneficial changes. Some diversity experts have genuine expertise and offer evidence-based advice.[60] The criticisms I make here should not be taken as a blanket dismissal of all activities taking place in the diversity space, or of everything being recommended.

But with the DEI industry projected to reach US$24.4 billion by 2030,[61] it is also important that there can be good-faith questioning of whether organizations are spending their money and using their employees' time wisely. A cautionary tale comes from an episode involving the prestigious scientific journal *Nature Communications*. Towards the end of 2020, it published a study that used a large database of scientific articles to analyse about three million mentor–mentee pairings within US institutions. Among other results, the researchers reported that female mentees with proportionately more male mentors early in their careers went on to have greater scientific impact. The authors conclude: 'Our gender-related findings suggest that current diversity policies promoting female–female mentorships, as well-intended as they may be, could hinder the careers of women who remain in academia in unexpected ways. Female scientists, in fact, may benefit from opposite-gender mentorships in terms of their publication potential and impact throughout their post-mentorship careers.'[62]

This is exactly what we might expect from networks of advice, information and opportunities opening up across gender lines, as we saw in chapter 5. It is also consistent with other evidence. Dobbin and Kalev describe same-gender and same-race mentoring programmes as 'a recipe for failure', in part because they leave the white men 'with real clout' mentoring other white men.[63]

However, because the article seemed to imply that women were inferior mentors, it violated the new, more demanding concept of inclusion towards which DEI has now shifted. A social media campaign against the article erupted, led by scientists without evident expertise in the area.[64] Before long, *Nature Communications* had posted an Editor's Note alerting readers 'that this paper is subject to criticisms . . . targeted to the authors' interpretation of their data that gender plays a role in the success of mentoring relationships between junior and senior researchers, in a way that undermines the role of female mentors and mentees'. A month later, the article was retracted.[65]

Yes, there were valid criticisms of the article to be made, and everyone is entitled to publicly make them. But every scientific study has its limitations, and none were egregious enough in this case to merit retraction (which is usually reserved for situations such as clear error or data fraud). The research team's retraction notice bears the familiar hallmarks of the DEI hostage note, expressing 'deep regret that the publication of our research has both caused pain on an individual level and triggered such a profound response among many in the scientific community'. In case it isn't obvious, individual experiences of psychic pain are entirely irrelevant to what should remain part of the scientific record. An added poignant twist to this tale is that the person whose career was most damaged by the episode, the article's lead author, is a female Arabian computer scientist, who uses big data and machine learning to study race and gender inequalities.

I don't want to make too much of a single episode, but this is a red flag. If this is how an empirical challenge to a popular but ineffective diversity practice is handled in a scientific journal, where respect for open inquiry and the rigorous testing of evidence and arguments should be paramount, it suggests a widespread need to lift our game. A recent report by the UK's Free Speech Union, based on a representative survey of British workers, found that 36 per cent reported that they had seen staff penalized by their employer because they had challenged some aspect of DEI training. Well over half said they had to conceal their views about its contents.[66] We all deserve that workplace diversity policies be based on evidence, not what makes the noisiest progressives comfortable.

Or what is least disruptive to the status quo. The Patriarchy Inc. account helps us see why many common approaches are too superficial to be effective. This involves paying attention to the 'Inc.' part. As I described earlier, when the corporate strategy is to have no more employees than can dance on the head of a pin, conformity to norms of overwork and constant availability intensify, confounding men's and women's efforts to lead more egalitarian lives.

DEI strategies also ignore the steep hierarchies built into the opportunities they seek to equalize. For example, in 2024, the media spotlight turned on the gender pay gap reported by Goldman Sachs International (UK), which had hit a six-year high of 54 per cent in the previous year. A bank spokesperson said: 'Importantly, this gender pay gap report does not account for pay in similar role or tenure, but we know that we need to do more to increase representation of women at the senior-most levels of the firm.'[67] But, dispensing with flawed Market-Thinking, chances are the real problem is that these mostly male senior leaders are taking more than they deserve, at the expense of women, people of colour and those from the 'wrong' background. If so, putting more women in overpaid roles would be like robbing Petra or Vivek to pay Paula rather than Paul, and we can't assume the benefits will 'trickle down'. Consider Virgin Money UK. In 2023, as part of its submission to the Women in Finance Charter, it reported meeting its 45 per cent target for women in senior management three years ahead of schedule, putting it in a star position among signatories to the Charter.[68] Yet that same year, its median gender pay gap in hourly wages was 35 per cent.[69]

Circling back to the Women in Finance Charter with which this chapter began, this is all rather awkward territory. This is because financialization – the 'wide-ranging reversal of the role of finance from a secondary, supportive activity to a principal driver of the economy'[70] – has shaped many of these broad economic trends. Studies of inequality in OECD countries 'have repeatedly identified financial activity as a significant factor in widening inequality', as Ken-Hou Lin and Megan Tobias Neely explain in *Divested: Inequality in the Age of Finance*.[71] This now immensely powerful sector has rung in a self-serving ideology of shareholder value maximization that has facilitated and rationalized deteriorating worker conditions and security for many, while lining the pockets of the elite, mostly male, few. As I finished writing this chapter, the European Banking Authority released its latest report on 'high earners' with remuneration of one million euros or more in the 2022 financial year. That number had risen by 20 per cent since the previous year. Of those high earners, 92 per cent were men.[72] It is therefore rather ironic that the Women in Finance Charter's official champion, the UK Treasury, appears to have had an outsized role in kick-starting the advancement of financialization in the 1970s.[73]

It is perfectly in keeping with the values of DEI for the UK Treasury to promote the 'harnessing' of women in the belief that this will help grow the bloodsucking finance sector. But it is important to keep in mind that such ambitions have little to do with diversity, equality and inclusion.

9

A NEW VISION

I BEGAN THIS BOOK AS I LIKE TO START ALL PROJECTS: with a complaint. We are being distracted by visions of gender equality that reduce the concept to a shell, or husk.

In the vision offered by the Different But Equal perspective, gender equality looks a lot like patriarchy, rebranded as the natural consequence of evolved differences. A salutary example of where the Different But Equal-ers' denuded version of the concept can take us comes from a global gender equality index developed by Evolutionary Psychologists David Geary and Gijsbert Stoet. Their aim was to avoid creating yet another politically biased measure of gender equality, as they saw it, that overlooks male disadvantage and imports contentious (i.e., feminist 'equal = the same') political values.

To that end, the index compares the sexes across just three dimensions: access to primary and secondary education; life satisfaction; and life span.[1] The researchers stripped out what are standard-issue inputs to global gender equality measures, such as labour market participation and income, and political power. After all, they argue, in practical terms, household income is more important than individual contributions. The earnings gender gap may simply represent 'a strategic and desired division of labor within families, rather than a disadvantage to women'.[2] Likewise, they suggest women may be poorly represented in government because they have relatively little taste for high-level politics. Besides, that kind of activity 'is only relevant to the tiny proportion of people who choose a political career'.[3] They also excluded measures of skewed sex ratios that reflect preferences for sons over daughters, claiming that including them 'undervalues the health and survival of actually living persons' and represents only 'a very indirect measure' of negative attitudes towards females.[4] (They even cite the somewhat fringe philosophical argument that since existence is but a valley of tears, it's better never to have been born.)[5]

'Gender equality', in this conception, is compatible with men enjoying legislative authority over girls' and women's lives; with women being economically dependent on husbands, fathers or a male-dominated state; and with females being so devalued by economic, social and political structures that a country can be haunted by large numbers of 'missing girls'. These are not exactly politically neutral positions.[6]

Labelling their creation the Basic Index of Gender Inequality (BIGI), Stoet and Geary concluded that Bahrain, an archipelago in the Persian Gulf to the east of Saudi Arabia, was the most gender-equal nation in the world in 2019.[7] Here is a snapshot of Bahrain at the time. Men hold 85 per cent of parliamentary positions and 96 per cent of ministerial positions. Indeed, up until 2002, only men enjoyed the right to vote and stand as political candidates. Bahraini men hold two thirds of professional and technical roles, and make up almost four in five legislators, senior officials and managers. Men's labour force participation is about twice that of women, their earned income roughly triple. Bahraini women do not have equal rights of nationality, divorce, guardianship, inheritance, or protection from child marriage. If a woman is a man's wife, he can legally rape her. In some other circumstances, a rapist can neatly extricate himself from his legal problem by marrying his victim.[8]

The vision of gender equality implied by the BIGI was published in a reputable journal of science and reported in mainstream news media.[9]

Turning now to the vision offered by DEI, gender equality is a way of making good by doing good. A salutary illustration of the corporate hypocrisy to which this perspective can lead came from the ridesharing company Uber Technologies Inc. In 2015, founder Travis Kalanick, then also its CEO, proudly announced that the company was 'embarking on a new global partnership with UN Women with the goal of accelerating economic opportunity for women'. In its press release, Uber committed to creating a million jobs for women on the Uber platform by 2020, as part of a 'shared vision of equality and women's empowerment'.[10]

As for what that equality and empowerment might look like, Uber is notorious for spending millions of dollars fighting regulation to set minimum standards for wages and conditions.[11] Trade unions and women's rights groups pointed out that increasing women's access to insecure, poorly paid, potentially unsafe jobs is not most people's idea of female empowerment.[12] 'Women already make up a high proportion of the precarious workforce,' the International Transport Workers' Federation wrote in a press release, 'and increasing informal, piecemeal work contributes significantly to women's economic disempowerment and marginalization across the globe.'[13] (UN Women ended up politely declining the partnership.)

While Uber was committing to increasing the number of women among the ranks of its poor-quality independent contractor jobs, it was offering a far from inclusive environment for women among the 'good jobs' of its core employees, as an eye-opening blog post by former Uber software engineer Susan Fowler later revealed.[14] Fowler alleges that on her first day as a member of a site reliability engineering team, her new manager propositioned her over company chat. When she complained, neither the human resources department nor upper management were willing to punish a supposedly inadvertent mistake by a star performer even though Fowler's was not the first such complaint. She was then told she could either move to another team or accept that she would probably get a poor performance evaluation from that manager. This turned out to be part of a broader pattern of widespread sexism. Fowler's blog post went viral, the scandal contributing to the ousting of Kalanick in June 2017.[15] An investigation into Uber by the Equal Employment Opportunity Commission revealed a Hobbesian workplace culture that licensed sexual harassment and permitted retaliation against people who complained about it.[16]

Time to replace these shells and husks with Mill's vivid

conception and living belief. Gender equality is not whatever 'natural state' the Pleistocene designed us for. It is not what will make the bottom line fatter. The time has come for a new mainstream vision of gender equality, based on what the Patriarchy Inc. account has shown us.

Returning to where we began, divisions of labour help us tackle the challenges of reproduction, survival and flourishing. We make our contributions (*who does what*) and get a bundle of rewards in return (*who gets what*). Both parts of this equation powerfully shape well-being – that is, 'what people are able to do and to be, and thus the kind of life they are effectively able to lead', as political philosopher Ingrid Robeyns puts it.[17] She means important opportunities and experiences such as physical health, bodily integrity and safety; being respected; the ability to pursue paid work, care for family and combine the two; social relationships, networks and support; gaining education and knowledge and putting them to use; mental well-being, leisure, control over one's time; political participation.[18]

We have seen again and again how Patriarchy Inc. interferes with what we can do and be and what we get in return. Putting this together with a proposal from Robeyns for assessing when Western societies will be 'gender just' points us to a very simple vision of gender equality.[19] It is liberation from a gender system that constrains our freedom to achieve well-being and that biases what we get in return.

This vision of gender equality should be acceptable even to people who still subscribe to the Different But Equal perspective, or its Different And Unequal variants. Well-being encompasses both stereotypically feminine and masculine activities and experiences, which means that we can and should care just as much about Patriarchy Inc.'s detrimental effects on boys and men as its consequences for girls and women. This new vision of gender equality is also sensitive to feminist objections about masculine norms being treated as the gold standard of how life should be lived. What's more, this definition of gender equality stipulates *freedom* to achieve the many dimensions of well-being, not the precise mix women and men should strive for. So even those who think I've overestimated the contribution of the gender system to the division of labour can get on board. Nobody sensible thinks that gender roles are rigidly set by biology, or that nature's whisperings dictate how society should be arranged. We are the kind of creatures who construct social identities, roles and institutions. We should look for ways to reconstruct gendered identities, roles and institutions in ways that enhance well-being.[20]

This vision should also be palatable to supporters of the DEI approach, so long as they genuinely care about doing good (rather than just appearing virtuous or making money). We will, however, need to kick the habit of talking about the economy as if we humans serve merely as a large support team to keep it growing. For instance, a report from the McKinsey Global Institute, titled *The Power of Parity: How Advancing Women's Equality Can Add $12 Trillion to Global Growth*, sternly warned that '[i]f women . . . do not achieve their full economic potential, the global economy will suffer'.[21] But of course, the economy exists for *us*, for *our* well-being, not the other way around.

An efficient, productive economy that supports well-being means an economy with policies that support care, helping children develop into well-adjusted, healthy, non-aggressive, and educated citizens.[22] It means an economy that doesn't squander the human capital of anyone, of either sex, who can't meet the ideal worker norm. It means workplaces in which people are appointed based on genuine merit rather than stereotypes, and rewarded for competence and contributions rather than ruthlessness, dominance and self-interest.

An economy that supports well-being also means one in which exploitation of employer power is kept in check to ensure a living wage. This view was expressed by none other than Adam Smith, set out in his classic book *An Inquiry into the Nature and Causes of the Wealth of Nations*. Should wages fall below subsistence levels, 'it would be impossible for [the worker] to bring up a family, and the race of such workmen could not last beyond the first generation'. Moreover, Smith appreciated that there would be something deeply amiss about an economy that left the majority unable to thrive. 'No society can surely be flourishing and happy,' he wrote, 'of which the far greater part of the members are poor and miserable.' And in an observation with which certain contemporary titans of business might wish to familiarize themselves, he also pointed out that such a situation would be grossly unfair: 'It is but equity, besides, that they who feed, clothe, and lodge the whole body of the people, should have such a share of the produce of their own labour as to themselves be tolerably well fed, clothed, and lodged.'[23]

Finally, an economy that supports everyone's well-being is

also one that equitably meets everyone's needs and interests. In most sectors, that will be a tall order so long as one or other gender is in the minority. Adding to illustrations of the point from medical research, a recent analysis of nearly 5,000 films released between 2000 and 2022 across 95 consumer markets suggested that those with more female scriptwriters enjoyed a box office premium, particularly in markets where women have more purchasing power. Moreover, portrayal of female subjectivity – women as full human beings with thoughts and feelings – was stronger in films with higher representation of women within screenwriting teams. These films were more likely to pass the so-called Bechdel test (whether the movie features two named female characters who have a conversation about a topic other than a male love interest), and included more female dialogue.[24] Obviously, watching a film that doesn't pass the Bechdel test isn't life-threatening (with the possible exception of *Beavis and Butt-Head Do the Universe*). However, it is an example of men's greater power to define feminine roles – part of the elaborate social process of mindshaping.

In other words, this new vision of gender equality reminds advocates of the DEI approach – or licenses action in those who never forgot – what diversity, equality and inclusion are actually *for*: creating a more just society.

The Patriarchy Inc. account also illuminates pathways to move us towards that goal. I offer several suggestions here, with the gay abandon of someone who will not be held accountable for implementing them.

My first suggestion is to continue reorienting societies and workplaces around the assumption that most workers will have caring responsibilities for significant periods of their working lives. Schultz calls this aspiration the 'reasonable work week':

> a new social ideal and a new set of norms about working time in which most people are able to work regular, predictable schedules for a number of hours (or a range of hours) that lies somewhere comfortably between the two poles of overwork and underutilization and that gives people the ability to plan and to participate meaningfully in important life endeavours in addition to employment.[25]

Experts are on hand to supply suggestions of social and employment policy levers that can be pulled to better support both women and men who combine caring responsibilities with wage work. These would rejig both spheres of life: examples include state-subsidized training accounts to help keep caregivers' skills up to date, extended local care services, greater employee power to control schedules and hours, guaranteed work hours, a high minimum wage, state-supported childcare and parental leave.[26] The long-term promise of generous 'use it or lose it' leave for dads is that it will lead to a reduction in workplace discrimination against women, and against men who work flexibly in order to care, and will help equalize women's and men's opportunities to work and care, respectively.[27]

It sounds expensive, I know. But roads, airports and power stations are also costly yet we pay for them as a society because they are necessary. And we also don't expect people to build and run them for free. Raising children and caring for elderly, disabled or unwell family aren't indulgent hobbies. Without caring, 'there could be no society', as legal theorist Martha Fineman points out. 'Caretaking labor provides the citizens, the workers, the voters, the consumers, the students, and others who populate society and its institutions.'[28] A reasonable work week would also enhance well-being more broadly. Research into work–family conflict finds that single men and women living alone can find long work hours challenging. They have no one else with whom to share household responsibilities, and report that work demands leave them without enough time to maintain friendships or establish romantic relationships.[29] Labour market expert Heejung Chung, prosecuting the policy case for the four-day work week, argues that:

> [W]orking long hours in our societies, rather than being a necessary function of one's job, has persisted largely as a performance tool to signify one's productivity, commitment, and self-worth. It is, further, a root cause of many problems we face in society today, including issues around workers' and their families' well-being, labour market inequality, decline in social cohesion, and the stigmatisation of disadvantaged workers.[30]

In addition to enhancing gender equality, Chung has marshalled evidence of additional benefits of shorter work hours: workers with a bouncier spring in their step and better-rested neurons; a lower burden on health-care systems; happier kids and families; the energy for more active leisure pursuits than watching TV; more time for community activities; and a slower lifestyle that helps reduce carbon emissions.

My second piece of counsel is to mindshape the gender system out of jobs. We need to be aware that jobs 'are not gender-neutral − rather they are created as appropriate for either men or women . . . "sexed" jobs and new occupations are struggled over and negotiated to establish their gender coding'.[31] High-status jobs are likely to be 'reserved' for men through a subtle process of cultivating so-called 'masculine defaults' that link standards, values and competence to masculine gender roles.[32] As we saw with the example of programming, prototypes, such as the idea of the mathematically gifted but socially unskilled loner computer-geek, can be used to hoard valuable jobs for (some) men. Genuine commitment to diversity, equality and inclusion means setting aside definitions of 'fit' and success that exclude women and other marginalized groups, but that are irrelevant or counterproductive from the perspective of organizational purpose or societal good.

Tackling this means looking at formal systems, such as how people are selected and recruited, policies, training and on-boarding, how performance is evaluated and managed, authority structures and the ways decisions are made. It also entails scrutinizing an organization's informal systems: who are the role models and the heroes? What are the rituals, unwritten norms or tacit assumptions embedded in language? What advice do veterans of the organization pass on to junior employees?[33] A classic ethnographic study of life on an offshore deepwater oil production platform built by Shell in the Gulf of Mexico, conducted by Ely and Meyerson and published in 2010, remains one of the most remarkable illustrations of how transformative this de-gendering can be.[34]

As you might expect, oil rigs are workplaces where a masculinity contest culture usually pervades. One offshore installation manager vividly captured the typical culture by describing his co-workers as behaving 'like a pack of lions':

> The guy that was in charge was the one who could basically out-perform and out-shout and out-intimidate all the others. That's just how it worked out here on drilling rigs and in production. So those people went to the top, over other people's bodies in some cases. Intimidation was the name of the game. . . . They decided who the driller was by fighting. If the job came open, the one that was left standing was the driller.[35]

In keeping with the tenet of 'show no weakness', one veteran of the industry recalls getting just 15 minutes to process seeing a fellow worker die on the oil rig.[36]

In the 1990s, Shell made an original move with a major strategy to enhance safety and effectiveness. In doing so, an environment was created in which men no longer had to prove how tough and infallible they were. For the first time, workers 'readily acknowledged their physical limitations, publicly admitted their mistakes, and openly attended to their own and others' feelings', as Ely and Meyerson noted. In this once macho environment, a deck mechanic was overheard at lunch explaining why he sent a classical music tape of Mozart and

Chopin to the home of a co-worker with a baby: 'because it's real important for them babies to listen to music like that. Real soothing.' When a researcher tipped back in his chair in a meeting, he was politely told, 'That's not safe.' The men openly and unapologetically displayed their fear when they had to be evacuated following the 9/11 terrorist attacks. As one production operator described the unexpected change:

> [We had to be taught] how to be more lovey-dovey and more friendly with each other and to get in touch with the more tender side of each other type of thing. And all of us just laughed at first. It was like, man, this is never going to work, you know? But now you can really tell the difference. Even though we kid around and joke around with each other, there's no malice in it. We are a very different group now than we were when we first got together – kinder, gentler people.[37]

As part of the safety strategy, the men slated to work on the new deep-water platforms underwent intensive therapy. But leaders also promoted organizational change through more conventional routes. One tack taken by leaders was to promote 'all in this together' collectivist goals – like keeping co-workers safe. These had previously been undermined by poor relations with management, status hierarchies, and a culture of competition, harassment, lack of trust and collaboration, and retaliation. Production goals were now presented in relative rather than absolute terms: 'every drop as fast as possible' and 'not a penny more than it takes'; rather than *this many* barrels a day. New recruits were told they could shut down anything if they felt it was unsafe.

A second prong of attack was to align definitions of competence with the skills that tasks required, rather than allow masculine norms of aggression, toughness, infallibility and emotional detachment to stand in for genuine expertise and ability. 'Coworkers who behaved too aggressively failed to move up in the company,' interviewees explained.

A third important change was undoing the culture of scapegoating and cover-ups, and promoting instead an environment in which it was all right to admit mistakes and gaps in knowledge. The company even set up a 'Millionaire Club' to celebrate workers whose mistakes had cost the company a million dollars, to communicate that to err is human and that the company would forgive.

Previously, platform workers saw the company as indifferent to their safety and well-being. 'You were only a hat and shoes,' as one poetic worker put it.[38] But the concerted changes appeared to have profound effects, demonstrated both by improved company statistics on safety and by the men's incorporation of stereotypically feminine traits into their self-narratives of what it meant to be a man. To put it in mindshaping terms, Shell's comprehensive overhaul of policies, practices, rituals and language deliberately shaped men's minds to match a new model of the ideal worker. It was a success. 'The corporate-wide changes resulted in an 84% decline in the company's accident rate; in the same period, the company's level of productivity (number of barrels), efficiency (cost per barrel), and reliability (production 'up' time) came to exceed the industry's previous benchmark.'[39] In the process, the strategy also inadvertently reshaped masculine identity – the personal changes on workers' gender identities were perhaps no less profound. Asked by the researchers to reflect on what being a man meant to them, 'most described manliness in non- or even counter-stereotypical terms', often emphasizing 'humility, feelings, approachability, and compassion'.[40]

Reshaping gendered identities is no small task. As three gender scholars point out, 'critical social identities are forged on the job: core identities of what it means to be a good worker, a good man or woman, and a good person'. For professionals, they point out, work devotion is also an important way of signalling class. As we saw from the studies of overworking 'Iron Man' surgeons and overdelivering consultants, 'any proposal to redefine work is profoundly threatening to people whose identities have been forged around the old way of doing it'.[41]

Although we need more research into how best to reforge identities, rather than trying to encourage men to be more 'like women', a promising approach is to offer alternative models. In the surgeon study, the hospital employees who managed to bring about successful reform of very long working hours: 'countered the traditional narrative of surgeons as "working machines" who "don't eat and don't sleep" with a new narrative of surgeons who were "well-organized" and "efficient" workers who "know how to prioritize tasks" in order to hand off patient care efficiently'.[42]

There are already plenty of positive masculine norms to work with, such as the 'good-natured ribbing' by which boys and men 'express a cloaked form of affection with each other'. When my son failed one of the multiple tests involved in getting an Australian driving licence, my efforts to soothe and sympathize him into a more cheerful state failed dismally. But just a short time into the journey home from the testing centre, following a rapid exchange of text messages with his mates, the dark cloud hovering over him lifted. He even smiled. Curious to know how a male teenager had succeeded in cheering up my son where his own mother, trained in psychology, had failed, I asked what the emotionally restorative message had said. It was *You fuckwit*. Other positive aspects of traditional masculinity include heroism, a 'healthy dose' of self-reliance, breadwinning, courage, and an expectation that men will care for and protect family and members of their community.[43]

Positive masculinity is already there for the cultivating in our workplaces. For example, interviews with people working in the UK construction industry – a mix of first-aiders, health and safety officers, and site managers and foremen – revealed plenty of 'feminine' sensitivity and concern about the well-being of coworkers. In one such example, an interviewee explained: 'We had a particular issue [a few months ago] and the lad who he was working with rang us up first thing in morning, about 9 o'clock got a phone call and he said "y'know this lad he's not right, he's not" – anyway, we fetched him back and y'know, he was on the verge of a nervous breakdown. But that were because the person he were working with knew . . . that's because you know that person.' Said another, with a view to intervention, 'I can spot if someone has a face on them, I can spot it straight away.'[44]

It's not always going to be obvious when formal and informal systems reflect bona fide competence and demands, and when they are gender-biased. (There's a good chance that the communities that are the most biased will be the least aware of it.) But probing is especially warranted when masculine defaults appear to contribute to the undermining of basic organizational goals like not breaking the law, not going bankrupt, not bringing about nervous breakdowns in employees, not creating an unsafe work environment and not causing a worldwide financial crisis. Masculine contest cultures put women in a triple bind, can result in abusive and harassing environments for other culturally lower-status groups, and effectively mark out what are often relatively well-paid jobs as male territory. But these cultures are not necessarily even good for men. As the Shell example illustrates, the costs for them can also be high, even lethal.

My third suggestion is that we need to be more alert to how deeply embedded the gender system is in childhood.[45] Stereotypical toys being explicitly and symbolically labelled as 'for boys' or 'for girls' is just straightforward sexism, and this should be unacceptable in any society that claims to be committed to gender equality.[46] Some school cultures code educational underachievement as masculine, and that harms boys.[47] From baby bedrooms stocked with gendered toys before infants have even shown any such preferences,[48] to persistent and visible divisions of labour in homes, schools, politics and workplaces, young people's gender identities form in a developmental landscape that is deeply grooved by gender. Different But Equal-ers are right that people's preferences are relevant for understanding the gendered division of labour.[49] But when the direction those preferences take are eased and deterred by the valleys and hills of the gender system – destination patriarchy – that is unjust. Equality demands more than passive non-discrimination.

Consider a 'natural experiment' that arose when Germany suspended both its compulsory military service and its social sector civilian service alternative in 2011. By comparing men's experiences and occupational choices before and after, the researchers estimated that participating in social sector civilian service – a gender-atypical learning experience for the men – raised their chances of taking up a female-dominated occupation by 12 percentage points.[50] As Richard Reeves points out, there is plenty of scope for programmes aiming to get more young women into STEM to be complemented by similar active efforts to encourage more young men into health, education, administration and literacy fields.[51]

A fourth big-ticket item for increasing gender equality comes courtesy of Dobbin and Kalev, whose work points to the importance of 'democratizing career systems' for increasing diversity in management. Put simply, they mean that the opportunities of recruitment, flexible work, mentoring, networks and training need to be deliberately extended to a wider group of employees. Broader recruitment strategies can make candidate pools more diverse. Democratizing flexible work policies helps ensure that more employees, not just 'high value' ones, have more control over their work schedules. Formal mentoring programmes, offered beyond those identified as future stars, and that cross lines of gender and race, are effective because '[p]eople get ahead by working alongside, or being mentored by, people who have clout'.[52]

Self-managed teams, in which employees from different roles and divisions work together in an egalitarian way, help to open up networks to employees who would otherwise tend to be siloed from more powerful employees who can help their careers and give them the chance to shine. This is likely to break down stereotypes far more effectively than diversity training. The practice was developed to enhance performance, but also appears to be effective in promoting diversity. Similarly, expanding training to a wider range of roles, and cross-training – rotating workers through several different jobs – was also initially developed with business interests in mind. (Specifically, enhancing flexibility, productivity and skills.) But it also turns out to 'advance managerial diversity by giving staffers exposure to a wider range of jobs and people, a basic resource for promotion'.[53] Cross-training new recruits can challenge young people's stereotypical assumptions about what roles will best suit them, increasing gender and racial diversity in those positions.

Notably, none of these practices involve 'fixing' women, singling them out in divisive ways for extra 'help', drawing on condescending gender stereotypes, or 'educating' those who interact with them. Instead, to use Relations-Thinking concepts, they involve organizations being more egalitarian about who benefits from organizational resources.

More generally, we need to think more critically about *who gets what*. In our new vision, gender equality means that the pay-offs people receive in return for their labour contributions are equitable, not gender-biased by tacit assumptions that things that men tend to do are more skilled and important.

The criterion here is not just that women and men should receive the same pay for doing exactly the same work, but that 'jobs or other social positions that are numerically dominated by either women or men should not systematically be rewarded lower pay-offs without any plausible justification', as Robeyns puts it.[54]

Of course, what counts as an equitable pay-off is an immensely difficult question.[55] But we need to reject the comforts of Market-Thinking. Relations-Thinking tells us we should be constantly sceptical about who is getting hold of resources, at whose expense, and how those resource-rich opportunities are closed off from outsiders. We need to re-examine the gendered mindshaping that causes us to undervalue caregiving and part-time work and overvalue 12-hour days at the office and selling complex financial products you don't quite understand. We need to appreciate that sensitively taking care of a confused elderly person with multiple health-care needs is skilled and demanding work, not just women doing what comes naturally to them. Relations-Thinking also exposes the exploitative flows of resources to people at the top of organizational hierarchies, at the expense of those nearer the bottom. Women, especially working-class and racial-minority women, are often overrepresented among the exploited, and underrepresented among the exploiters. They can't individually 'lean in' their way to more equitable pay-offs.

This brings us to reforms the DEI approach never talks

about, but that would help increase gender equality.[56] One is to increase job security. The use of casual (zero-hour) contracts and outsourced independent contractors shifts a key business risk (that one might need fewer employees next month) from firms, and especially shareholders, onto workers. Treating workers as temps excludes them from many benefits, including access to cross-training, mentoring and flexible work. This trend conflicts with the democratizing of career systems – practices that, unlike anti-bias training, do actually promote diversity. High-intensity competition and churn in managerial and professional roles promote greedy jobs that undermine gender-egalitarian households.[57]

We need employment regulations, such as minimum wages and working conditions, that allow for family life and financial security for families, enforceable by regulators with teeth and resources. This enables companies to be both ethical and competitive. Reforming pay-for-performance reward systems and executive pay tied to stock option schemes, which 'end up redirecting organizational resources away from lower-level employees or dependent suppliers and toward top managers and executives', would help close gender pay gaps.[58]

It is probably obvious why leaders are not lobbying for such changes or pushing for initiatives like these in DEI strategies. But when organizations boast of their commitment to diversity, equality and inclusion, the rest of us can ask . . . why not?

Finally, we need to ask awkward questions about why our governments seem so much more willing to provide welfare for companies than for children. For instance, several economically minded commentators have pointed out that imposing a financial transaction tax on stocks and bonds and derivative trading – the so-called Robin Hood tax – would not just discourage the kind of speculative trading that fuels unhealthy market volatility. It could also serve to pay back some of the debt owed to taxpayers by the industry because of the global financial crisis.[59]

According to one set of UK-based calculations, the estimated sum raised by a financial transactions tax of just 0.01 per cent:

> [W]ould have paid for the uprating of benefits, tax credits and public sector pensions in line with the Retail Price Index, retaining the health in pregnancy grant (£150 million) and Sure Start maternity grants, restoring the cuts in tax credits and housing benefit. It would have avoided freezing child benefit, obviated the requirement that single parents whose youngest child starts school look for paid employment, avoided the squeeze on Disability Living Allowance, and still provided £15,000 million or so to maintain the public services that are critical for gender equality.[60]

More funding for those public services would also mean that paid care workers, mostly women, could enjoy higher wages, more training and better work conditions. I'm *just saying*.

It would be comforting to think that we could achieve gender equality with the DEI approach of Fixing the Women, Creating Equal Opportunities and Valuing the Feminine, sold to powerful stakeholders with business-case arguments. It would be even more reassuring to think that in post-industrial countries, women and men are now mostly Different But Equal, and that gender inequality is a blight largely confined to poorer countries, history books and the fevered imaginations of feminist scholars.

Regrettably, both these conflicting visions of gender equality are sorely off track.

Time for a new vision, and a new path.

ACKNOWLEDGEMENTS

SEVERAL TIMES DURING THE WRITING OF THIS BOOK, my partner and I would have a conversation that ran roughly as follows. He would kindly ask how the book was going and, with fear in my eyes, I would reply, 'There are a lot of theories in this book. A *lot.*' Then he would say something sensible, like 'Well, can you take some of them out?' To which *I* would respond with great affront, as if I had just been accused of greedily helping myself to more than my fair share of the fruits of the humanities, social and evolutionary sciences, 'No, I can't. I need them all.' It is nonetheless a pleasure to acknowledge, beyond the endnotes, my considerable intellectual debt to others. Since academics sometimes label their theories and concepts in awful and unapproachable ways, I've performed the writerly equivalent of blending the vegetables into the sauce to make their presence more palatable. I apologize for any nuance that has been lost in the purée.

Many academics, including several whose names will by now be familiar, also provided immensely helpful feedback on ancestral versions of chapters. I am deeply grateful to Dustin Avent-Holt, Maria Charles, John Dupré, Deborah Figart, Cecilia Ridgeway, Ingrid Robeyns, Donald Tomaskovic-Devey, Kim Sterelny, Melissa Wheeler, Tadeusz Zawidzki, and especially Kit Fine, Ione Fine, Nick Haslam, Holly Lawford-Smith and Carsten Murawski, all of whom heroically read entire draft manuscripts and provided invaluable comments.

A special thanks also to Matriarchy Ink – my mother, Anne Fine, and sister, Ione Fine, both of whom were wellsprings of much-appreciated encouragement and editorial assistance.

I am also grateful beyond measure to my editors on both sides of the Atlantic, Poppy Hampson and Amy Cherry, without whose excellent editorial skills, direction and endurance this book would be vastly the poorer. My heartfelt gratitude also to my agent, Andrew Gordon, whose wisdom and judgement served as important positive selective forces in the evolution of the book. I thank everyone at Atlantic Books who has helped bring this book into being, particularly my copy-editor, Jane Selley, for her meticulous work on the manuscript. I also thank Margaret Cameron, the head of the School of Historical & Philosophical Studies at the University of Melbourne, for her support, and Leila Zohali and Cynthia Troup for their assistance with the endnotes and bibliography.

As the number of words written increased, so too did the demands on those who live with me. My deepest gratitude and appreciation is reserved for Carsten Murawski, whose unwavering kindness, patience, encouragement and support far exceeds what I deserve. Hopefully, by dedicating a book about patriarchy to him, I haven't deepened the debt.

NOTES

Full bibliographical details of the texts referred to in these notes can be found in the bibliography (p. 278).

Introduction

1.   Deloitte (2023b, figure 3).
2.   Bank size defined by market capitalization. Data from Fine et al. (forthcoming).
3.   Office for National Statistics (2018, figure 3).
4.   See Baker & Cornelson (2018), who found that the majority of occupational sex segregation in the US labour market remained statistically unexplained, even after taking account of women and men choosing different occupations based on sensory, motor and spatial job attributes, interest in 'people' and 'things', competition and mortality risk, among others.
5.   E.g., Stoet & Geary (2018; 2022).
6.   Screenwriting statistic from Thomson et al. (2024), based on credited screenwriters of 4,749 feature films from 95 countries released between 2000 and 2022. For computer and mathematical science doctorates in the US, see National Center for Science and Engineering Statistics et al. (2023).
7.   For example, in the UK in 2022/23, 96 per cent of worker

fatalities and 75 per cent of deaths linked to exposure to work-place hazards were of men (Health and Safety Executive, n.d.).

8. Specifically, household production, which refers to 'the production of goods and services by the members of a household, for their own consumption, using their own capital and their own unpaid labor. Goods and services produced by households for their own use include accommodation, meals, clean clothes, and child care'. Ironmonger (2001, 2).

9. Calculated from Office for National Statistics (2024c), March 2024 dataset.

10. E.g., Craig & Powell (2018); Craig & Mullan (2013).

11. See Chafetz (1988, 108), who observes that 'virtually all [social science theories concerned with gender differences and gender inequality] have recognized that the family and the economy constitute the central arenas wherein gender stratification is produced and sustained'.

12. As England et al. (2020) report, in the US, progress towards gender equality has slowed or stalled since the 1980s/90s on a number of indicators: employment; educational attainment; segregation in fields of study; earnings; occupational segregation.

13. E.g., Cotter et al; (2011a; 2011b); England (2010). For data on historical changes and cross-cultural variation in multidimensional gender ideologies, see, for example, Begall et al. (2023); Scarborough et al. (2019); Grunow et al. (2018); Knight & Brinton (2017).

14. Following the convention introduced by Buller (2006), I capitalize the 'E' and the 'P' of Evolutionary Psychology to distinguish this research programme, and its core assumptions, from the broader field of inquiry exploring the effects of evolution on the human brain and behaviour.

15. Evans et al. (2018, tables 13 and 14).

16. Plan International Australia (2023).

17. Wittenberg-Cox (2014, figure 1-1).

18. Lanz & Brown (2020, ix, emphasis on 'feminine energy' and 'e-quality' removed).

19. Georgeac & Rattan (2023). The remaining 18 per cent offered no case at all.

20. Ipsos & Global Institute for Women's Leadership (2019, 50).
21. King's Global Institute for Women's Leadership & Ipsos (2024, 12).
22. Dynata & Thrive Insights (2021, 17) on behalf of TDC Global.
23. Risman (2004).
24. Mill (1859, 72). Mill was describing the effects of 'the mischievous operation of the absence of free discussion'. Although there is certainly plenty of disagreement when it comes to gender equality, there is arguably less in the way of free and productive discussion across competing views.
25. Anderson (2012, 45).

1 Divisions

1. Information about this case drawn from Smith (2008).
2. Quoted in Smith (2008, 4).
3. This was the Equal Opportunity Act 1977 (Victoria).
4. Quoted in Smith (2008, 10).
5. In an important legal judgment, the Equal Opportunity Board disagreed.
6. These arguments draw on O'Connor (2019).
7. Smith (1776).
8. This will be discussed more extensively in chapters 6 and 7.
9. Pirlott & Schmitt (2014, 199, references removed). They argue, for example, that 'the suggestion that gendered sexual culture [sex differences in cognition, affect, behaviour, knowledge and skills] involves a large degree of learning does not undermine the basic evolutionary blueprint underlying these sex-specific roles' (p.201).
10. Wood & Eagly (2012); Eagly & Wood (1999).
11. Van Anders (2013).
12. E.g., Schmitt (2015, 222).
13. As Wood and Eagly note, '[s]ocialization builds on characteristically human evolved traits such as the predisposition to imitate others and to engage in social processes of emulation, collaborative learning, and teaching' Wood & Eagly (2012, 66, references removed). However, the insight that we should expect

cultural evolutionary processes to give rise to even arbitrary divisions of labour comes from O'Connor (2019, 95–6).

14. Schmitt (2023a, 68, references removed).

15. This and the following drawn from useful accounts in Buller (2006), Confer et al. (2010), Downes (2005; 2013), Laland & Brown (2011) and Schmitt (2015).

16. These functional mechanisms are also sometimes referred to as 'modules'. For a useful discussion of confusion over the meaning of that term, see Pietraszewski & Wertz (2022).

17. Heyes (2018).

18. E.g., Henrich (2016).

19. See Brown & Richerson (2014).

20. Sterelny (2008; 2014).

21. Hrdy (2011); see also Burkart et al. (2017).

22. See Fuentes (2021).

23. See, for example, Hrdy (2011), Sterelny (2014, chap. 4).

24. Sterelny (2014, 18).

25. Sterelny (2008).

26. Legare (2017, 7877).

27. Brown & Richerson (2014, 111).

28. The classic example is the genetic evolution of lactose tolerance beyond early childhood in populations that adopted cultural practices of herding and milking (see, for example, Henrich, 2016, chap. 6).

29. Murdock & Provost (1973).

30. With thanks to Kim Sterelny for this point.

31. Brown (1970).

32. Bird & Codding (2015, 2).

33. A point made by O'Connor (2019, 95–6).

34. Murdock and Provost (1973).

35. Bird & Codding (2015).

36. O'Connor (2019).

37. O'Connor (2019, 4). Using game theory models, O'Connor demonstrates that we can expect gender roles to emerge even under very minimal conditions.

38. The first two points are made by Cross et al. (2023). For discussion of, and data regarding, relations between economies

and cultural values, see https://www.worldvaluessurvey.org/
WVSContents.jsp?CMSID=Findings.

39. Everything I know about termites I learned from this website:
https://www.britannica.com/animal/termite/Nests.

40. US Bureau of Labor Statistics (n.d.).

41. This is a play on one of feminism's most famous quotations, from
Simone de Beauvoir's (1949) *The Second Sex*: 'One is not born,
but rather becomes, a woman'.

42. Zawidzki (2013). The term (and related concept) was first
introduced by Mameli (2001). 'Mindshaping occurs when a
mechanism aims to make a target match, in relevant respects, a
model . . . The model can be an individual agent, but it can also
be something more abstract, like a possible pattern of activity, or
even a purely fictional agent'. Zawidzki (2013, 31–2).

43. Horner & Whiten (2005).

44. Hardcastle (2003, 41–2).

45. There is debate, however, as to what kinds of behaviours
imitation is important for, and how it comes about. See Heyes
(2021).

46. Sterelny (2014).

47. Parkinson (2012).

48. Parkinson (2012, 296).

49. The following is based on Kline's taxonomy of teaching, cited in
Legare (2017).

50. Zawidzki (2018, 741).

51. Sterelny (2019, 376).

52. Boyd (2019). With thanks to Kim Sterelny for alerting me to
this point.

53. Sterelny (2019).

54. Sterelny (2019, 377).

55. See discussion in Legare (2017).

56. E.g., Eriksson et al. (2021).

57. For an overview of the different philosophical positions within
proposals of the narrative self, see Schechtman (2011, 394).

58. Sterelny (2021).

59. Zawidzki (2013, 58–9).

60. This could even include the 'installation' of culturally inherited

specialized mechanisms for mindshaping processes, acquired over the course of childhood development through social interactions. See Heyes (2018).

61. See Fausto-Sterling (2021).
62. Quinn et al. (2002). This preference is only seen for same-race female faces, and not in newborns.
63. Yamaguchi (2000); Younger & Fearing (1999).
64. Serbin et al. (2002); Zosuls et al. (2009). This literature reviewed in Martin & Ruble (2010), and also discussed in Fine (2010).
65. Bussey (2011, 608, 607).
66. Bussey (2011, 608).
67. Drawing from Bussey & Bandura (1999).
68. Martin & Ruble (2004). For same-sex imitation, see, for example, Bussey & Bandura (1984), Bussey & Perry (1982), Shutts et al. (2010).
69. Hayes et al. (2018).
70. Goodale (1974, see 38–40). Thanks to Kim Sterelny for alerting me to this example.
71. Lew-Levy et al. (2020).
72. Edwards (1993, 337).
73. This argument, including the example that follows, draws on Fine et al. (2017).
74. Berger et al. (2001).
75. Griffiths (2002, 74–5) has pointed out that 'selection cannot favor a trait that compensates for the loss of a developmental input that is, as a matter of fact, reliably available. Evolution does not anticipate future contingencies.'
76. Fine et al. (2017). O'Connor (2019) makes the same point about her account of the cultural evolution of the gendered division of labour.
77. Fuentes (2021, S21). See also Kuhn & Stiner (2006), and Haas et al. (2020, 4). Following Kuhn & Stiner (2006), Wood & Eagly (2012, 59) also suggest that a male–female hunter–gatherer division of labour developed during the late Pleistocene.
78. Haas et al. (2020, 4).
79. E.g., Henrich (2016). In addition, given arguments that division of labour between hunters and gatherers would have arisen

perhaps 80–90,000 years ago, it is not obvious why these activities wouldn't have come to be organized around sex (and age) during this time period, as they were subsequently and in contemporary hunter-gatherer forager societies. Thanks to K. Sterelny for this point, and see O'Connell (2006).

80. Henrich (2016, 44).

81. In particular, it would be difficult to control for the possibility that babies had been subtly conditioned to imitate those of the same sex.

82. Henrich (2016, see 310).

83. For example, although I'm not aware of studies looking at sex differences in babies' interest in infants, a large study of 224 5-week-old babies, using the Neonatal Behavioral Assessment Scale, did not find a sex difference in tracking of face versus inanimate red ball (Bedford et al. 2015). For critiques of the much-cited study of sex differences in newborn looking preferences for a face versus a mobile (Connellan et al. 2000), see Nash & Grossi (2007); Fine (2010; 2020a).

84. Benenson et al. (2011) found that more 6- to 9-month-old infant boys (32 per cent) than girls (0 per cent) were likely to hit a balloon after seeing adult models do so, and the increase was correlated only with time spent looking at the male model. However, to my knowledge this result has not been replicated, and Dinella et al. (2017) found no evidence of gender differences in interest in toys linked to their propulsion properties.

85. See useful discussion in Brown & Richerson (2014).

86. Richerson et al. (2021, 7–8).

2   Sex and Status

1. Ho (2009, 118).

2. Ho (2009, 118).

3. Ridgeway (2019, 2). The book presents the evidence and arguments of what is known as Status Construction Theory.

4. See Rhodes & Baron (2019).

5. Bodenhausen et al. (2012, 319).
6. Bodenhausen et al. (2012, 319).
7. See Sterelny (2021, table 2.1).
8. Sterelny (2021, 56).
9. Sterelny (2021, 7).
10. Henrich & Gil-White (2001). See also Cheng (2020).
11. The answers to these questions are, respectively: always; yes, but not all three on the same day; and no. You are welcome.
12. Ridgeway (2019, 3).
13. Ridgeway (2019, 4).
14. Thanks to Kim Sterelny for this point.
15. Heck et al. (2022, 594).
16. Heck et al. (2022, 594), references removed.
17. Ridgeway (2019, 30).
18. Reviewed in Ridgeway (2019, chap. 5).
19. Whipple (1939, loc. 305).
20. Ridgeway & Nakagawa (2017, 133).
21. Ridgeway & Diekema (1989).
22. Boehm et al. (1993).
23. See Ridgeway (2019, chap. 4).
24. Ridgeway et al. (1998).
25. Ridgeway (2019, 85). Ridgeway goes on to note that studies also find that other biasing factors, in addition to a material resource like pay, can give rise to status beliefs about the group with the advantage (see p.86).
26. The classic contemporary book of this genre is Tilly (1998).
27. Ridgeway (2019, 128–9).
28. The filename of the cartoon is Office-Sexism-Women-Business-Relationships-Cartoons-Punch-Magazine-Riana-Duncan-1988. 01.08.11.tif. It can be found at https://magazine.punch.co.uk/gallery-image/Riana-Duncan-Cartoons/GooooBxiFqQLTUiM/IooooeHEXGJ_wImQ.
29. E.g., see Saini (2024).
30. Simpson (2004, 359, 360).
31. Block (2023, 49).
32. Ridgeway (2019).
33. Thompson (1825, 206, 198). Although Anna Doyle Wheeler is

not named as an author, her contribution is acknowledged in an 'Introductory Letter to Mrs. Wheeler'.

34. Costa Dias et al. (2020); Gough & Noonan (2013); Kleven et al. (2019); Grimshaw & Rubery (2015).

35. Vagni & Breen (2021). No earnings penalty was estimated for the highest earning mothers.

36. Australian Human Rights Commission (2014).

37. McGoogan (2018) (21 July 2018). 37 per cent said that if the law allowed it, they would advertise men-only jobs.

38. For example, an analysis of Danish data found that mothers, compared with fathers, experienced a 20 per cent earnings penalty over the two decades following the birth of the first child. This wasn't solely due to reduced labour market participation and fewer hours worked. Earnings also fell because of lower wages, adverse effects on occupational rank, reduced probability of being a manager, and a shift to the lower-paid but 'family-friendly' public sector (Kleven et al., 2019).

39. Wood et al. (2020).

40. In the rather unlikely event that you wish to read more about the history of Australian superannuation, see Parliament of Australia (2014).

41. This percentage has been gradually increasing since the scheme began, and in 2023–4 was at 11 per cent.

42. In Australia, the government pension is means-tested, but otherwise the same for everyone.

43. Kitchen et al. (2021).

44. For committee membership over its 12-year duration, see Hooper (August 2006).

45. Hargita (2016, 228).

46. OECD (2021, figure 1.1).

47. See European Commission: Directorate-General for Justice and Consumers & Sierminska (2017).

48. The female-to-male ratio for mean net wealth was a bit higher, 0.73, but in countries with considerable wealth inequality, the mean tends to be skewed by the very wealthy.

49. Using median net wealth, see European Commission:

Directorate-General for Justice and Consumers & Sierminska (2017, table 5A and 6A).

50. Chang (2010).

51. In 2022, 28.9 per cent of households were single with no kids, and an additional 8.1 per cent were single parents (USA Facts, 2022).

52. Office for National Statistics (2024a).

53. Chang (2010, 7).

54. See chap. 2 and figure 2.10 of Chang (2010).

55. Toossi & Joyner (2018).

56. Brown (2012, 251–2).

57. For example, 1–4 years following divorce, 42 per cent of divorced mothers can't afford a week's holiday away from home every year, compared with 11 per cent of divorced dads (Brown, 2016, see figure 12).

58. 85 per cent of lone-parent families are headed by a mother (Office for National Statistics 2024a).

59. Social Metrics Commission (2023).

60. Sierminska (2018, 58).

61. Chang (2010). See also Blumenthal & Rothwell (2018).

3 (Re)producing Fathers

1. Padavic et al. (2020, 79–80).

2. Padavic et al. (2020, 81).

3. Ely et al. (2014).

4. Gino et al. (2015, 12358).

5. In Italy, an innovative 'solution' to this risk is the *dimissioni in bianco* ('blank resignations') – an undated letter of resignation that employers can conveniently pull out if an employee becomes pregnant – estimated in 2011 to have affected 800,000 women (Davies, 2013).

6. Hakim (2000).

7. Hakim (2002, 435).

8. See table 3, Hakim (2002, 436).

9. Goldin (2021).

10. Goldin (2021, 21).
11. Hakim (2000, 454).
12. Hobson & Fahlén (2009, 229).
13. See figure 3, Hobson & Fahlén (2009, 223).
14. E.g., see Greenhaus et al. (2012), who found that among US business professionals, links between the centrality of work, job level and salary, with work hours, were stronger in women than in men.
15. Kalleberg (2011).
16. Messing (2021, 106, 107).
17. Hanna et al. (2020, 637).
18. Galea et al. (2022).
19. Galea et al. (2022, 127).
20. See Gerson (2023).
21. Reeves (2023, sec. Culture lags economics).
22. Gerson (2023, 1424–5).
23. Gerson (2023, 1425).
24. Gerson (2023, 1426). See also Goldin (2021) on the obstacle to gender egalitarian households posed by greedy jobs.
25. Gerson (2023, 1427).
26. Stanfors & Goldscheider (2017, 189).
27. Rosenbaum et al. (2018).
28. For example: 'Women's mate preferences center, in part, on cues to a man's ability and willingness to provide resources' (Schmitt 2023a, 66).
29. Gettler (2014, 157).
30. This can be heard in the *Working Fathers* podcast trailer. More information about the podcast, created by myself, Dan Halliday, Melissa Wheeler and Annabelle Baldwin, is available at https://blogs.unimelb.edu.au/shaps-research/2023/07/17/working-fathers-introduction/. The podcast was funded by the Faculty of Arts and the School of Historical & Philosophical Studies at the University of Melbourne, and supported by external partners the Women's Leadership Institute Australia and the Trawalla Foundation.
31. Hewlett (1991, 168).
32. Seccombe (1986, 57).
33. Seccombe (1986, 65, references removed).
34. Seccombe (1986, 66 footnote 9, references removed), referencing

the work of Abbott, E. (1969). *Women in industry: A study in American Economic History.* Arno Press, New York.

35. Seccombe (1986, 65).
36. Seccombe (1986, 74).
37. See also Walby (1986).
38. Seccombe (1986, 57).
39. This and the following draws on Bueskens (2018).
40. Bueskens (2018, 9).
41. Siegel (1994, 1093).
42. Glenn (2010).
43. Walby (1986, loc. 1596).
44. Walby (1986, loc. 3592).
45. Borgkvist et al. (2018, 709), fillers and repetition omitted from quotation.
46. Acker (1990).
47. See Williams et al. (2016).
48. Borgkvist et al. (2021, 2081).
49. Haas & Hwang (2019).
50. Haas & Hwang (2019, 64).
51. Williams at al. (2016, 522, reference removed).
52. Shows & Gerstel (2009).
53. Shows & Gerstel (2009, 177).
54. Shows & Gerstel (2009, 178).
55. Shows & Gerstel (2009, 179).
56. Kellogg (2011).
57. Kellogg (2011, 135).
58. Cooper (2000, 382).
59. Cooper (2000, 394).
60. Cooper (2000, 398, 400).
61. Cooper (2000, 397).
62. Cooper (2000, 395).
63. Padavic et al. (2020, 83–4).
64. Padavic et al. (2020, 84).
65. Ely & Padavic (2020, 62).
66. Padavic et al. (2020, 63).
67. Padavic et al. (2020, 79).
68. Padavic et al. (2020, 86).

69. A point made by Strazdins et al. (2017), who also conducted the research on children's attitudes.

4 Beyond Market-Thinking

1. European Banking Authority (2021, 5).
2. Godechot (2017, sec. Avoiding simple ideas, entering the bank).
3. Here Godechot (2017, sec. Avoiding simple ideas, entering the bank) references Lordon, F. (2000). 'La force des idées simples. Misère épistémique des comportements économiques'. *Politix. Revue des sciences sociales du politique*, 13(52), 183–209.
4. Sloan (2024).
5. Sloan (2023).
6. Sloan (2024).
7. Lyons & Butler (2024). X post available at https://twitter.com/mattjcan/status/1762235731811164187, accessed on 9 May 2024.
8. https://twitter.com/mattjcan/status/1762339596208308651, accessed on 9 May 2024.
9. https://twitter.com/mattjcan/status/1762400947630952824, accessed on 9 May 2024.
10. Workplace Gender Equality Agency (2024). This is the median total remuneration gender pay gap (%) for the mining industry.
11. Explanation drawn from Avent-Holt & Tomaskovic-Devey (2014) and Figart et al. (2005).
12. See discussion in Folbre (1994).
13. For example, 'associating gender and race-ethnicity solely with discriminatory practices assumes that basic wage-determination models remain unchanged. Discrimination becomes a special case of market failure. In contrast, the underpinning of our approach is the belief that gendered relations in society have fundamental effects on wages as well as other economic outcomes'. Figart et al. (2005, sec. Feminist Methodology and Economic Theory). See also Avent-Holt & Tomaskovic-Devey (2014).
14. Cowper-Coles et al. (2021, 6). The report additionally notes the importance of equal pay for work of equal value.
15. Feiner & Roberts (1990, 178).

16. Strassmann (2009).
17. Tomaskovic-Devey & Avent-Holt (2019, 163).
18. Discussed extensively in England & Folbre (1999); England et al. (2002).
19. Tomaskovic-Devey & Avent-Holt (2019, 196).
20. See figure 3, Krippner (2005). Krippner defines financialization 'as a pattern of accumulation in which profits accrue primarily through financial channels rather than through trade and commodity production. "Financial" here refers to activities relating to the provision (or transfer) of liquid capital in expectation of future interest, dividends, or capital gains' (pp.174–5, reference removed).
21. Data from the US Bureau of Labor Statistics, as of 26 January 2024: https://www.bls.gov/cps/cpsaat11.htm.
22. Lin & Neely (2017).
23. For example, the UK's Office for National Statistics (2024b) reported a median gender pay gap of 34.3 per cent for the UK financial services sector (excluding insurance and pensions), the largest of good- and reasonable-quality estimates across all industries. See table 4.12 of the 2023 provisional edition of the gender pay-gap estimates.
24. Chiu (2023).
25. See figures 1 and 2, Deloitte (2023a). The survey was sent to 2,487 firms.
26. Masterson (2024).
27. Sherman & Clayton (2023).
28. Qiu (2023).
29. Krugman (2023).
30. Farnsworth (2021).
31. Last updated 6 February 2024. https://goodjobsfirst.org/amazon-tracker/.
32. Farnsworth (2013).
33. Farnsworth (2013, 54).
34. Women's Budget Group (2016); Women's Budget Group & Runnymede (2016). See also discussion in Criado-Perez (2020).
35. Workplace Gender Equality Agency (2024).
36. Avent-Holt & Tomaskovic-Devey (2023, 220).

37. Tomaskovic-Devey et al. (2009). This was the case both for average pay and for inequality between the highest and lowest earners.

38. Joshi et al. (2015).

39. Cha & Weeden (2014); Chung (2022b).

40. Steinberg (1990, 458).

41. Examples from Steinberg (1990).

42. For a striking example, see Otis & Wu (2018).

43. Levanon & Grusky (2016, 594).

44. Cited in Folbre (2006, 23).

45. Shorter (1975, 181). In addition, as Shorter explains, poor rural women would send out their own children to wet nurses at very low rates so that they could themselves take on paid nursing work at a higher rate.

46. Shorter (1975, 185).

47. Shorter (1975, 185, 186).

48. Nelson (1999, 44).

49. Lovell (2006).

50. Tomaskovic-Devey (2014, 57), referring to the work of Nelson & Bridges (1999).

51. Tomaskovic-Devey & Avent-Holt (2019, 117–18).

52. Soit (2022). That VC, current as of 2024, is Professor Duncan Maskell.

53. Rowlands & Boden (2020).

54. Hare (2021).

55. Penner et al. (2022).

56. Nelson & Bridges (1999, 2).

57. Nelson & Bridges (1999, 324).

58. Nelson & Bridges (1999, 309, 310).

59. Palmer & Eveline (2012, 269).

60. Palmer & Eveline (2012, 264).

61. Palmer & Eveline (2012, 268).

62. Palmer & Eveline (2012, 256). For example, a survey of aged-care personal carers found that only 26 per cent expressed satisfaction with their pay, compared with 72 per cent of female employees with equivalent levels of education in the Australian workforce (Martin, 2007).

63. Royal Commission into Aged Care Quality and Safety (2020).
64. Royal Commission into Aged Care Quality and Safety (2021).
65. Fair Work Commission (2024).
66. The Fair Work Act 2009 – Sec. 157. Available at https://classic.austlii.edu.au/au/legis/cth/consol_act/fwa2009114/s157.html.
67. https://www.fwc.gov.au/documents/decisionssigned/pdf/2024fwcfb150.pdf, p.57.
68. Palmer & Eveline (2012, 268).

5   Border Control

1. Consumer Financial Protection Bureau (2016).
2. Egan (2016).
3. Reckard (2013).
4. Polonsky v. Wells Fargo Bank & Company, et. al. Los Angeles Superior Court. No. BC634475 (2016). Accessed 6 January 2024. https://www.nakedcapitalism.com/wp-content/uploads/2016/09/Polonsky-v.-Wells-Fargo-Bank-Co.-BC634475-California-Superior-Court-Los-Angeles-County.pdf.
5. See Fine et al. (2020).
6. Cited in Carbone (2022).
7. US Attorney's Office, Central District of California (2023).
8. Cowley (2023).
9. US Attorney's Office, Central District of California (2023); Mayer (2023).
10. Carbone et al. (2019).
11. Mackert (2012). These themes draw from Albiston & Green (2018); Roscigno et al. (2007).
12. Weeden (2002).
13. This idea finds some empirical support in Weeden (2002).
14. See Mills (1998).
15. Stoker et al. (2012).
16. Kübler et al. (2018). The CVs spanned a range of competitiveness, counterbalanced across gender.
17. See table 1 of Kübler et al. (2018).
18. Ceci et al. (2023).
19. Ceci et al. (2023, 59).

20. See Albiston & Green (2018).

21. Greenwald & Pettigrew (2014, 673, emphasis removed).

22. E.g., Nielsen (2018). See also Cheryan & Markus (2020).

23. Patton et al. (2017).

24. Roth (2015, 56).

25. Roth (2004b, 201).

26. Roth (2004a).

27. Roth (2015, 67). See chap. 3, especially figure 3.1.

28. Roth (2004a, 226).

29. 'Hedge Fund Industry'. BarclayHedge. Accessed 27 July 2024. https://www.barclayhedge.com/solutions/assets-under-management/hedge-fund-assets-under-management/hedge-fund-industry.

30. For large hedge funds (Harjani, 2014).

31. Taub (2024).

32. Neely (2021; 2018).

33. According to an analysis by the Knight Foundation in 2021, only 2.2 per cent of US-based hedge fund assets were managed by women, and 3.4 per cent by minorities (Lerner et al., 2021, see figure 2).

34. Luscombe (2022).

35. Bourdieu (1977, 80).

36. Neely (2018, 373).

37. Giazitzoglu & Muzio (2021, 78).

38. Giazitzoglu & Muzio (2021, 79).

39. See table 2, Rivera & Tilcsik (2016).

40. Rivera & Tilcsik (2016, 1121).

41. Halrynjo & Mangset (2022).

42. Halrynjo & Mangset (2022, 944).

43. McDowell (2010, 653; 1997).

44. Westwood (1998, 809).

45. Fortado (2017).

46. Neely (2020, 286, 287).

47. Neely (2020, 288).

48. Davis & Kim (2015, 211).

49. Smithers et al. (2023).

50. Carbone (2022, 169).

51. Carbone et al. (2019, 1117), first citing the work of Fusaro & Miller (2009), then Dallas (2012).
52. Lardner (2002), quoted in Dallas (2012, 37).
53. Carbone et al. (2019, 1105).
54. Carbone et al. (2019, 1105).
55. Egan et al. (2022). Wells Fargo Advisors is one of several financial services businesses operated by parent company Wells Fargo.
56. US Congress, Senate. Committee on Banking, Housing and Urban Affairs. Hearing, 'An Examination of Wells Fargo's Unauthorized Accounts and the Regulatory Response'. 20 September 2016. Available at https://www.youtube.com/watch?v=xJhkX74D10M. Quoted at approx. 6.50. For full information on this hearing see https://www.banking.senate.gov/hearings/an-examination-of-wells-fargos-unauthorized-accounts-and-the-regulatory-response. In January 2020, Stumpf received a $17.5 million fine from the federal regulator, and a lifetime ban from the banking industry (Cowley & Flitter, 2020).
57. Berdahl et al. (2018, 430, 433).
58. Berdahl et al. (2018, 423-24, references omitted).
59. Tomaskovic-Devey & Avent-Holt (2019, 199), citing the work of Battiston et al. (2012); Vitali et al. (2011).
60. Sojo et al. (2020).
61. Schultz (2018, 35).
62. Verified Petition, People v. The Weinstein Company, et al. New York State Supreme Court. No. 450293 (2018). https://ag.ny.gov/sites/default/files/weinstein_company.pdf. Quoted from 9–10.
63. People v. The Weinstein Company (2018), at 14.
64. People v. The Weinstein Company (2018), at 11. As of this writing, the civil case against Weinstein remains ongoing and he has denied any non-consensual sexual activity. Kantor, Jodi and Megan Twohey. 2020. 'Judge, Expressing Skepticism, Upends $25 Million Harvey Weinstein Settlement'. New York Times, 14 July 2020. https://www.nytimes.com/2020/07/14/us/harvey-weinstein-settlement.html.
65. Schultz (2018, 24).
66. Schultz (2018, 47).
67. Sawer (2013).

68. Jabour (2013). The menu came to light thanks to a staff member and chef working at the Brisbane restaurant that hosted the dinner, and was subsequently condemned by opposition party leaders in news reports.
69. Lake (2013).
70. Weaving et al. (2023).
71. Australian Human Rights Commission (2022). Respondents were asked if they had experienced a list of behaviours likely to constitute sexual harassment.
72. Sojo et al. (2016).
73. Cortina & Areguin (2021, 295).
74. Schultz (2018, 53).
75. Jacobs & Siddiqui (2016).
76. House of Commons Treasury Committee (2024, 37, 27).

6   Differences

1. Quoted in, and details of incident drawn from, Lewis (2017).
2. Damore (2017, 3).
3. Levin (2017).
4. Pichai (2017).
5. Saini (2017); Soh (2017).
6. See, for example, Brooks (2017), George (2017), Lee (2017) and range of views from scientists collated at Heterodox Academy (2017).
7. Fine & Herbert (2017).
8. Janicke et al. (2016).
9. Stewart-Williams & Halsey (2021, 7).
10. Stewart-Williams & Halsey (2021, 7, references removed).
11. Stewart-Williams & Halsey (2021, 7, references removed).
12. Global Education Monitoring Report Team (2020, figure 12.2). Globally, the tertiary education enrollment gender ratio favours women, and particularly strongly in Tunisia, Algeria, and Europe and North America.
13. Charmes (2022).
14. Schmitt (2017).

15. Lippa et al. (2010).
16. See discussion in Henrich et al. (2023) and Davis et al. (2021).
17. Example provided in Schwartz & Rubel-Lifschitz (2009), referring to Schwartz & Rubel (2005, app. D). Effect size is .59 in Finland and -.64 in Ethiopia. The variation is not as striking in other samples, but there are always many countries in which no significant sex differences in the importance of universalism are found.
18. Nivette et al. (2019).
19. See appendix table 1, Murphy et al. (2021).
20. Figure 3, Falk et al. (2018, 1670).
21. For ease of reading, I have added 'I' to the beginning of these statements.
22. Hofmann et al. (2023).
23. Hofmann et al. (2023, tables 3 & 4).
24. Soh (2020, 57). Similarly, Stewart-Williams & Halsey (2021, 6) write that 'several lines of evidence suggest that people's interests, career preferences and life priorities are shaped in part by prenatal hormones'.
25. This research programme and its findings are extensively discussed in Jordan-Young (2010; 2012). See also Fine (2010; 2015).
26. White & Speiser (2000).
27. See Jordan-Young (2010, 70–1; 2012).
28. See Hines (2020).
29. Jordan-Young (2010, 21); for a recent review of this perspective, see Hines (2020).
30. The following draws on Doell & Longino (1988).
31. Jordan-Young (2010, 288).
32. Examples cited by Jordan-Young (2010, 287) are: Wakshlak & Weinstock (1990); Leboucher (1989); Hendricks et al. (1982); Clemens et al. (1969).
33. Jordan-Young (2010, 289).
34. Dupré (2024); see also Fausto-Sterling (2021, figure 5).
35. Bussey (2011).
36. Jordan-Young (2010; 2012).
37. Jordan-Young (2012, 1741), emphasis in original removed.

38. Jordan-Young (2012, 1742), emphasis removed for first quotation.

39. Hines et al. (2016).

40. Neufeld et al. (2023).

41. My colleagues and I suggested the link between prenatal androgens and same-sex copying in Fine et al. (2017), and this was also suggested in Kung et al. (2024). Hines et al. (2016) have made the second suggestion.

42. Lew-Levy et al. (2020, 1290).

43. Beltz et al. (2011). The formal terms for the 6 General Occupational Interests are Realistic, Investigative, Artistic, Social, Enterprising and Conventional, respectively.

44. In this study, the Organizers dimension couldn't be used due to statistical issues.

45. The effect size for the sex difference was d=1.5 for Doer occupations, and between d=.81 and .97 for Helper, Creator and Persuader occupations. To give a rough idea of meaning, an effect size of 1 means there is approximately 62 per cent overlap between the populations, and if you were to choose a girl and boy at random, about 3 out of 4 times their preferences would be consistent with sex-typing (e.g., the girl would rate the Helper occupation more highly than the boy).

46. Su et al. (2009).

47. Beltz et al. (2011, 315).

48. Based on O*NET interest testing, retrieved from https://www. onetcenter.org/dl_tools/ipsf/Interest_Profiler.pdf on 23 April 2024. O*NET, sponsored by the US Department of Labor/ Employment and Training Administration, uses a framework called the O*NET Content Model to identify the mix of abilities, skills, knowledge, activities and tasks that make up occupations. One part of that mix is the 6 General Occupational Interests.

49. Valian (2014, 227).

50. Valian (2014, 226).

51. Valian (2014, 226).

52. Based on Charles & Grusky (2004, Tables A5.1 and A3.2).

53. E.g., Wong et al. (2013); Pasterski et al. (2005).

54. Shirazi et al. (2022, 343). As they explain, in the first trimester, androgen production in the gonads is stimulated by human

chorionic gonadotropin (hCG) produced by the placenta. As placental hCG drops, the hypothalamus normally takes over hormonal stimulation of gonadal hormone production (through the secretion of gonadotropin-releasing hormone), but there is a failure of this normal pattern in isolated gonadotropin-releasing-hormone deficiency.

55. Zucker et al. (2006). For items used in this study, see the questionnaire, available at https://osf.io/qw4rk.

56. E.g., Bleier (1988); Fausto-Sterling (2000); Fine (2010); Jordan-Young (2010); Grossi & Fine (2012).

57. Trarbach et al. (2007).

58. See citations in Shirazi et al. (2022).

59. Crowley & Whitcomb (1990).

60. In the supplementary materials, Shirazi et al. (2022) consider the possibility that androgen-related physical differences between the clinical and non-clinical group may explain their results. To investigate, they performed factor analysis on the questionnaire items, and found that the five items that clustered together as the factor explaining the most variation in responses did not include the two questions in which participants were asked whether they enjoyed playing baseball, marbles, dolls or football at ages 5 to 8 and ages 9 to 13. They then repeated the comparisons between men with and without the hormonal condition using just those five items, and still found a statistical difference between the groups. They conclude that this demonstrates that 'any effect of early gonadal hormones on [Childhood Gender Nonconformity] is not driven primarily by a difference in sports interest that could be related to differences in physical characteristics'. It would be more accurate to say that this analysis shows that the difference between the clinical and non-clinical group is not restricted to, or dependent on, differences in interest in the highly specific gender-typed activities of baseball, marbles, dolls and football. Supplementary materials accessed from https://osf.io/m8hn9 on 16 March 2024.

61. David Puts, quoted in Dolan (2022).

62. Shirazi et al. (2021).

63. Statistically, the difference between low-testosterone men and control women was about four and a half times larger than the difference between low-testosterone men and control men.
64. Geary (2024).

7 Girl, Uninterrupted?

1. Abbate (2012).
2. Abbate (2012, 128).
3. See Abbate (2012, 95–6).
4. Abbate (2012, 1).
5. See Donato (1990).
6. Abbate (2012, 53).
7. Abbate (2012, 1).
8. West et al. (2019, 78).
9. Mill (1869, 104–5). He attributed considerable credit for this work to his wife, Harriet Taylor Mill.
10. While it was once assumed by economists that only rich countries could afford to liberate their women, it now appears that freeing women helps make countries richer (Scott, 2020).
11. Balducci (2023). For other gender gaps, either no relationship with gender equality was discerned (e.g., basic maths ability) or the results were inconclusive (e.g., for science).
12. Schmitt et al. (2008, 168). In a later popular piece, Schmitt (2023b) cautioned that the presence of larger sex differences in Nordic countries 'doesn't mean the Nordic-sized sex differences are "natural" and all other nations just aren't reaching their true "sex difference potential."' However, the assumption remains that there can be a 'natural' expression of a gendered trait for a particular socio-ecological context. In Schmitt's (2015) framework for understanding sex differences in personality, there are 'obligate evolved sex differences' for traits 'adaptively designed to manifest relatively uniform sex differences across cultures' (p.223); 'facultative adaptations' that may be 'specially designed to be differentially sensitive to local ecological information' (p.225); and 'emergently-moderated sex differences'

in which both obligate and facultative adaptations can be accentuated or suppressed such as by strong religious norms or other external forces.

13. Schmitt et al. (2008, 179).
14. See discussions in Fine (2020b) and Wilson et al. (2003).
15. Stewart-Williams & Halsey (2021, 25). They argue that, contra Damore, sex differences in personality do not offer a good explanation of the STEM gap.
16. Stewart-Williams & Halsey (2021, 26).
17. Stern & Madison (2022, 695).
18. Specifically, Jordan-Young (2010) and Hines (2004). A tension in the inclusion of both these books is that Hines is a leading researcher working within the brain organization theory research programme critiqued by Jordan-Young. By way of disclosure, one of my own books, *Delusions of Gender*, was among those so dismissed.
19. See, for example, evidence and arguments in Fine (2017b, chaps. 5–7) presenting evidence and arguments that risk-taking is not a stable one-dimensional personality trait that can then be linked to high testosterone exposure; that the risk of many activities is inherently subjective and some activities may be objectively less risky for males than females; that syntheses of studies of sex differences across ages and domains reveal a complex pattern inconsistent with what we would expect from Evolutionary Psychology accounts; that there is androcentrism and confirmation bias in studies of risk-taking that bias towards findings of male risk-taking, including financial risk-taking; that the existence of sex differences in risk perceptions, economic risk-taking and competition is contingent on identity and cultural context; that testosterone levels are modulated by gender constructions in humans and are therefore not a 'pure' biological variable; and that studies attempting to link testosterone exposure to financial risk-taking have not yielded consistent or compelling findings. Jordan-Young & Karkazis (2019, chap. 5) expose the inconsistencies and statistical and methodological weaknesses glossed over in studies attempting to link testosterone to low- and high-status occupations and

risk-taking; the complexity and socially constructed nature of risk, and the need to incorporate social status and gender expectations into models of relationships between testosterone and economic risk-taking. Stanton et al. (2021, 1) conducted two double-blind placebo-controlled experimental studies and one correlational study of testosterone and economic risk-taking, and reported that '[b]roadly, the results of all three studies suggest no consistent relationship between testosterone and financial behavior or preferences'.

20. Stern & Madison (2022, 696–7, 700).
21. Stern & Madison (2022, 695).
22. Guo et al. (2024, 42).
23. See Else-Quest & Grabe (2012).
24. Jackson (2010).
25. E.g., Scarborough et al. (2019); Knight & Brinton (2017).
26. See Legare (2017).
27. Cross et al. (2023, 10, 3).
28. Schmitt (2023a, 100, references removed).
29. Purported examples of such accusations are provided in Schmitt (2023a, 71), but on my reading they do not make these claims. A potential source of confusion lies in the important distinction between mechanisms (which are proposed to be universal) and manifest behaviour (which is contingent, both developmentally and in expression). Zentner & Mitura reasonably observe that there is some disagreement as to how large cultural variation in sex differences in mate preferences can be before an Evolutionary Psychology account requires 'an unworkably large number of assumptions and hypotheses', and merely state that sex differences that are core to Evolutionary Psychology accounts – not necessarily their size – should be consistent across contexts (2012, 1176). Smith (2020) is a philosophy of biology article concerned with whether Evolutionary Psychologists can ever provide evidence for hypothesized mechanisms. (The conclusion is that they cannot.) Endendijk et al. (2020, 166) acknowledge that cross-cultural variation in sex differences is predicted for emergently moderated sex differences, but since this 'does not yield a testable hypothesis about whether increasing levels of

gender equality would suppress or accentuate gender differences in the norms of sexual behavior', they are only able to test the prediction of relatively uniform sex differences based on the obligate sex difference perspective. Wood & Eagly (2002) discuss when Evolutionary Psychologists do and don't predict variability cross-culturally.

30. The following discussion of Aristotle's theory and the Natural State Model draws on Sober (1980) and, in relation to Evolutionary Psychologists' psychological adaptations, Buller (2006).

31. Sober (1980, 361).

32. Schmitt (2015, 227). Though see note 12 of this chapter.

33. Defined in terms of health, education, employment, income, political representation and family size (Schwartz and Rubel-Lifschitz, 2009).

34. Schwartz & Rubel (2005, 1023).

35. Schwartz & Rubel-Lifschitz (2009, 171).

36. Schmitt says of this work: 'It is not that humans are adapted to anticipate this freedom and have special design features that facultatively respond to it, instead it is the case that sex differences in values may be obligate (or perhaps facultative) and the degree of psychological sex differences is an emergently-moderated response this [*sic*] to freedom' (2015a, 228, reference removed).

37. Laland & Brown (2011, 159).

38. Henrich et al. (2010, 61).

39. Women in Computer Science (n.d.).

40. Ensmenger (2010, 121, 136).

41. Ensmenger (2010, 125).

42. Abbate (2012, 98).

43. Brandon (1968, 332).

44. Ensmenger (2010, 127).

45. Valian (2014).

46. Ensmenger (2010, 129).

47. Abbate (2012, 111).

48. Kapin (2020).

49. Abbate (2012, 40).

50. Budge et al. (2023).

NOTES

51. Leichman (2023).
52. Richardson and the GenderSci Lab (2020). See also discussion in Else-Quest & Hamilton (2018) and the GenderSci Lab's other posts about the Gender Equality Paradox, available from https://www.genderscilab.org/blog/category/Gender+Equality+Paradox.
53. Charles & Grusky (2004, 4).
54. See Hook & Li (2020).
55. Wong & Charles (2020).
56. Block et al. (2022).
57. Richardson and the GenderSci Lab (2020).
58. Jordan-Young (2010).
59. McDowell (2004, 322).
60. Richardson and the GenderSci Lab (2020).
61. See Richardson (2011).
62. Caird (2010, 207).
63. See Tomaskovic-Devey & Avent-Holt (2019, 196).
64. NHS (n.d.).
65. Jordan Peterson, interview by Cathy Newman. *Channel 4 News* (UK). Aired 16 January 2018. https://www.youtube.com/watch?app=desktop&v=aMcjxSThD54.
66. Jordan Peterson, interview by Tara Brown. *60 Minutes Australia*. Aired 30 April 2018. https://9now.nine.com.au/60-minutes/pay-up/8478e7a7-5aa3-407d-bed4-179d4bb196f0.
67. Risman (2004, 433).
68. Schultz (1998, 1691).
69. Tomaskovic-Devey & Avent-Holt (2019, 226).

8 From Equality to DEI

1. HM Treasury & Virgin Money (2016, 6).
2. HM Treasury & Virgin Money (2016, 3).
3. HM Treasury (n.d.).
4. Chinwala et al. (2023, 4).
5. Chinwala et al. (2024).
6. Global Institute for Women's Leadership (2020), at about 25:14 minutes.

7. Blackford (2024, 191).
8. Blackford (2024, 223).
9. See Haslam (2016).
10. Lewis (2017).
11. Blackford (2024, 208–9).
12. Edelman et al. (2001).
13. This passage draws on Fine (2017a).
14. Sandberg (2010).
15. Sandberg (2013a).
16. This can be found at LeanIn.org.
17. 'Changing the World, Circle by Circle'. Lean In. Accessed 21 May. https://leanin.org/driving-change.
18. 'Allyship at Work'. Lean In. Accessed 29 August 2024. https://leanin.org/allyship-at-work. Examples from Allyship at Work, Workshop Presentation materials.
19. '50 Ways to Fight Bias'. Lean In. Accessed 29 August 2024. https://leanin.org/gender-bias-program-for-companies. Example from 'For Managers' set, available at https://leanin.org/gender-bias-cards/grid/sets#!
20. 'International Women's Day'. Lean In. Accessed 5 January 2024. https://www.internationalwomensday.com/?utm_source=leanin&utm_medium=referral&utm_campaign=iwd_2023.
21. Sandberg (2013b).
22. Giridharadas (2018, 30).
23. Another interesting example comes from the Australian legislation that makes provisions for affirmative action. First enacted as the Affirmative Action (Equal Opportunity for Women) Act 1986 (Cth), it then became the Equal Opportunity for Women in the Workplace Act 1999 (Cth), and then the Workplace Gender Equality Act 2012 (Cth). The revised legislation explicitly cites productivity and competitiveness as objectives of the Act (Thornton, 2015).
24. See rigorous analysis by Adams (2016), noting influence of studies by Catalyst, McKinsey and Credit Suisse.
25. For combined meta-analysis and thoughtful critique, see Hoobler et al. (2018). Fine et al. (forthcoming), based on content analysis of academic finance, found that the most

common sex/gender research question was instrumental, that is, concerned with how women could benefit other entities, such as shareholders.

26. Sojo et al. (2020).
27. Georgeac & Rattan (2023); Pasztor (2019).
28. Tatli (2011, 242).
29. Georgeac & Rattan (2023).
30. Ely & Meyerson (2000).
31. See references in Gardiner et al. (2023).
32. 'Build Your Skills'. Lean In. Accessed 29 August 2024. http://leanin.org/education.
33. Metz & Kumra (2019, 89–90).
34. Sandberg (2013a, Introduction).
35. Arruzza et al, (2019, 4).
36. Criado-Perez (2020, 314).
37. E.g., Arruzza et al. (2019); Geier & Curve Contributors (2014).
38. Dana (1915).
39. Gillard & Okonjo-Iweala (2021, 286).
40. Gardiner et al. (2023).
41. Kim et al. (2018).
42. Jones et al. (2023). The 12 dimensions of job quality were: skills (likelihood of work-related training); prospects for promotion; regularly working outside of contracted hours; working non-standard hours; annual pay increments; workplace pension; salaried (versus hourly wage); receives bonus; task discretion; control over start and finish times; formal access to flexible work; ability to informally vary hours.
43. Artz et al. (2018).
44. Sauer et al. (2021, 934).
45. See Fine (2010).
46. Lanz & Brown (2020, 79, 63, 65, 66). These claims about male and female brains drew on Ingalhalikar et al. (2014). For critiques, see, for example, Fine (2013), Joel & Tarrasch (2014).
47. 'Mark Carney: The "film star" Bank of England governor' (2016).
48. Carney (2016).
49. Shen & Joseph (2021).
50. Peters et al. (2018).

51. US Department of Treasury, Office of the Comptroller of the Currency (2020, 3).
52. Ely & Meyerson (2000, 109).
53. Ely & Meyerson (2000, 124, references removed).
54. Most recently and accessibly summarized in Dobbin & Kalev (2022).
55. Dobbin & Kalev (2018, 48).
56. See Dobbin & Kalev (2022).
57. E.g., Buss (2023).
58. Schultz (2010, 1215).
59. Kornberger et al. (2010, 786, 788, reference removed).
60. The Australian Workplace Gender Equality Agency is one such example. So is Dobbin & Kalev (2022).
61. Research & Markets (2024).
62. AlShebli et al. (2020a, 6).
63. Dobbin & Kalev (2022, 111).
64. Science News Staff (2020); Wessel (2020).
65. AlShebli et al. (2020b).
66. Harris (2024).
67. Franklin & Massoudi (2024).
68. Chinwala et al. (2023).
69. Virgin Money UK (2023).
70. Lin & Neely (2020, 10).
71. Lin & Neely (2020, 181, references removed).
72. European Banking Authority (2024, figure 3).
73. Davis & Walsh (2016).

9   A New Vision

1. For education, the largest deviation from parity in sex ratio for primary education, secondary education and literacy was used. For all ratios, the average was taken over five years of data.
2. Stoet & Geary (2019, 2).
3. Stoet & Geary (2019, 4).
4. Stoet & Geary (2019, 2).
5. Benatar (2006).

6. See discussion in Worsdale & Wright (2021).
7. As calculated in 2019, based on data from 2012–16. Countries were ranked in two ways: average absolute deviation from parity; and average deviation from parity. The former has the advantage that it prevents male-advantage and female-advantage from 'cancelling' each other out. Bahrain was ranked 1st using the former calculation and 12th using the second. Saudi Arabia, which was discussed in both the article and associated news media, was ranked 72nd using the former calculation and 3rd using the second method.
8. ESCWA et al. (2019); Millar (2002); World Economic Forum (2019, 81).
9. E.g., Hamill (2019), Pinkstone (2019).
10. Mlambo-Ngcuka & Kalanick (2015).
11. Wong & Paul (2020); see also Carbone et al. (2019).
12. Alter (2015).
13. International Transport Workers' Federation (2015, emphasis removed).
14. Fowler (2017); Tait (2020).
15. Conger (2019a); Isaac (2017).
16. Conger (2019b).
17. Robeyns (2017, 24).
18. Robeyns (2003). These are her proposed capabilities for assessing gender equality in Western societies.
19. Robeyns (2007).
20. For a general argument of this kind, see Barker (2015, chap. 7).
21. Woetzel et al. (2015, sec. Executive Summary).
22. E.g., Engster (2007).
23. Smith (1776, bk 1, chap. VIII).
24. Thomson et al. (2024). The box-office premium was not simply due to these features of films with female scriptwriters, as the association persisted even when these variables were controlled.
25. Schultz (2010, 1207).
26. Rubery (2015). See also discussion in Reeves (2022, chap. 12).
27. For discussion of the benefits of 'daddy leave', and arguments for its compatibility with liberalism, see Barclay (2013).
28. Fineman (2004, 48).

29. Wilkinson et al. (2017).
30. Chung (2022a, 556).
31. McDowell (2004, 322–3).
32. Cheryan & Markus (2020).
33. These suggestions are drawn from Treviño & Nelson's (2011, 153) multisystem ethical culture framework.
34. Ely & Meyerson (2010); see also Chen (2016).
35. Ely & Meyerson (2010, 14).
36. Chen (2016).
37. Ely & Meyerson (2010, 3, 12, 16, 15).
38. Ely & Meyerson (2010, 22, 23, 22).
39. Ely & Meyerson (2010, 9).
40. Ely & Meyerson (2010, 26).
41. Williams et al. (2016, 532).
42. Williams et al. (2016, 529), quoting Kellogg (2011, 161).
43. Kiselica & Englar-Carlson (2010, 278, reference removed).
44. Hanna et al. (2020, 640).
45. See, for example, the Let Toys Be Toys research, campaigns and 'silliest' gendered marketing awards at https://www.lettoysbetoys.org.uk/silliness-awards/.
46. For discussion of the ethics and science of gendered toy marketing, see Fine & Rush (2018).
47. E.g., Hsin (2018); Kolluri (2023).
48. Boe et al. (2018).
49. See Benatar (2012, chap. 6) for discussion of distinctions between different causes of gender disparities in labour market outcomes.
50. Hamjediers (2023).
51. Reeves (2022, chap. 11).
52. Dobbin & Kalev (2022, 85).
53. Dobbin & Kalev (2022, 123).
54. Robeyns (2007, 69).
55. Tomaskovic-Devey & Avent-Holt (2019, 5) define exploitation as 'when more powerful actors materially benefit at the expense of less powerful actors, taking increased shares of the resources available in the organization or in exchanges between organizations and their suppliers, customers, or governments. Exploitation is the dynamic face of successful claims-making'.

NOTES

For an interesting reconceptualization of the concept of exploitation, as an alternative to sociological and economic conceptions, see Avent-Holt (2015).

56. Suggestions are drawn from the final chapter of Tomaskovic-Devey & Avent-Holt (2019).
57. Goldin (2021).
58. Tomaskovic-Devey & Avent-Holt (2019, 241).
59. E.g., Oxfam International (2017).
60. Pearson & Elson (2015, 25).

BIBLIOGRAPHY

Abbate, Janet. 2012. *Recoding Gender: Women's Changing Participation in Computing*. Cambridge, Mass.; London: The MIT Press.

Acker, Joan. 1990. 'Hierarchies, Jobs, Bodies: A Theory of Gendered Organizations'. *Gender and Society* 4 (2): 139–58.

Adams, Renée B. 2016. 'Women on Boards: The Superheroes of Tomorrow?' *The Leadership Quarterly* 27 (3): 371–86. https://doi.org/10.1016/j.leaqua.2015.11.001.

Albiston, Catherine, and Tristin K. Green. 2018. 'Social Closure Discrimination'. *Berkeley Journal of Employment and Labor Law* 39 (Issue 1): 1–36.

AlShebli, Bedoor, Kinga Makovi, and Talal Rahwan. 2020a. 'RETRACTED ARTICLE: The Association between Early Career Informal Mentorship in Academic Collaborations and Junior Author Performance'. *Nature Communications* 11 (1): 5855. https://doi.org/10.1038/s41467-020-19723-8.

———. 2020b. 'Retraction Note: The Association between Early Career Informal Mentorship in Academic Collaborations and Junior Author Performance'. *Nature Communications* 11 (1): 6446. https://doi.org/10.1038/s41467-020-20617-y.

Alter, C. 2015. 'UN Women Breaks Off Partnership with Uber', 23 March 2015. https://time.com/3754537/un-women-breaks-off-partnership-with-uber/.

278

BIBLIOGRAPHY

Anders, Sari M. van. 2013. 'Beyond Masculinity: Testosterone, Gender/
Sex, and Human Social Behavior in a Comparative Context'.
Frontiers in Neuroendocrinology 34 (3): 198–210. https://doi.org/
10.1016/j.yfrne.2013.07.001.

Anderson, Elizabeth. 2012. 'Equality'. In *Oxford Handbook of Political
Philosophy*, David Estlund (ed.), Oxford Handbooks, Oxford
Academic.

Arruzza, Cinzia, Tithi Bhattacharya, and Nancy Fraser. 2019. *Feminism
for the 99 Percent: A Manifesto*. London; Brooklyn, NY: Verso.

Artz, Benjamin, Amanda H. Goodall, and Andrew J. Oswald. 2018. 'Do
Women Ask?' *Industrial Relations: A Journal of Economy and Society* 57
(4): 611–36. https://doi.org/10.1111/irel.12214.

Australian Human Rights Commission. 2014. 'Supporting Working
Parents: Pregnancy and Return to Work'. National Review –
Report. https://humanrights.gov.au/our-work/sex-discrimination/
publications/pregnancy-and-return-work-national-review-
report.

———. 2022. 'Time for Respect: Fifth National Survey on Sexual
Harassment in Australian Workplaces'. https://humanrights.gov.
au/sites/default/files/document/publication/2022.11.25_time_
for_respect_2022_final_digital.pdf.

Avent-Holt, Dustin. 2015. 'Reconceptualizing Exploitation: New
Directions for an Old Concept in Social Stratification'. *Social
Currents* 2 (3): 213–21. https://doi.org/10.1177/2329496515589854.

Avent-Holt, Dustin, and Donald Tomaskovic-Devey. 2014. 'A Relational
Theory of Earnings Inequality'. *American Behavioral Scientist* 58 (3):
379–99. https://doi.org/10.1177/0002764213503337.

———. 2023. 'Skill and Power at Work: A Relational Inequality
Perspective'. In *A Research Agenda for Skills and Inequality*, edited by
Michael Tåhlin, 217–32. Edward Elgar Publishing. https://doi.org/
10.4337/9781800378469.00019.

Baker, Michael, and Kirsten Cornelson. 2018. 'Gender-Based
Occupational Segregation and Sex Differences in Sensory, Motor,
and Spatial Aptitudes'. *Demography* 55 (5): 1749–75. https://doi.
org/10.1007/s13524-018-0706-3.

Balducci, Marco. 2023. 'Linking Gender Differences with Gender

Equality: A Systematic-Narrative Literature Review of Basic Skills and Personality'. *Frontiers in Psychology* 14 (February): 1105234. https://doi.org/10.3389/fpsyg.2023.1105234.

Barclay, Linda. 2013. 'Liberal Daddy Quotas: Why Men Should Take Care of the Children, and How Liberals Can Get Them to Do It'. *Hypatia* 28 (1): 163–78. https://doi.org/10.1111/j.1527-2001.2011.01255.x.

Barker, Gillian. 2015. *Beyond Biofatalism: Human Nature for an Evolving World.* New York (NY): Columbia University Press.

Battiston, Stefano, Domenico Delli Gatti, Mauro Gallegati, Bruce Greenwald, and Joseph E. Stiglitz. 2012. 'Liaisons Dangereuses: Increasing Connectivity, Risk Sharing, and Systemic Risk'. *Journal of Economic Dynamics & Control* 36 (8): 1121.

Bedford, Rachael, Andrew Pickles, Helen Sharp, Nicola Wright, and Jonathan Hill. 2015. 'Reduced Face Preference in Infancy: A Developmental Precursor to Callous-Unemotional Traits?' *Biological Psychiatry* 78 (2): 144–50. https://doi.org/10.1016/j.biopsych.2014.09.022.

Begall, Katia, Daniela Grunow, and Sandra Buchler. 2023. 'Multidimensional Gender Ideologies Across Europe: Evidence From 36 Countries'. *Gender & Society* 37 (2): 177–207. https://doi.org/10.1177/08912432231155914.

Beltz, Adriene M., Jane L. Swanson, and Sheri A. Berenbaum. 2011. 'Gendered Occupational Interests: Prenatal Androgen Effects on Psychological Orientation to Things versus People'. *Hormones and Behavior* 60 (4): 313–17. https://doi.org/10.1016/j.yhbeh.2011.06.002.

Benatar, David. 2006. *Better Never to Have Been: The Harm of Coming into Existence.* Oxford, New York: Clarendon Press; Oxford University Press.

———. 2012. *The Second Sexism: Discrimination against Men and Boys.* Malden, MA: Wiley-Blackwell.

Benenson, Joyce F., Robert Tennyson, and Richard W. Wrangham. 2011. 'Male More than Female Infants Imitate Propulsive Motion'. *Cognition* 121 (2): 262–7. https://doi.org/10.1016/j.cognition.2011.07.006.

BIBLIOGRAPHY

Berdahl, Jennifer L., Marianne Cooper, Peter Glick, Robert W. Livingston, and Joan C. Williams. 2018. 'Work as a Masculinity Contest'. *Journal of Social Issues* 74 (3): 422–48. https://doi.org/10.1111/josi.12289.

Berger, Joel, Jon E. Swenson, and Inga-Lill Persson. 2001. 'Recolonizing Carnivores and Naïve Prey: Conservation Lessons from Pleistocene Extinctions'. *Science* 291 (5506): 1036–9. https://doi.org/10.1126/science.1056466.

Bird, Rebecca Bliege, and Brian F. Codding. 2015. 'The Sexual Division of Labor'. In *Emerging Trends in the Social and Behavioral Sciences*, ed. Robert A. Scott and Stephan M. Kosslyn, 1st edn, 1–16. Wiley. https://doi.org/10.1002/9781118900772.etrds0300.

Blackford, Russell. 2023. *How We Became Post-Liberal: The Rise and Fall of Toleration*. London and New York: Bloomsbury Academic.

Bleier, Ruth. 1988. 'Sex Differences Research: Science or Belief?' In *Feminist Approaches to Science*, ed. Ruth Bleier, 2nd pr, 147–64. The Athene Series. New York Oxford Toronto Sydney Frankfurt Kronberg-Taunus: Pergamon Press.

Block, Katharina, Maria I. T. Olsson, Toni Schmader, Colette Van Laar, Sarah E. Martiny, Carolin Schuster, Sanne Van Grootel, Loes Meeussen, and Alyssa Croft. 2022. 'The Gender Gap in the Care Economy is Larger in Highly Developed Countries: Socio-Cultural Explanations for Paradoxical Findings'. https://doi.org/10.31234/osf.io/k6g5d.

Block, Per. 2023. 'Understanding the Self-Organization of Occupational Sex Segregation with Mobility Networks'. *Social Networks* 73 (May): 42–50. https://doi.org/10.1016/j.socnet.2022.12.004.

Blumenthal, Anne, and David W. Rothwell. 2018. 'The Measurement and Description of Child Income and Asset Poverty in Canada'. *Child Indicators Research* 11 (6): 1907–33. https://doi.org/10.1007/s12187-017-9525-0.

Bodenhausen, Galen V., Sonia K. Kang, and Destiny Peery. 2012. 'Social Categorization and the Perception of Social Groups'. In *The SAGE Handbook of Social Cognition*, ed. Susan T. Fiske and C. Neil Macrae, 311–29. Los Angeles, Calif: SAGE Publications Ltd.

Boe, Josh L., and Rebecca J. Woods. 2018. 'Parents' Influence on Infants' Gender-typed Toy Preferences'. *Sex Roles* 79: 358–73. https://doi.org/10.1007/s11199-017-0858-4.

Boehm, Christopher, Harold B. Barclay, Robert Knox Dentan, Marie-Claude Dupre, Jonathan D. Hill, Susan Kent, Bruce M. Knauft, Keith F. Otterbein, and Steve Rayner. 1993. 'Egalitarian Behavior and Reverse Dominance Hierarchy'. *Current Anthropology* 34 (3): 227–54. https://doi.org/10.1086/204166.

Borgkvist, Ashlee, Vivienne Moore, Shona Crabb, and Jaklin Eliott. 2021. 'Critical Considerations of Workplace Flexibility "for All" and Gendered Outcomes: Men Being Flexible about Their Flexibility'. *Gender, Work & Organization* 28 (6): 2076–90. https://doi.org/10.1111/gwao.12680.

Borgkvist, Ashlee, Vivienne Moore, Jaklin Eliott, and Shona Crabb. 2018. '"I Might Be a Bit of a Front Runner": An Analysis of Men's Uptake of Flexible Work Arrangements and Masculine Identity'. *Gender, Work & Organization* 25 (6): 703–17. https://doi.org/10.1111/gwao.12240.

Bourdieu, Pierre. 1977. *Outline of a Theory of Practice*. Trans. Richard Nice. 1st edn. Cambridge University Press. https://doi.org/10.1017/CBO9780511812507.

Boyd, Robert. 2019. *A Different Kind of Animal: How Culture Transformed Our Species*. The University Center for Human Values Series. Princeton: Princeton University Press.

Brandon, R. H. 1968. 'The Problem in Perspective'. In *Proceedings of the 1968 23rd ACM National Conference*, 332–4. New York: ACM Press. https://dl.acm.org/doi/pdf/10.1145/800186.810594.

Brooks, David. 2017. 'Sundar Pichai Should Resign as Google's C.E.O.' *New York Times*, 11 August 2017. https://www.nytimes.com/2017/08/11/opinion/sundar-pichai-google-memo-diversity.html.

Brown, Gillian R., and Peter J. Richerson. 2014. 'Applying Evolutionary Theory to Human Behaviour: Past Differences and Current Debates'. *Journal of Bioeconomics* 16 (2): 105–28. https://doi.org/10.1007/s10818-013-9166-4.

Brown, Judith K. 1970. 'A Note on the Division of Labor by Sex'.

BIBLIOGRAPHY

American Anthropologist 72 (5): 1073–8. https://doi.org/10.1525/aa.1970.72.5.02a00070.

Brown, Laurie. 2016. 'Divorce: For Richer, for Poorer'. AMP.NATSEM Income and Wealth Report Issue 39. https://corporate.amp.com.au/content/dam/corporate/newsroom/files/December%2013%20-%20AMP.NATSEM39%20-%20For%20Richer,%20For%20Poorer%20-%20Report%20-%20FINAL.pdf.

Brown, Tyson. 2012. 'The Intersection and Accumulation of Racial and Gender Inequality: Black Women's Wealth Trajectories'. *The Review of Black Political Economy* 39 (2): 239–58. https://doi.org/10.1007/s12114-011-9100-8.

Budge, Jason, Maria Charles, Yariv Feniger, and Halleli Pinson. 2023. 'The Gendering of Tech Selves: Aspirations for Computing Jobs among Jewish and Arab/Palestinian Adolescents in Israel'. *Technology in Society* 73 (May): 102245. https://doi.org/10.1016/j.techsoc.2023.102245.

Bueskens, Petra. 2018. *Modern Motherhood and Women's Dual Identities: Rewriting the Sexual Contract*. Routledge Research in Gender and Society 67. London; New York, NY: Routledge.

Buller, David J. 2006. *Adapting Minds: Evolutionary Psychology and the Persistent Quest for Human Nature*. Cambridge, Mass.: MIT Press.

Burkart, Judith M., Carel Van Schaik, and Michael Griesser. 2017. 'Looking for Unity in Diversity: Human Cooperative Childcare in Comparative Perspective'. *Proceedings of the Royal Society B: Biological Sciences* 284 (1869): 20171184. https://doi.org/10.1098/rspb.2017.1184.

Buss, David M. 2023. 'Sexual Violence Laws: Policy Implications of Psychological Sex Differences'. *Evolution and Human Behavior* 44 (3): 278–83. https://doi.org/10.1016/j.evolhumbehav.2023.01.003.

Bussey, Kay. 2011. 'Gender Identity Development'. In *Handbook of Identity Theory and Research*, ed. Seth J. Schwartz, Koen Luyckx, and Vivian L. Vignoles, 603–28. New York, NY: Springer New York. https://doi.org/10.1007/978-1-4419-7988-9_25.

Bussey, Kay, and Albert Bandura. 1984. 'Influence of Gender Constancy and Social Power on Sex-Linked Modeling'. *Journal*

of Personality and Social Psychology 47 (6): 1292–1302. https://doi.
org/10.1037/0022-3514.47.6.1292.

———. 1999. 'Social Cognitive Theory of Gender Development and
Differentiation'. *Psychological Review* 106 (4): 676–713. https://doi.
org/10.1037/0033-295X.106.4.676.

Bussey, Kay, and David G. Perry. 1982. 'Same-Sex Imitation: The
Avoidance of Cross-Sex Models or the Acceptance of Same-Sex
Models?' *Sex Roles* 8 (7). https://doi.org/10.1007/BF00287572.

Caird, Mona. 2010. 'Suppression of Variant Types'. In *The Morality
of Marriage: And Other Essays on the Status and Destiny of Woman*,
195–211. Cambridge Library Collection – British and Irish History,
19th Century. Cambridge: Cambridge University Press. https://
doi.org/10.1017/CBO9780511704468.013.

Carbone, June. 2022. 'Board Diversity: People or Pathways?' *Law and
Contemporary Problems* 85 (1): 167–213.

Carbone, June, Naomi Cahn, and Nancy Levit. 2019. 'Women,
Rule-Breaking, and the Triple Bind'. *The George Washington Law
Review* 87 (5): 1105–62.

Carney, Mark. 2016. 'Opening Remarks to the "Empowering
Productivity: Harnessing the Talents of Women in Financial
Services" Report Launch'. Presented at the Gadhia Review launch,
Bank of England, London, 22 March. https://www.bis.org/
review/r160405a.pdf.

Ceci, Stephen J., Shulamit Kahn, and Wendy M. Williams. 2023.
'Exploring Gender Bias in Six Key Domains of Academic Science:
An Adversarial Collaboration'. *Psychological Science in the Public
Interest* 24 (1): 15–73. https://doi.org/10.1177/15291006231163179.

Cha, Youngjoo, and Kim A. Weeden. 2014. 'Overwork and the Slow
Convergence in the Gender Gap in Wages'. *American Sociological
Review* 79 (3): 457–84. https://doi.org/10.1177/
0003122414528936.

Chafetz, Janet Saltzman. 1988. 'The Gender Division of Labor and
the Reproduction of Female Disadvantage: Toward an Integrated
Theory'. *Journal of Family Issues* 9 (1): 108–31. https://doi.org/
10.1177/019251388009001006.

Chang, Mariko Lin. 2010. *Shortchanged: Why Women Have Less Wealth and What Can Be Done About It.* Oxford; New York: Oxford University Press.

Charles, Maria, and David B. Grusky. 2004. *Occupational Ghettos: The Worldwide Segregation of Women and Men.* Stanford, California: Stanford University Press.

Charmes, Jacques. 2022. 'Variety and Change of Patterns in the Gender Balance between Unpaid Care-Work, Paid Work and Free Time across the World and over Time: A Measure of Wellbeing?' *Wellbeing, Space and Society* 3: 100081. https://doi.org/10.1016/j.wss.2022.100081.

Chen, Angus. 2016. 'Invisibilia: How Learning To Be Vulnerable Can Make Life Safer'. *NPR*, 28 July 2016. https://www.kcur.org/2016-07-28/invisibilia-how-learning-to-be-vulnerable-can-make-life-safer.

Cheng, Joey T. 2020. 'Dominance, Prestige, and the Role of Leveling in Human Social Hierarchy and Equality'. *Current Opinion in Psychology* 33 (June): 238–44. https://doi.org/10.1016/j.copsyc.2019.10.004.

Cheryan, Sapna, and Hazel Rose Markus. 2020. 'Masculine Defaults: Identifying and Mitigating Hidden Cultural Biases'. *Psychological Review* 127 (6): 1022–52. https://doi.org/10.1037/rev0000209.

Chinwala, Yasmine, Jennifer Barrow, and Sheenam Singhal. 2023. 'HM Treasury Women in Finance Charter: Annual Review 2022'. New Financial: Rethinking capital markets. https://assets.publishing.service.gov.uk/government/uploads/system/uploads/attachment_data/file/1142828/HMT_WIFC_Review_2022.pdf.

———. 2024. 'HM Treasury Women in Finance Charter: Annual Review 2023'. New Financial: Rethinking capital markets. https://assets.publishing.service.gov.uk/media/65fb084d9316f5001164c432/HMT_WIFC_Review_2023.pdf.

Chiu, Bonnie. 2023. 'Outperforming Female Fund Managers Still Struggle To Access Capital'. *Forbes*, 2 November 2023. https://www.forbes.com/sites/bonniechiu/2023/11/02/outperforming-female-fund-managers-still-struggle-to-access-capital/?sh=6c8008f44a2e.

Chung, Heejung. 2022a. 'A Social Policy Case for a Four-Day Week'. *Journal of Social Policy* 51 (3): 551–66. https://doi.org/10.1017/S0047279422000186.

———. 2022b. *The Flexibility Paradox: Why Flexible Working Leads to (Self-)Exploitation*. Bristol, UK: Polity Press.

Clemens, L. G., M. Hiroi, and R. A. Gorski. 1969. 'Induction and Facilitation of Female Mating Behavior in Rats Treated Neonatally with Low Doses of Testosterone Propionate'. *Endocrinology* 84 (6): 1430–38. https://doi.org/10.1210/endo-84-6-1430.

Confer, Jaime C., Judith A. Easton, Diana S. Fleischman, Cari D. Goetz, David M. G. Lewis, Carin Perilloux, and David M. Buss. 2010. 'Evolutionary Psychology: Controversies, Questions, Prospects, and Limitations'. *American Psychologist* 65 (2): 110–26. https://doi.org/10.1037/a0018413.

Conger, Kate. 2019a. 'Uber Founder Travis Kalanick Leaves Board, Severing Last Tie'. *New York Times*, 24 December 2019. https://www.nytimes.com/2019/12/24/technology/uber-travis-kalanick.html.

———. 2019b. 'Uber Settles Federal Investigation into Workplace Culture'. *New York Times*, 18 December 2019. https://www.nytimes.com/2019/12/18/technology/uber-settles-eeoc-investigation-workplace-culture.html.

Connellan, Jennifer, Simon Baron-Cohen, Sally Wheelwright, Anna Batki, and Jag Ahluwalia. 2000. 'Sex Differences in Human Neonatal Social Perception'. *Infant Behavior and Development* 23 (1): 113–18. https://doi.org/10.1016/S0163-6383(00)00032-1.

Consumer Financial Protection Bureau. 2016. 'Consumer Financial Protection Bureau Fines Wells Fargo $100 Million for Widespread Illegal Practice of Secretly Opening Unauthorized Accounts'. https://www.consumerfinance.gov/about-us/newsroom/consumer-financial-protection-bureau-fines-wells-fargo-100-million-widespread-illegal-practice-secretly-opening-unauthorized-accounts/.

Cooper, Marianne. 2000. 'Being the "Go-To Guy": Fatherhood, Masculinity, and the Organization of Work in Silicon Valley'. *Qualitative Sociology* 23 (4): 379–405. https://doi.org/10.1023/A:1005522707921.

Cortina, Lilia M., and Maira A. Areguin. 2021. 'Putting People

Down and Pushing Them Out: Sexual Harassment in the Workplace'. *Annual Review of Organizational Psychology and Organizational Behavior* 8 (1): 285–309. https://doi.org/10.1146/annurev-orgpsych-012420-055606.

Costa Dias, Monica, Robert Joyce, and Francesca Parodi. 2020. 'The Gender Pay Gap in the UK: Children and Experience in Work'. *Oxford Review of Economic Policy* 36 (4): 855–81. https://doi.org/10.1093/oxrep/graa053.

Cotter, David, Joan M. Hermsen, and Reeve Vanneman. 2011. 'The End of the Gender Revolution? Gender Role Attitudes from 1977 to 2008'. *American Journal of Sociology* 117 (1): 259–89. https://doi.org/10.1086/658853.

———. 2011. 'Reframing Gender Equality: Explaining the Stalled Gender Revolution'. *Work in Progress: Sociology on the Economy, Work and Inequality* (blog). 3 November 2011. https://workinprogress.oowsection.org/2011/11/03/reframing-gender-equality-explaining-the-stalled-gender-revolution/.

Cowley, Stacy. 2023. 'Former Wells Fargo Executive Avoids Prison in Sham Accounts Scandal'. *New York Times*, 15 September 2023. https://www.nytimes.com/2023/09/15/business/wells-fargo-former-executive-avoids-prison.html/.

Cowper-Coles, Minna, Miriam Glennie, Aleida Mendes Borges, and Caitlin Schmid. 2021. 'Bridging the Gap? An Analysis of Gender Pay Gap Reporting in Six Countries'. King's College London: The Global Instititute for Women's Leadership. https://www.kcl.ac.uk/giwl/assets/bridging-the-gap-an-analysis-of-gender-pay-gap-reporting-in-six-countries-summary-and-recommendations.pdf.

Craig, L., and K. Mullan. 2013. 'Parental Leisure Time: A Gender Comparison in Five Countries'. *Social Politics: International Studies in Gender, State & Society* 20 (3): 329–57. https://doi.org/10.1093/sp/jxt002.

Craig, Lyn, and Abigail Powell. 2018. 'Shares of Housework Between Mothers, Fathers and Young People: Routine and Non-Routine Housework, Doing Housework for Oneself and Others'. *Social Indicators Research* 136 (1): 269–81. https://doi.org/10.1007/s11205-016-1539-3.

Criado-Perez, Caroline. 2020. *Invisible Women: Exposing Data Bias in a World Designed for Men*. London: Vintage.

Cross, C. P., L. G. Boothroyd, and C. A. Jefferson. 2023. 'Agent-Based Models of the Cultural Evolution of Occupational Gender Roles'. *Royal Society Open Science* 10 (6): 221346. https://doi.org/10.1098/rsos.221346.

Crowley, William F., and Randall W. Whitcomb. 1990. 'Gonadotropin-Releasing Hormone Deficiency in Men: Diagnosis and Treatment with Exogenous Gonadotropin-Releasing Hormone'. *American Journal of Obstetrics and Gynecology* 163 (5): 1752–8. https://doi.org/10.1016/0002-9378(90)91440-N.

Dallas, Lynne L. 2012. 'Short-Termism, the Financial Crisis, and Corporate Governance'. *Journal of Corporation Law* 37:265.

Damore, James. 2017. 'Google's Ideological Echo Chamber'. https://s3.documentcloud.org/documents/3914586/Googles-Ideological-Echo-Chamber.pdf.

Dana, Charles. 1915. 'Suffrage a Cult of Sex and Self'. *New York Times*, 27 June 1915. https://www.nytimes.com/1915/06/27/archives/suffrage-a-cult-of-self-and-sex-the-average-zealot-has-the-mental-a.html.

Davies, Lizzie. 2013. 'Italian Election Brings "Female Question" to Fore'. *Guardian*, 1 February 2013. https://www.theguardian.com/world/2013/jan/31/italian-election-female-question-employment.

Davis, Aeron, and Catherine Walsh. 2016. 'The Role of the State in the Financialisation of the UK Economy'. *Political Studies* 64 (3): 666–82. https://doi.org/10.1111/1467-9248.12198.

Davis, Gerald F., and Suntae Kim. 2015. 'Financialization of the Economy'. *Annual Review of Sociology* 41 (January): 203–21. https://doi.org/10.1146/annurev-soc-073014-112402.

Davis, Helen E., Jonathan Stack, and Elizabeth Cashdan. 2021. 'Cultural Change Reduces Gender Differences in Mobility and Spatial Ability among Seminomadic Pastoralist-Forager Children in Northern Namibia'. *Human Nature* 32 (1): 178–206. https://doi.org/10.1007/s12110-021-09388-7.

Deloitte. 2023a. 'VC Human Capital Survey (Fourth Edition)'. https://

BIBLIOGRAPHY

www2.deloitte.com/content/dam/Deloitte/us/Documents/audit/
us-audit-human-capital-survey-report-2023.pdf.

———. 2023b. 'Women in Financial Services Leadership, 2023 Global
Update'. Deloitte Insights. https://www2.deloitte.com/uk/en/
insights/industry/financial-services/women-leaders-financial-
services.html.

Dinella, Lisa M., Erica S. Weisgram, and Megan Fulcher. 2017.
'Children's Gender-Typed Toy Interests: Does Propulsion
Matter?' *Archives of Sexual Behavior* 46 (5): 1295–1305. https://doi.
org/10.1007/s10508-016-0901-5.

Dobbin, Frank, and Alexandra Kalev. 2018. 'Why Doesn't Diversity
Training Work? The Challenge for Industry and Academia'.
Anthropology Now 10 (2): 48–55. https://doi.org/10.1080/1942820
0.2018.1493182.

———. 2022. *Getting to Diversity: What Works and What Doesn't.*
Cambridge, Mass.; London: The Belknap Press of Harvard
University Press.

Doell, Ruth G., and Helen E. Longino. 1988. 'Sex Hormones and
Human Behavior: A Critique of the Linear Model'. *Journal
of Homosexuality* 15 (3–4): 55–78. https://doi.org/10.1300/
J082v15n03_03.

Dolan, Eric W. 2022. 'Study Finds Early Exposure to Testosterone
Predicts Gender-Role Behaviors in Boys'. *PsyPost*, 2 June 2022.
https://www.psypost.org/study-finds-early-exposure-to-
testosterone-predicts-gender-role-behaviors-in-boys/.

Donato, Katherine M. 1990. 'Programming for Change? The Growing
Demand for Women Systems Analysts'. In *Job Queues, Gender Queues:
Explaining Women's Inroads into Male Occupations*, written and edited
by Barbara F. Reskin and Patricia A. Roos, 167–82. Philadelphia:
Temple University Press.

Downes, Stephen M. 2005. 'Integrating the Multiple Biological Causes
of Human Behavior'. *Biology & Philosophy* 20 (1): 177–90. https://
doi.org/10.1007/s10539-004-2319-z.

———. 2013. 'Evolutionary Psychology Is Not the Only Productive
Evolutionary Approach to Understanding Consumer Behavior'.

Journal of Consumer Psychology 23 (3): 400–3. https://doi.
org/10.1016/j.jcps.2013.03.005.

Dupré, John. 2024. 'Lecture 5: Human Nature and Human Kinds'.
Presented at the Gifford Lectures, University of Edinburgh,
8 February. https://www.youtube.com/watch?v=qOcqk1eUGIE.

Dynata, and Thrive Insights. 2021. 'Allyship and Gender Equality
Research: Measuring the Perceptions of Men in the Workplace, and
the Motivators and Barriers to Gender Equality and Diversity &
Inclusion Training Initiatives'. TDC Global. https://8993753.fs1.
hubspotusercontent-na1.net/hubfs/8993753/Gated%20content/
TDC%20Global%20-%20Allyship%20and%20Gender%20
Equality%202021.pdf?__hstc=60726962.3361186afbd9720
489c328006354e3ed.1708042945799.1708042945799.
1708042945799.1&__hssc=60726962.4.1708042945799&__
hsfp=190980063.

Eagly, Alice H., and Wendy Wood. 1999. 'The Origins of Sex
Differences in Human Behavior: Evolved Dispositions Versus Social
Roles'. *American Psychologist*, 54 (6), 408–23. https://doi.org/
10.1037/0003-066X.54.6.408.

Edelman, Lauren B., Sally Riggs Fuller, and Iona Mara-Drita. 2001.
'Diversity Rhetoric and the Managerialization of Law'. *The
American Journal of Sociology* 106 (6): 1589–1641.

Edwards, Carolyn Pope. 1993. 'Behavioral Sex Differences in Children
of Diverse Cultures: The Case of Nurturance to Infants'. In *Juvenile
Primates: Life History, Development, and Behavior*, 327–38. New York:
Oxford University Press.

Egan, Mark, Gregor Matvos, and Amit Seru. 2022. 'When Harry Fired
Sally: The Double Standard in Punishing Misconduct'. *Journal of
Political Economy* 130 (5): 1184–1248. https://doi.org/10.1086/
718964.

Egan, Matt. 2016. 'Workers Tell Wells Fargo Horror Stories'. *CNN*, 9
September 2016, sec. Business. https://money.cnn.com/2016/
09/09/investing/wells-fargo-phony-accounts-culture.

Else-Quest, Nicole M., and Shelly Grabe. 2012. 'The Political Is
Personal: Measurement and Application of Nation-Level Indicators
of Gender Equity in Psychological Research'. *Psychology of*

Women Quarterly 36 (2): 131–44. https://doi.org/10.1177/
0361684312441592.

Else-Quest, Nicole M., and Veronica Hamilton. 2018. 'Measurement and Analysis of Nation-Level Gender Equity in the Psychology of Women'. In *APA Handbook of the Psychology of Women: Perspectives on Women's Private and Public Lives (Vol. 2).*, ed. Cheryl B. Travis, Jacquelyn W. White, Alexandra Rutherford, Wendi S. Williams, Sarah L. Cook, and Karen Fraser Wyche, 545–63. Washington: American Psychological Association.

Ely, Robin J., and Debra E. Meyerson. 2000. 'Theories of Gender in Organizations: A New Approach to Organizational Analysis and Change'. *Research in Organizational Behavior* 22:103–51. https://doi.org/10.1016/S0191-3085(00)22004-2.

———. 2010. 'An Organizational Approach to Undoing Gender: The Unlikely Case of Offshore Oil Platforms'. *Research in Organizational Behavior* 30 (January): 3–34. https://doi.org/10.1016/j.riob.2010.09.002.

Ely, Robin J., and Irene Padavic. 2020. 'What's Really Holding Women Back?' *Harvard Business Review*. March–April. 58–67. https://hbr.org/2020/03/whats-really-holding-women-back.

Ely, Robin J., Pamela Stone, and Colleen Ammerman. 2014. 'Rethink What You "Know" about High-Achieving Women'. *Harvard Business Review*, December, 101–9.

Endendijk, Joyce J., Anneloes L. Van Baar, and Maja Deković. 2020. 'He Is a Stud, She Is a Slut! A Meta-Analysis on the Continued Existence of Sexual Double Standards'. *Personality and Social Psychology Review* 24 (2): 163–90. https://doi.org/10.1177/1088868319891310.

England, Paula. 2010. 'The Gender Revolution: Uneven and Stalled'. *Gender & Society* 24 (2): 149–66. https://doi.org/10.1177/0891243210361475.

England, Paula, Michelle Budig, and Nancy Folbre. 2002. 'Wages of Virtue: The Relative Pay of Care Work'. *Social Problems* 49 (4): 455–73. https://doi.org/10.1525/sp.2002.49.4.455.

England, Paula, and Nancy Folbre. 1999. 'The Cost of Caring'. *The ANNALS of the American Academy of Political and Social Science* 561 (1):

39–51. https://doi.org/10.1177/0002716299956100103.

England, Paula, Andrew Levine, and Emma Mishel. 2020. 'Progress Toward Gender Equality in the United States Has Slowed or Stalled'. *Proceedings of the National Academy of Sciences* 117 (13): 6990–7. https://doi.org/10.1073/pnas.1918891117.

Engster, Daniel. 2007. *The Heart of Justice: Care Ethics and Political Theory.* Oxford: Oxford University Press.

Ensmenger, Nathan. 2010. 'Making Programming Masculine'. In *Gender Codes*, ed. Thomas J. Misa, 115–41. Wiley.

Eriksson, Kimmo, Pontus Strimling, Michele Gelfand, Junhui Wu, Jered Abernathy, Charity S. Akotia, Alisher Aldashev, et al. 2021. 'Perceptions of the Appropriate Response to Norm Violation in 57 Societies'. *Nature Communications* 12 (1): 1481. https://doi.org/10.1038/s41467-021-21602-9.

ESCWA, UNFPA, UN Women, and UNDP. 2019. 'Bahrain: Gender Justice and the Law'. https://www.undp.org/sites/g/files/zskgke326/files/migration/arabstates/Bahrain.Summary.19.Eng.pdf.

European Banking Authority. 2021. 'EBA Report on High Earners: Data as of End of 2019'. EBA/REP/2-21/23. 28 May 2024. https://www.eba.europa.eu/sites/default/documents/files/document_library/Publications/Reports/2021/1018449/Report%20on%20High%20Earners%202019.pdf.

———. 2024. 'EBA Report on High Earners: Data as of End 2022'. EBA/Rep/2024/07. European Banking Authority. https://www.eba.europa.eu/sites/default/files/2024-04/5fe011e7-56a3-4308-9827-6a9b11fe710b/Report%20on%20high%20earners%20-%20data%20from%202022.pdf.

European Commission: Directorate-General for Justice and Consumers, and Eva Sierminska. 2017. *Wealth and gender in Europe.* Publications Office. www.doi.org/10.2838/39491.

Evans, Mark, Virginia Haussegger, Max Halupka, and Pia Rowe. 2018. 'From Girls to Men: Social Attitudes to Gender Equality in Australia'. The University of Canberra: 50/50 by 2030 Foundation. https://www.broadagenda.com.au/wp-content/uploads/attachments/From-Girls-to-Men.pdf.

Fair Work Commission. 2024. 'Work Value Case – Aged Care Industry Decision Issues'. https://www.fwc.gov.au/about-us/news-and-media/news/work-value-case-aged-care-industry-decision-issued-0.

Falk, Armin, Anke Becker, Thomas Dohmen, Benjamin Enke, David Huffman, and Uwe Sunde. 2018. 'Global Evidence on Economic Preferences'. *The Quarterly Journal of Economics* 133 (4): 1645–92. https://doi.org/10.1093/qje/qjy013.

Farnsworth, Kevin. 2013. 'Public Policies for Private Corporations: The British Corporate Welfare State'. *Renewal*, 2013.

———. 2021. 'Business and the (Corporate) Welfare State'. In *Handbook of Business and Public Policy*, ed. Aynsley Kellow, Tony Porter, and Karsten Ronit, 278–97. Edward Elgar Publishing. https://doi.org/10.4337/9781788979122.00024.

Fausto-Sterling, Anne. 2000. *Sexing the Body: Gender Politics and the Construction of Sexuality*. New York: Basic Books.

———. 2021. 'A Dynamic Systems Framework for Gender/Sex Development: From Sensory Input in Infancy to Subjective Certainty in Toddlerhood'. *Frontiers in Human Neuroscience* 15 (April): 613789. https://doi.org/10.3389/fnhum.2021.613789.

Feiner, Susan F., and Bruce B. Roberts. 1990. 'Hidden by the Invisible Hand: Neoclassical Economic Theory and the Textbook Treatment of Race and Gender'. *Gender & Society* 4 (2): 159–81. https://doi.org/10.1177/089124390004002003.

Figart, Deborah M., Ellen Mutari, and Marilyn Power. 2005. *Living Wages, Equal Wages: Gender and Labor Market Policies in the United States*. London: Taylor & Francis e-Library.

Fine, Cordelia. 2010. *Delusions of Gender: How Our Minds, Society, and Neurosexism Create Difference*. New York: W. W. Norton.

———. 2013. 'New Insights into Gendered Brain Wiring, or a Perfect Case Study in Neurosexism?' *The Conversation*, 4 December 2013. https://theconversation.com/new-insights-into-gendered-brain-wiring-or-a-perfect-case-study-in-neurosexism-21083.

———. 2015. 'Neuroscience, Gender, and "Development To" and "From": The Example of Toy Preferences'. In *Handbook of Neuroethics*, ed. Jens Clausen and Neil Levy, 1737–55. Dordrecht: Springer Netherlands.

—————. 2017a. 'Business as Usual?' *The Monthly*, March 2017. https://www.themonthly.com.au/issue/2017/march/1488286800/cordelia-fine/business-usual#mtr.

—————. 2017b. *Testosterone Rex: Myths of Sex, Science, and Society*. New York, NY: W. W. Norton.

—————. 2020a. 'Trumped-up Charges of "Feminist Bias" Are Bad for Science'. *Aeon*, 28 July 2020. https://aeon.co/essays/trumped-up-charges-of-feminist-bias-are-bad-for-science.

—————. 2020b. 'Constructing Unnecessary Barriers to Constructive Scientific Debate: A Response to Buss and von Hippel (2018)'. *Archives of Scientific Psychology* 8 (1): 5–10. https://doi.org/10.1037/arc0000070.

Fine, Cordelia, John Dupré, and Daphna Joel. 2017. 'Sex-Linked Behavior: Evolution, Stability, and Variability'. *Trends in Cognitive Sciences* 21 (9): 666–73. https://doi.org/10.1016/j.tics.2017.06.012.

Fine, Cordelia, and Joe Herbert. 2017. 'Is Testosterone the Key to Sex Differences in Human Behaviour? The Debate'. *The Psychologist*, 8 September 2017. https://www.bps.org.uk/psychologist/testosterone-key-sex-differences-human-behaviour.

Fine, Cordelia, and Emma Rush. 2018. '"Why Do All the Girls Have to Buy Pink Stuff?" The Ethics and Science of the Gendered Toy Marketing Debate'. *Journal of Business Ethics* 149 (4): 769–84.

Fine, Cordelia, Victor Sojo, and Holly Lawford-Smith. 2020. 'Why Does Workplace Gender Diversity Matter? Justice, Organizational Benefits, and Policy'. *Social Issues and Policy Review* 14 (1): 36–72. https://doi.org/10.1111/sipr.12064.

Fine, Cordelia, Nitin Yadav, and Carsten Murawski. Forthcoming. 'No Interest: Male Dominance and the Marginalization of Women in Academic Finance'. *Feminist Economics*. Accepted 21 May 2024.

Fineman, Martha. 2004. *The Autonomy Myth: A Theory of Dependency*. New York; London: The New Press.

Folbre, Nancy. 1994. *Who Pays for the Kids?: Gender and the Structure of Constraint*. London: Routledge.

—————. 2006. 'Demanding Quality: Worker/Consumer Coalitions and "High Road" Strategies in the Care Sector'. *Politics & Society* 34 (1): 11–32. https://doi.org/10.1177/0032329205284754.

Fortado, Lindsay. 2017. 'Hedge Funds Run by Women Outperform'. *Financial Times*, 11 March 2017. https://www.ft.com/content/146a6c5c-0417-11e7-aa5b-6bb07f5c8e12.

Fowler, Susan. 2017. 'Reflecting on One Very, Very Strange Year at Uber'. 19 February 2017. https://www.susanjfowler.com/blog/2017/2/19/reflecting-on-one-very-strange-year-at-uber.

Franklin, Joshua, and Arash Massoudi. 2024. 'Goldman Sachs's UK Gender Pay Gap Widest in Six Years'. *Financial Times*, 4 May 2024. https://www.ft.com/content/112d86f7-5c18-491d-bc25-ec8419edb889.

Fuentes, Agustín. 2021. 'Searching for the "Roots" of Masculinity in Primates and the Human Evolutionary Past'. *Current Anthropology* 62 (S23): S13–25. https://doi.org/10.1086/711582.

Fusaro, Peter C., and Ross M. Miller. 2009. *What Went Wrong at Enron: Everyone's Guide to the Largest Bankruptcy in US History*. QFinance. A&C Black Publishers Ltd.

Galea, Natalie, Abigail Powell, Fanny Salignac, Louise Chappell, and Martin Loosemore. 2022. 'When Following the Rules is Bad for Wellbeing: The Effects of Gendered Rules in the Australian Construction Industry'. *Work, Employment and Society* 36 (1): 119–38. https://doi.org/10.1177/0950017020978914.

Gardiner, Anna, Anna Chur-Hansen, Deborah Turnbull, and Carolyn Semmler. 2023. 'Qualitative Evaluations of Women's Leadership Programs: A Global, Multi-Sector Systematic Review'. *Australian Journal of Psychology* 75 (1): 2213781. https://doi.org/10.1080/00049530.2023.2213781.

Geary, David C. 2024. 'Sex Differences in the Brain and the Mind'. *Quillette*, 18 January 2024. https://quillette.com/2024/01/18/sex-differences-in-the-brain-and-the-mind/.

Geier, Kathleen, and Curve Contributors. 2014. 'Does Feminism Have a Class Problem?' *The Nation*, 11 June 2014. https://www.thenation.com/article/archive/does-feminism-have-class-problem/.

George, Bill. 2017. 'Google Engineer Deserved to Be Fired by the CEO'. *Harvard Business School Working Knowledge*, 14 September 2017. https://hbswk.hbs.edu/item/op-ed-why-google-engineer-deserved-to-be-fired-by-the-ceo.

Georgeac, Oriane A. M., and Aneeta Rattan. 2023. 'The Business Case for Diversity Backfires: Detrimental Effects of Organizations' Instrumental Diversity Rhetoric for Underrepresented Group Members' Sense of Belonging'. *Journal of Personality and Social Psychology* 124 (1): 69–108. https://doi.org/10.1037/pspi0000394.

Gerson, Kathleen. 2023. 'Why No One Can "Have It All" and Why That Matters for Everyone'. *Sociological Forum* 38 (4): 1423–31. https://doi.org/10.1111/socf.12959.

Gettler, Lee T. 2014. 'Applying Socioendocrinology to Evolutionary Models: Fatherhood and Physiology'. *Evolutionary Anthropology: Issues, News, and Reviews* 23 (4): 146–60. https://doi.org/10.1002/evan.21412.

Giazitzoglu, Andreas, and Daniel Muzio. 2021. 'Learning the Rules of the Game: How Is Corporate Masculinity Learned and Enacted by Male Professionals from Nonprivileged Backgrounds?' *Gender, Work & Organization* 28 (1): 67–84. https://doi.org/10.1111/gwao.12561.

Gillard, Julia, and Ngozi Okonjo-Iweala. 2021. *Women and Leadership: Real Lives, Real Lessons.* Sydney: Penguin Books.

Gino, Francesca, Caroline Ashley Wilmuth, and Alison Wood Brooks. 2015. 'Compared to Men, Women View Professional Advancement as Equally Attainable, but Less Desirable'. *Proceedings of the National Academy of Sciences* 112 (40): 12354–59. https://doi.org/10.1073/pnas.1502567112.

Giridharadas, Anand. 2018. *Winners Take All: The Elite Charade of Changing the World.* New York: Alfred A. Knopf.

Glenn, Evelyn Nakano. 2010. *Forced to Care: Coercion and Caregiving in America.* Cambridge, Mass.: Harvard University Press.

Global Education Monitoring Report Team. 2020. 'Global Education Monitoring Report 2020: Inclusion and Education: All Means All'. Paris: UNESCO. https://doi.org/10.54676/JJNK6989.

Global Institute for Women's Leadership. 2020. 'Four Years of the Women in Finance Charter'. 11 September. https://www.youtube.com/watch?v=gBeluJfB5X4.

Godechot, Olivier. 2017. *Wages, Bonuses and Appropriation of Profit in the*

BIBLIOGRAPHY

Financial Industry: The Working Rich. Trans. Susannah Dale. London; New York: Routledge, Taylor & Francis Group.

Goldin, Claudia Dale. 2021. *Career & Family: Women's Century-Long Journey toward Equity.* Princeton: Princeton University Press.

Goodale, Jane C. 1974. *Tiwi Wives: A Study of the Women of Melville Island, North Australia.* Seattle: University of Washington Press.

Gough, Margaret, and Mary Noonan. 2013. 'A Review of the Motherhood Wage Penalty in the United States'. *Sociology Compass* 7 (4): 328–42. https://doi.org/10.1111/soc4.12031.

Greenhaus, Jeffrey H., Ann C. Peng, and Tammy D. Allen. 2012. 'Relations of Work Identity, Family Identity, Situational Demands, and Sex with Employee Work Hours'. *Journal of Vocational Behavior* 80 (1): 27–37. https://doi.org/10.1016/j.jvb.2011.05.003.

Greenwald, Anthony G., and Thomas F. Pettigrew. 2014. 'With Malice toward None and Charity for Some: Ingroup Favoritism Enables Discrimination'. *American Psychologist* 69 (7): 669–84. https://doi.org/10.1037/a0036056.

Griffiths, Paul E. 2002. 'What Is Innateness?'. *Monist* 85 (1): 70–85. https://doi.org/10.5840/monist20028518.

Grimshaw, Damian, and Jill Rubery. 2015. 'The Motherhood Pay Gap: A Review of the Issues, Theory and International Evidence'. *Conditions of Work & Employment Working Papers*, no. 57 (March), 1–67.

Grossi, Giordana, and Cordelia Fine. 2012. 'The Role of Fetal Testosterone in the Development of the "Essential Difference" Between the Sexes: Some Essential Issues'. In *Neurofeminism*, ed. Robyn Bluhm, Anne Jaap Jacobson, and Heidi Lene Maibom, 73–104. London: Palgrave Macmillan UK.

Grunow, Daniela, Katia Begall, and Sandra Buchler. 2018. 'Gender Ideologies in Europe: A Multidimensional Framework'. *Journal of Marriage and Family* 80 (1): 42–60. https://doi.org/10.1111/jomf.12453.

Guo, Jiesi, Herbert W. Marsh, Philip D. Parker, and Xiang Hu. 2024. 'Cross-Cultural Patterns of Gender Differences in STEM: Gender Stratification, Gender Equality and Gender-Equality Paradoxes'.

Educational Psychology Review 36 (2). https://doi.org/10.1007/s10648-024-09872-3.

Haas, Linda, and C. Philip Hwang. 2019. 'Policy Is Not Enough – the Influence of the Gendered Workplace on Fathers' Use of Parental Leave in Sweden'. *Community, Work & Family* 22 (1): 58–76. https://doi.org/10.1080/13668803.2018.1495616.

Haas, Randall, James Watson, Tammy Buonasera, John Southon, Jennifer C. Chen, Sarah Noe, Kevin Smith, Carlos Viviano Llave, Jelmer Eerkens, and Glendon Parker. 2020. 'Female Hunters of the Early Americas'. *Science Advances* 6 (45): eabd0310. https://doi.org/10.1126/sciadv.abd0310.

Hakim, Catherine. 2000. *Work–Lifestyle Choices in the 21st Century: Preference Theory*. New York: Oxford University Press.

———. 2002. 'Lifestyle Preferences as Determinants of Women's Differentiated Labor Market Careers'. *Work and Occupations* 29 (4): 428–59. https://doi.org/10.1177/0730888402029004003.

Halrynjo, Sigtona, and Marte Mangset. 2022. 'Parental Leave vs. Competition for Clients: Motherhood Penalty in Competitive Work Environments'. *Journal of Family Research* 34 (3): 932–57. https://doi.org/10.20377/jfr-751.

Hamill, Jasper. 2019. 'Men Are More Disadvantaged than Women in the UK, US and Most of Europe, Scientists Claim'. *Metro*, 4 January 2019. https://metro.co.uk/2019/01/04/men-disadvantaged-women-uk-us-europe-scientists-claim-8309361/.

Hamjediers, Maik. 2023. 'Gender-Atypical Learning Experiences of Men Reduce Occupational Sex Segregation: Evidence From the Suspension of the Civilian Service in Germany'. *Gender & Society* 37 (4): 524–52. https://doi.org/10.1177/08912432231177650.

Hanna, Esmée, Brendan Gough, and Steven Markham. 2020. 'Masculinities in the Construction Industry: A Double-edged Sword for Health and Wellbeing?' *Gender, Work & Organization* 27 (4): 632–46. https://doi.org/10.1111/gwao.12429.

Hardcastle, Valerie Cray. 2003. 'The Development of the Self'. In *Narrative and Consciousness Literature, Psychology and the Brain*, ed. Gary D. Fireman, Ted E. McVay, and Owen J. Flanagan. Oxford

BIBLIOGRAPHY

University Press. https://doi.org/10.1093/acprof:oso/9780195140057.001.0001.

Hare, Julie. 2021. 'The Vice-Chancellor Who Negotiated His Salary down to $484,000'. *Australian Financial Review*, 18 June 2021. https://www.afr.com/work-and-careers/leaders/the-vice-chancellor-who-negotiated-his-salary-down-to-484-000-20210514-p57r1z4.

Hargita, C. Starla. 2016. 'Disrupting the Hegemonic Temporality of Superannuation'. *Australian Feminist Law Journal* 42 (2): 223–40. https://doi.org/10.1080/13200968.2016.1253134.

Harjani, Ansuya. 2014. 'Hedge Fund Manager Pay Rises to $2.4 Million'. *CNBC*, 6 November 2014. https://www.cnbc.com/2014/11/06/hedge-fund-manager-pay-rises-to-24-million.html.

Harris, Thomas. 2024. 'The EDI Tax: How Equity, Diversity and Inclusion Is Hobbling British Businesses'. Free Speech Union. https://freespeechunion.org/the-edi-tax-how-equity-diversity-and-inclusion-is-hobbling-british-businesses.

Haslam, Nick. 2016. 'Concept Creep: Psychology's Expanding Concepts of Harm and Pathology'. *Psychological Inquiry* 27 (1): 1–17. https://doi.org/10.1080/1047840X.2016.1082418.

Hayes, Amy Roberson, Rebecca S. Bigler, and Erica S. Weisgram. 2018. 'Of Men and Money: Characteristics of Occupations That Affect the Gender Differentiation of Children's Occupational Interests'. *Sex Roles* 78 (11–12): 775–88. https://doi.org/10.1007/s11199-017-0846-8.

Health and Safety Executive. (n.d.) 'Gender: Information on Work-Related Injuries and Ill Health by Gender'. Accessed 27 July 2024. https://www.hse.gov.uk/statistics/gender/index.htm.

Heck, Isobel A., Kristin Shutts, and Katherine D. Kinzler. 2022. 'Children's Thinking about Group-Based Social Hierarchies'. *Trends in Cognitive Sciences* 26 (7): 593–606. https://doi.org/10.1016/j.tics.2022.04.004.

Hendricks, Shelton E., James R. Lehman, and Gaylon Oswalt. 1982. 'Responses to Copulatory Stimulation in Neonatally Androgenized Female Rats'. *Journal of Comparative and Physiological Psychology* 96 (5): 834–45. https://doi.org/10.1037/h0077931.

Henrich, Joseph. 2016. *The Secret of Our Success: How Culture Is Driving Human Evolution, Domesticating Our Species, and Making Us Smarter.* Princeton: Princeton University Press.

Henrich, Joseph, Damián E. Blasi, Cameron M. Curtin, Helen Elizabeth Davis, Ze Hong, Daniel Kelly, and Ivan Kroupin. 2023. 'A Cultural Species and Its Cognitive Phenotypes: Implications for Philosophy'. *Review of Philosophy and Psychology* 14 (2): 349–86. https://doi.org/10.1007/s13164-021-00612-y.

Henrich, Joseph, and Francisco J. Gil-White. 2001. 'The Evolution of Prestige: Freely Conferred Deference as a Mechanism for Enhancing the Benefits of Cultural Transmission'. *Evolution and Human Behavior* 22 (3): 165–96. https://doi.org/10.1016/S1090-5138(00)00071-4.

Henrich, Joseph, Steven J. Heine, and Ara Norenzayan. 2010. 'The Weirdest People in the World?' *Behavioral and Brain Sciences* 33 (2–3): 61–83. https://doi.org/10.1017/S0140525X0999152X.

Heterodox Academy. 2017. 'The Google Memo: What Does the Research Say about Gender Differences?' 11 August 2017. https://heterodoxacademy.org/blog/the-google-memo-what-does-the-research-say-about-gender-differences/.

Hewlett, Barry S. 1991. *Intimate Fathers: The Nature and Context of Aka Pygmy Paternal Infant Care.* Ann Arbor: University of Michigan Press.

Heyes, Cecilia. 2018. *Cognitive Gadgets: The Cultural Evolution of Thinking.* Cambridge, Mass.: The Belknap Press of Harvard University Press.

———. 2021. 'Imitation'. *Current Biology* 31 (5): R228–32. https://doi.org/10.1016/j.cub.2020.11.071.

Hines, Melissa. 2004. *Brain Gender.* Oxford: Oxford University Press.

———. 2020. 'Human Gender Development'. *Neuroscience & Biobehavioral Reviews* 118 (November): 89–96. https://doi.org/10.1016/j.neubiorev.2020.07.018.

Hines, Melissa, Vickie Pasterski, Debra Spencer, Sharon Neufeld, Praveetha Patalay, Peter C. Hindmarsh, Ieuan A. Hughes, and Carlo L. Acerini. 2016. 'Prenatal Androgen Exposure Alters Girls' Responses to Information Indicating Gender-Appropriate

BIBLIOGRAPHY

Behaviour'. *Philosophical Transactions of the Royal Society B: Biological Sciences* 371 (1688): 20150125. https://doi.org/10.1098/rstb.2015.0125.

HM Treasury. (n.d.) 'Women in Finance Charter: A Pledge for Gender Balance across Financial Services'. Accessed 1 June 2024. https://assets.publishing.service.gov.uk/media/5a7f44e9ed915d74e62296df/women_in_finance_charter.pdf.

HM Treasury, and Virgin Money. 2016. 'Empowering Productivity: Harnessing the Talents of Women in Financial Services'. HM Treasury. https://uk.virginmoney.com/virgin/assets/pdf/Virgin-Money-Empowering-Productivity-Report.pdf.

Ho, Karen Zouwen. 2009. *Liquidated: An Ethnography of Wall Street.* Durham: Duke University Press.

Hobson, Barbara, and Susanne Fahlén. 2009. 'Competing Scenarios for European Fathers: Applying Sen's Capabilities and Agency Framework to Work–Family Balance'. *The ANNALS of the American Academy of Political and Social Science* 624 (1): 214–33. https://doi.org/10.1177/0002716209334435.

Hofmann, Roxana, Dmitri Rozgonjuk, Christopher J. Soto, Fritz Ostendorf, and René Mõttus. 2023. 'There Are a Million Ways to Be a Woman and a Million Ways to Be a Man: Gender Differences across Personality Nuances and Nations'. https://doi.org/10.31234/osf.io/cedwk.

Hoobler, Jenny M., Courtney R. Masterson, Stella M. Nkomo, and Eric J. Michel. 2018. 'The Business Case for Women Leaders: Meta-Analysis, Research Critique, and Path Forward'. *Journal of Management* 44 (6): 2473–99. https://doi.org/10.1177/0149206316628643.

Hook, J. L., and M. Li. 2020. *Gendered Tradeoffs.* The Palgrave Handbook of Family Policy. Springer. https://doi.org/10.1007/978-3-030-54618-2_11.

Hooper, Wayne (August 2006). The Senate Select Committee on Superannuation 1991–2003. Papers on Parliament No. 45. Canberra: Parliament of Australia. https://www.aph.gov.au/About_Parliament/Senate/Powers_practice_n_procedures/~/~/link.aspx?_id=DD1579E4C2D844E4A7654B2C9F075323.

Horner, Victoria, and Andrew Whiten. 2005. 'Causal Knowledge and Imitation/Emulation Switching in Chimpanzees (Pan Troglodytes) and Children (Homo Sapiens)'. *Animal Cognition* 8 (3): 164–81. https://doi.org/10.1007/s10071-004-0239-6.

House of Commons Treasury Committee. 2024. 'Sexism in the City: Sixth Report of Session 2023–24'. https://committees.parliament. uk/publications/43731/documents/217019/default/.

Hrdy, Sarah Blaffer. 2011. *Mothers and Others: The Evolutionary Origins of Mutual Understanding*. Cambridge, Mass.: Belknap Press of Harvard University Press.

Hsin, Amy. 2018. 'Hegemonic Gender Norms and the Gender Gap in Achievement: The Case of Asian Americans'. *Sociological Science* 5:752–74. https://doi.org/10.15195/v5.a32.

Ingalhalikar, Madhura, Alex Smith, Drew Parker, Theodore D. Satterthwaite, Mark A. Elliott, Kosha Ruparel, Hakon Hakonarson, Raquel E. Gur, Ruben C. Gur, and Ragini Verma. 2014. 'Sex Differences in the Structural Connectome of the Human Brain'. *Proceedings of the National Academy of Sciences* 111 (2): 823–8. https:// doi.org/10.1073/pnas.1316909110.

International Transport Workers' Federation. 2015. 'UN Women + Uber = A Vision For Precarious Work'. https://time.com/wp-content/uploads/2015/03/no-to-un-women-uber-partnership.pdf.

Ipsos, and The Global Institute for Women's Leadership. 2019. 'International Women's Day 2019: Global Attitudes towards Gender Equality'. King's College London. https://www.kcl.ac.uk/ giwl/assets/iwd-giwl-main.pdf.

Ironmonger, Duncan. 2001. 'Household Production and the Household Economy'. Research Paper Number 833. Department of Economics, The University of Melbourne. https://www.researchgate.net/ profile/D-Ironmonger/publication/5177551_Household_ Production_and_the_Household_Economy/links/54179ebb0cf 2218008bee9f4/Household-Production-and-the-Household-Economy.pdf.

Isaac, Mike. 2017. 'Inside Uber's Aggressive, Unrestrained Workplace Culture'. *New York Times*, 22 February 2017. https://www.nytimes. com/2017/02/22/technology/uber-workplace-culture.html.

Jabour, Bridie. 2013. 'Julia Gillard's "Small Breasts" Served up on Liberal Party Dinner Menu'. *Guardian*, 12 June 2013. https://www.theguardian.com/world/2013/jun/12/gillard-menu-sexist-liberal-dinner.

Jackson, Robert Max. 2010. *Destined for Equality: The Inevitable Rise of Women's Status*. Cambridge, Mass.: Harvard University Press.

Jacobs, Ben, and Sabrina Siddiqui. 2016. '"You Can Do Anything": Trump Brags on Tape about Using Fame to Get Women'. *Guardian*, 8 October 2016. https://www.theguardian.com/us-news/2016/oct/07/donald-trump-leaked-recording-women.

Janicke, Tim, Ines K. Häderer, Marc J. Lajeunesse, and Nils Anthes. 2016. 'Darwinian Sex Roles Confirmed across the Animal Kingdom'. *Science Advances* 2 (2): e1500983. https://doi.org/10.1126/sciadv.1500983.

Joel, Daphna, and Ricardo Tarrasch. 2014. 'On the Mis-Presentation and Misinterpretation of Gender-Related Data: The Case of Ingalhalikar's Human Connectome Study'. *Proceedings of the National Academy of Sciences* 111 (6). https://doi.org/10.1073/pnas.1323319111.

Jones, Laura, Rose Cook, and Sara Connolly. 2023. 'Parenthood and Job Quality: Is There a Motherhood Penalty in the UK?' *Social Indicators Research* 170 (2): 765–92. https://doi.org/10.1007/s11205-023-03214-6.

Jordan-Young, Rebecca M. 2010. *Brain Storm: The Flaws in the Science of Sex Differences*. Cambridge, Mass.: Harvard University Press.

———. 2012. 'Hormones, Context, and "Brain Gender": A Review of Evidence from Congenital Adrenal Hyperplasia'. *Social Science & Medicine* 74 (11): 1738–44. https://doi.org/10.1016/j.socscimed.2011.08.026.

Jordan-Young, Rebecca M., and Katrina Alicia Karkazis. 2019. *Testosterone: An Unauthorized Biography*. Cambridge, Mass.: Harvard University Press.

Joshi, Aparna, Jooyeon Son, and Hyuntak Roh. 2015. 'When Can Women Close the Gap? A Meta-Analytic Test of Sex Differences in Performance and Rewards'. *Academy of Management Journal* 58 (5): 1516–45. https://doi.org/10.5465/amj.2013.0721.

Kalleberg, Arne L. 2011. *Good Jobs, Bad Jobs: The Rise of Polarized and Precarious Employment Systems in the United States, 1970s to 2000s*. New York: Russell Sage Foundation.

Kapin, Allyson. 2020. 'Sexual Harrassment in Silicon Valley: Still Rampant as Ever'. *Forbes*, 15 September 2020. https://www.forbes.com/sites/allysonkapin/2020/09/15/sexual-harassment-in-silicon-valley-still-rampant-as-ever/?sh=1d5b81212cc4.

Kellogg, Katherine C. 2011. *Challenging Operations: Medical Reform and Resistance in Surgery*. Chicago: University of Chicago Press.

Kim, Jae Yun, Gráinne M. Fitzsimons, and Aaron C. Kay. 2018. 'Lean In Messages Increase Attributions of Women's Responsibility for Gender Inequality'. *Journal of Personality and Social Psychology* 115 (6): 974–1001. https://doi.org/10.1037/pspa0000129.

King's Global Institute for Women's Leadership, and Ipsos. 2024. 'International Women's Day 2024: Global Attitudes towards Women's Leadership'. King's College London. https://www.kcl.ac.uk/giwl/assets/iwd-2024-survey-global-findings.pdf.

Kiselica, Mark S., and Matt Englar-Carlson. 2010. 'Identifying, Affirming, and Building upon Male Strengths: The Positive Psychology/Positive Masculinity Model of Psychotherapy with Boys and Men'. *Psychotherapy: Theory, Research, Practice, Training* 47 (3): 276–87. https://doi.org/10.1037/a0021159.

Kitchen, Alison, Linda Elkins, and Grant Wardell-Johnson. 2021. 'The Gender Superannuation Gap: Addressing the Options'. KPMG. https://assets.kpmg.com/content/dam/kpmg/au/pdf/2021/addressing-gender-superannuation-gap.pdf.

Kleven, Henrik, Camille Landais, and Jakob Egholt Søgaard. 2019. 'Children and Gender Inequality: Evidence from Denmark'. *American Economic Journal: Applied Economics* 11 (4): 181–209. https://doi.org/10.1257/app.20180010.

Knight, Carly R., and Mary C. Brinton. 2017. 'One Egalitarianism or Several? Two Decades of Gender-Role Attitude Change in Europe'. *American Journal of Sociology* 122 (5): 1485–1532. https://doi.org/10.1086/689814.

Kolluri, Suneal. 2023. '"Chill Dudes" and "Academic-Type Students": Relational Masculinity and Straddling Culture at an Urban High

School'. *American Journal of Education* 129 (3): 355–81. https://doi. org/10.1086/724361.

Kornberger, M., C. Carter, and A. Ross-Smith. 2010. 'Changing Gender Domination in a Big Four Accounting Firm: Flexibility, Performance and Client Service in Practice'. *Accounting, Organizations and Society* 35 (8): 775–91. https://doi.org/10.1016/j. aos.2010.09.005.

Krippner, G. R. 2005. 'The Financialization of the American Economy'. *Socio-Economic Review* 3 (2): 173–208. https://doi.org/10.1093/ SER/mwi008.

Krugman, Paul. 2023. 'How Bad Was the Silicon Valley Bank Bailout?' *New York Times*, 14 March 2023. https://www.nytimes. com/2023/03/14/opinion/silicon-valley-bank-bailout.html.

Kübler, Dorothea, Julia Schmid, and Robert Stüber. 2018. 'Gender Discrimination in Hiring across Occupations: A Nationally-Representative Vignette Study'. *Labour Economics* 55:215–29. https://doi.org/10.1016/j.labeco.2018.10.002.

Kuhn, Steven L., and Mary C. Stiner. 2006. 'What's a Mother to Do?: The Division of Labor among Neandertals and Modern Humans in Eurasia'. *Current Anthropology* 47 (6): 953–81. https://doi.org/ 10.1086/507197.

Kung, Karson T. F., Krisya Louie, Debra Spencer, and Melissa Hines. 2024. 'Prenatal Androgen Exposure and Sex-Typical Play Behaviour: A Meta-Analysis of Classic Congenital Adrenal Hyperplasia Studies'. *Neuroscience & Biobehavioral Reviews* 159 (April): 105616. https://doi.org/10.1016/j.neubiorev.2024.105616.

Lake, Marilyn. 2013. 'How the PM's Gender Took over the Agenda'. *Sydney Morning Herald*, 25 June 2013. https://www.smh.com.au/ opinion/how-the-pms-gender-took-over-the-agenda-20130624- 2oson.html.

Laland, Kevin N., and Gillian R. Brown. 2011. *Sense and Nonsense: Evolutionary Perspectives on Human Behaviour*. New York: Oxford University Press.

Lanz, Kate, and Paul Brown. 2020. *All the Brains in the Business: The Engendered Brain in the 21st Century Organisation*. Cham, Switzerland: Palgrave Macmillan.

Lardner, James. 2002. 'Why Should Anyone Believe You'. *Business 2.0* 3 (3): 40.

Leboucher, Gérard. 1989. 'Maternal Behavior in Normal and Androgenized Female Rats: Effect of Age and Experience'. *Physiology & Behavior* 45 (2): 313–19. https://doi.org/10.1016/0031-9384(89)90133-9.

Lee, Cynthia. 2017. 'I'm a Woman in Computer Science. Let Me Ladysplain the Google Memo to You'. *Vox*, 11 August 2017. https://web.archive.org/web/20170811161145/https://www.vox.com/the-big-idea/2017/8/11/16130452/google-memo-women-tech-biology-sexism.

Legare, Cristine H. 2017. 'Cumulative Cultural Learning: Development and Diversity'. *Proceedings of the National Academy of Sciences* 114 (30): 7877–83. https://doi.org/10.1073/pnas.1620743114.

Leichman, Abigail Klein. 2023. 'State of High-Tech Industry in Israel Report: Ups but More Downs'. *Israel21c*, 29 June 2023. https://www.israel21c.org/state-of-high-industry-in-israel-report-ups-but-more-downs/.

Lerner, Josh, Rahat Dewan, Jake Ledbetter, and Alex Billias. 2021. 'Knight Diversity of Asset Managers Research Series: Industry'. Knight Foundation / Bella Private Markets. https://knightfoundation.org/wp-content/uploads/2021/12/KDAM_Industry_2021.pdf.

Levanon, Asaf, and David B. Grusky. 2016. 'The Persistence of Extreme Gender Segregation in the Twenty-First Century'. *American Journal of Sociology* 122 (2): 573–619. https://doi.org/10.1086/688628.

Levin, Sam. 2017. 'Google "Segregates" Women into Lower-Paying Jobs, Stifling Careers, Lawsuit Says'. *Guardian*, 15 September 2017. https://www.theguardian.com/technology/2017/sep/14/google-women-promotions-lower-paying-jobs-lawsuit.

Lewis, Paul. 2017. '"I See Things Differently": James Damore on His Autism and the Google Memo'. *Guardian*, 17 November 2017. https://www.theguardian.com/technology/2017/nov/16/james-damore-google-memo-interview-autism-regrets.

Lew-Levy, Sheina, Adam H. Boyette, Alyssa N. Crittenden, Barry S. Hewlett, and Michael E. Lamb. 2020. 'Gender-Typed and

Gender-Segregated Play Among Tanzanian Hadza and Congolese BaYaka Hunter-Gatherer Children and Adolescents'. *Child Development* 91 (4): 1284–1301. https://doi.org/10.1111/cdev.13306.

Lin, Ken-Hou, and Megan Tobias Neely. 2017. 'Gender, Parental Status, and the Wage Premium in Finance'. *Social Currents* 4 (6): 535–55. https://doi.org/10.1177/2329496516686622.

———. 2020. *Divested: Inequality in the Age of Finance*. New York: Oxford University Press.

Lippa, Richard A., Marcia L. Collaer, and Michael Peters. 2010. 'Sex Differences in Mental Rotation and Line Angle Judgments Are Positively Associated with Gender Equality and Economic Development Across 53 Nations'. *Archives of Sexual Behavior* 39 (4): 990–7. https://doi.org/10.1007/s10508-008-9460-8.

Lovell, Vicky. 2006. *Solving the Nursing Shortage through Higher Wages*. Washington: Institute for Women's Policy Research (IWPR).

Luscombe, Belinda. 2022. 'How Hedge Funds' Lack of Diversity Affects All of Us'. *Time*, 5 January 2022. https://time.com/6132594/hedged-out-book-hedge-fund-inequality/.

Lyons, Kate, and Josh Butler. 2024. 'Gender Pay Gap: Katy Gallagher Calls on Dutton to Reject Matt Canavan's Comments Calling Report "Useless Data"'. *Guardian*, 27 February 2024. https://www.theguardian.com/australia-news/2024/feb/27/gender-pay-gap-australia-katy-gallagher-matt-canavan-comments-peter-dutton.

Mackert, Juergen. 2012. 'Social Closure'. *Oxford Bibliographies in Sociology*. Oxford University Press. https://doi.org/10.1093/obo/9780199756384-0084.

Mameli, Matteo. 2001. 'Mindreading, Mindshaping, and Evolution'. *Biology & Philosophy* 16 (5): 595–626. https://doi.org/10.1023/A:1012203830990.

'Mark Carney: The "Film Star" Bank of England Governor'. 2016. BBC, October. https://www.bbc.com/news/business-23050597.

Martin, Bill. 2007. 'Good Jobs, Bad Jobs?: Understanding The Quality of Aged Care Jobs, and Why It Matters'. *Australian Journal of Social Issues* 42 (2): 183–97. https://doi.org/10.1002/j.1839-4655.2007.tb00048.x.

Martin, Carol Lynn, and Diane Ruble. 2004. 'Children's Search for Gender Cues: Cognitive Perspectives on Gender Development'. *Current Directions in Psychological Science* 13 (2): 67–70. https://doi.org/10.1111/j.0963-7214.2004.00276.x.

——. 2010. 'Patterns of Gender Development'. *Annual Review of Psychology* 61 (1): 353–81. https://doi.org/10.1146/annurev.psych.093008.100511.

Masterson, Victoria. 2024. 'Women Founders and Venture Capital – Some 2023 Snapshots'. World Economic Forum. https://www.weforum.org/agenda/2024/03/women-startups-vc-funding/.

Mayer, Grace. 2023. 'Ex-Wells Fargo Exec Who Pushed Bankers to Open Fake Accounts Will Plead Guilty. She'll Pay a $17 Million Fine – and Faces More than a Year in Prison'. *Business Insider*, 17 March 2023. https://www.businessinsider.com/wells-fargo-executive-guilty-bank-scandal-fake-accounts-prison-fine-2023-3.

McDowell, Linda. 2004. 'Thinking Through Work: Gender, Power, and Space'. In *Reading Economic Geography*, ed. Trevor J. Barnes, Jamie Peck, Eric Sheppard, and Adam Tickell, 1st edn, 315–28. Wiley. https://doi.org/10.1002/9780470755716.ch20.

——. 2010. 'Capital Culture Revisited: Sex, Testosterone and the City'. *International Journal of Urban and Regional Research* 34 (3): 652. https://doi.org/10.1111/j.1468-2427.2010.00972.x.

McGoogan, Cara. 2018. 'Third of Bosses Avoid Hiring Women Who Could Have Children Soon'. *Telegraph*, 21 July 2018. https://www.telegraph.co.uk/women/business/third-bosses-avoid-hiring-women-could-have-children-soon/.

Messing, Karen. 2021. *Bent out of Shape: Shame, Solidarity, and Women's Bodies at Work*. Toronto: Between the Lines.

Metz, Isabel, and Savita Kumra. 2019. 'Why Are Self-Help Books with Career Advice for Women Popular?' *Academy of Management Perspectives* 33 (1): 82–93. https://doi.org/10.5465/amp.2016.0152.

Mill, John Stuart. 1859. *On Liberty*. London and Felling-on-Tyne; New York and Melbourne: The Walter Scott Publishing Co., Ltd.

——. 1869. *The Subjection of Women*. London: Longmans, Green, Reader, and Dyer. https://www.gutenberg.org/cache/epub/27083/pg27083-images.html.

BIBLIOGRAPHY

Millar, Stuart. 2002. 'First Free Vote for Bahraini Women'. *Guardian*, 25 October 2002. https://www.theguardian.com/world/2002/oct/25/gender.stuartmillar.

Mills, Albert J. 1998. 'Cockpits, Hangars, Boys and Galleys: Corporate Masculinities and the Development of British Airways'. *Gender, Work & Organization* 5 (3): 172–88. https://doi.org/10.1111/1468-0432.00055.

Mlambo-Ngcuka, Phumzile, and Travis Kalanick. 2015. 'UN Women + Uber = A Vision For Equality'. Uber Newsroom. https://www.uber.com/en-AU/newsroom/un-women-uber-a-vision-for-equality-2/.

Murdock, George P., and Caterina Provost. 1973. 'Factors in the Division of Labor by Sex: A Cross-Cultural Analysis'. *Ethnology* 12 (2): 203. https://doi.org/10.2307/3773347.

Murphy, Sara A., Peter A. Fisher, and Chet Robie. 2021. 'International Comparison of Gender Differences in the Five-Factor Model of Personality: An Investigation across 105 Countries'. *Journal of Research in Personality* 90 (February): 104047. https://doi.org/10.1016/j.jrp.2020.104047.

NHS (n.d.) 'Working for the NHS in England'. https://www.healthcareers.nhs.uk/we-are-the-nhs/nursing-careers/international-recruitment/working-nhs-england.

Nash, Alison, and Giordana Grossi. 2007. 'Picking Barbie's Brain: Inherent Sex Differences in Scientific Ability?' *Journal of Interdisciplinary Feminist Thought* 2 (1): Article 5.

National Center for Science and Engineering Statistics, Directorate for Social, Behavioral and Economic Sciences, and National Science Foundation. 2023. 'Diversity and STEM: Women, Minorities, and Persons with Disabilities 2023'. Special Report NSF 23-315. National Science Foundation. https://ncses.nsf.gov/wmpd.

Neely, Megan Tobias. 2018. 'Fit to Be King: How Patrimonialism on Wall Street Leads to Inequality'. *Socio-Economic Review* 16 (2): 365–85. https://doi.org/10.1093/ser/mwx058.

———. 2020. 'The Portfolio Ideal Worker: Insecurity and Inequality in the New Economy'. *Qualitative Sociology* 43 (2): 271–96. https://doi.org/10.1007/s11133-020-09444-1.

————. 2021. *Hedged Out: Inequality and Insecurity on Wall Street*. Taylor and Francis.

Nelson, Julie A. 1999. 'Of Markets And Martyrs: Is It OK To Pay Well For Care?' *Feminist Economics* 5 (3): 43–59. https://doi.org/ 10.1080/135457099337806.

Nelson, Robert L., and William P. Bridges. 1999. *Legalizing Gender Inequality: Courts, Markets, And Unequal Pay for Women in America*. New York: Cambridge University Press.

Neufeld, Sharon A. S., Marcia L. Collaer, Debra Spencer, Vickie Pasterski, Peter C. Hindmarsh, Ieuan A. Hughes, Carlo Acerini, and Melissa Hines. 2023. 'Androgens and Child Behavior: Color and Toy Preferences in Children with Congenital Adrenal Hyperplasia (CAH)'. *Hormones and Behavior* 149 (March): 105310. https://doi. org/10.1016/j.yhbeh.2023.105310.

Nielsen, M. W. 2018. 'Scientific Performance Assessments through a Gender Lens: A Case Study on Evaluation and Selection Practices in Academia'. *Science and Technology Studies* 31 (1): 2–30.

Nivette, Amy, Alex Sutherland, Manuel Eisner, and Joseph Murray. 2019. 'Sex Differences in Adolescent Physical Aggression: Evidence from Sixty-three Low- and Middle-income Countries'. *Aggressive Behavior* 45 (1): 82–92. https://doi.org/10.1002/ab.21799.

O'Connell, James F. 2006. 'How Did Modern Humans Displace Neanderthals? Insights from Hunter-Gatherer Ethnography and Archaeology'. In *When Neanderthals and Modern Humans Met*, ed. Nicholas John Conard, 43–64. Tübingen Publications in Prehistory. Tübingen: Kerns.

O'Connor, Cailin. 2019. *The Origins of Unfairness: Social Categories and Cultural Evolution*. Oxford: Oxford University Press.

OECD. 2021. 'Towards Improved Retirement Savings Outcomes for Women'. Paris: OECD Publishing. https://doi.org/10.1787/ f7b48808-en.

Office for National Statistics. 2018. 'Understanding the Gender Pay Gap in the UK'. https://www.ons.gov.uk/employmentand labourmarket/peopleinwork/earningsandworkinghours/articles/ understandingthegenderpaygapintheuk/2018-01-17.

————. 2024a. 'Families and Households in the UK: 2023'. https://

www.ons.gov.uk/peoplepopulationandcommunity/birthsdeaths
andmarriages/families/bulletins/familiesandhouseholds/2023#
living-alone.

———. 2024b. 'Gender Pay Gap'. https://www.ons.gov.uk/
employmentandlabourmarket/peopleinwork/earningsand
workinghours/datasets/annualsurveyofhoursandearningsashe
genderpaygaptables.

———. 2024c. 'Time Use in the UK'. https://www.ons.gov.uk/
peoplepopulationandcommunity/personalandhouseholdfinances/
incomeandwealth/datasets/timeuseintheuk.

Otis, Eileen, and Tongyu Wu. 2018. 'The Deficient Worker: Skills,
Identity, and Inequality in Service Employment'. *Sociological
Perspectives* 61 (5): 787–807. https://doi.org/10.1177/
0731121418766899.

Oxfam International. 2017. 'Top Financiers Call on Europe to Agree
Robin Hood Tax'. https://www.oxfam.org/en/press-releases/
top-financiers-call-europe-agree-robin-hood-tax.

Padavic, Irene, Robin J. Ely, and Erin M. Reid. 2020. 'Explaining the
Persistence of Gender Inequality: The Work–Family Narrative as
a Social Defense against the 24/7 Work Culture'. *Administrative
Science Quarterly* 65 (1): 61–111. https://doi.org/10.1177/
0001839219832310.

Palmer, Elyane, and Joan Eveline. 2012. 'Sustaining Low Pay in Aged
Care Work'. *Gender, Work & Organization* 19 (3): 254–75. https://
doi.org/10.1111/j.1468-0432.2010.00512.x.

Parkinson, Brian. 2012. 'Piecing Together Emotion: Sites and
Time-Scales for Social Construction'. *Emotion Review* 4 (3): 291–8.
https://doi.org/10.1177/1754073912439764.

Parliament of Australia. 2014. 'Major Superannuation and Retirement
Income Changes in Australia: A Chronology'. https://www.
aph.gov.au/About_Parliament/Parliamentary_Departments/
Parliamentary_Library/pubs/rp/rp1314/SuperChron.

Pasterski, Vickie L., Mitchell E. Geffner, Caroline Brain, Peter
Hindmarsh, Charles Brook, and Melissa Hines. 2005. 'Prenatal
Hormones and Postnatal Socialization by Parents as Determinants
of Male-Typical Toy Play in Girls With Congenital Adrenal

Hyperplasia'. *Child Development* 76 (1): 264–78. https://doi.org/10.1111/j.1467-8624.2005.00843.x.

Pasztor, Sabrina K. 2019. 'Exploring the Framing of Diversity Rhetoric in "Top-Rated in Diversity" Organizations'. *International Journal of Business Communication* 56 (4): 455–75. https://doi.org/10.1177/2329488416664175.

Patton, Elizabeth W., Kent A. Griffith, Rochelle D. Jones, Abigail Stewart, Peter A. Ubel, and Reshma Jagsi. 2017. 'Differences in Mentor–Mentee Sponsorship in Male vs Female Recipients of National Institutes of Health Grants'. *JAMA Internal Medicine* 177 (4): 580. https://doi.org/10.1001/jamainternmed.2016.9391.

Pearson, Ruth, and Diane Elson. 2015. 'Transcending the Impact of the Financial Crisis in the United Kingdom: Towards Plan F – a Feminist Economic Strategy'. *Feminist Review* 109 (1): 8–30. https://doi.org/10.1057/fr.2014.42.

Penner, Andrew M., Trond Petersen, Are Skeie Hermansen, Anthony Rainey, István Boza, Marta M. Elvira, Olivier Godechot, et al. 2022. 'Within-Job Gender Pay Inequality in 15 Countries'. *Nature Human Behaviour* 7 (2): 184–9. https://doi.org/10.1038/s41562-022-01470-z.

Peters, Kim, Niklas K. Steffens, and Thekla Morgenroth. 2018. 'Superstars Are Not Necessarily Role Models: Morality Perceptions Moderate the Impact of Competence Perceptions on Supervisor Role Modeling'. *European Journal of Social Psychology* 48 (6): 725–46. https://doi.org/10.1002/ejsp.2372.

Pichai, Sundar. 2017. 'Note to Employees from CEO Sundar Pichai'. *Google* (blog). 8 August 2017. https://blog.google/outreach-initiatives/diversity/note-employees-ceo-sundar-pichai/.

Pietraszewski, David, and Annie E. Wertz. 2022. 'Why Evolutionary Psychology Should Abandon Modularity'. *Perspectives on Psychological Science* 17 (2): 465–90. https://doi.org/10.1177/1745691621997113.

Pinkstone, Joe. 2019. 'Men "Face MORE Discrimination than Women": Global Study Claims Males Receive the Raw End of the Deal with Harsher Punishments for the Same Crime, Compulsory Military

Service and More Deaths at Work'. *Daily Mail*, 1 July 2019. https://www.dailymail.co.uk/sciencetech/article-6564767/Men-face-discrimination-women.html.

Pirlott, Angela G., and David P. Schmitt. 2014. 'Gendered Sexual Cultures'. In *Culture Reexamined: Broadening Our Understanding of Social and Evolutionary Influences*, ed. Adam B. Cohen, 191–215. Washington: American Psychological Association.

Plan International Australia. 2023. 'Gender Compass: A Segmentation of Australia's Views on Gender Equality'. https://www.plan.org.au/wp-content/uploads/2023/09/GenderCompass_Report.pdf.

Qiu, Linda. 2023. 'No, "Wokeness" Did Not Cause Silicon Valley Bank's Collapse'. *New York Times*, 15 March 2023. https://www.nytimes.com/2023/03/15/us/politics/silicon-valley-bank-collapse-woke-fact-check.html.

Quinn, Paul C., Joshua Yahr, Abbie Kuhn, Alan M. Slater, and Olivier Pascalis. 2002. 'Representation of the Gender of Human Faces by Infants: A Preference for Female'. *Perception* 31 (9): 1109–21. https://doi.org/10.1068/p3331.

Reckard, E. Scott. 2013. 'Wells Fargo's Pressure-Cooker Sales Culture Comes at a Cost.' *Los Angeles Times*, 21 December 2013. https://www.latimes.com/business/la-fi-wells-fargo-sale-pressure-20131222-story.html#page=1.

Reeves, Richard. 2023. *Of Boys and Men: Why the Modern Male Is Struggling, Why It Matters, and What to Do about It*. London: Swift Press.

Research and Markets. 2024. 'Global Diversity and Inclusion (D&I) Strategic Research Report 2024: Market to Read $24.4 Billion by 2030 – Top Diversity, Equity, and Inclusion Trends for 2033 and Beyond'. *PR Newswire*, 1 March 2024. https://finance.yahoo.com/news/global-market-diversity-inclusion-d-100100759.html. https://www.prnewswire.com/news-releases/global-diversity-and-inclusion-di-strategic-research-report-2024-market-to-reach-24-4-billion-by-2030---top-diversity-equity-and-inclusion-trends-for-2023-and-beyond-302077414.html.

Rhodes, Marjorie, and Andrew Baron. 2019. 'The Development of Social Categorization'. *Annual Review of Developmental*

Psychology 1 (December): 359–86. https://doi.org/10.1146/annurev-devpsych-121318-084824.

Richardson, Angelique. 2011. 'Against Finality: Darwin, Mill and the End of Essentialism'. *Critical Quarterly* 53 (4): 21–44. https://doi.org/10.1111/j.1467-8705.2011.02020.x.

Richardson, Sarah, and the GenderSci Lab. 'Gender Stereotypes, Gendered Self-Expression, and Gender Segregation in Fields of Study: A Q&A with Professor Maria Charles'. GenderSci Blog, 14 February 2020. https://genderscilab.org/blog/gender-stereotypes-gendered-self-expression-and-gender-segregation-in-fields-of-study-a-qampa-with-professor-maria-charles.

Richerson, Peter J., Sergey Gavrilets, and Frans B. M. De Waal. 2021. 'Modern Theories of Human Evolution Foreshadowed by Darwin's *Descent of Man*'. *Science* 372 (6544): eaba3776. https://doi.org/10.1126/science.aba3776.

Ridgeway, Cecilia L. 2019. *Status: Why Is It Everywhere? Why Does It Matter?* New York: Russell Sage Foundation.

Ridgeway, Cecilia, and David Diekema. 1989. 'Dominance and Collective Hierarchy Formation in Male and Female Task Groups'. *American Sociological Review* 54 (1): 79–93. https://doi.org/10.2307/2095663.

Ridgeway, Cecilia L., Elizabeth Heger Boyle, Kathy J. Kuipers, and Dawn T. Robinson. 1998. 'How Do Status Beliefs Develop? The Role of Resources and Interactional Experience'. *American Sociological Review* 63 (3): 331–50. https://doi.org/10.2307/2657553.

Ridgeway, Cecilia L., and Sandra Nakagawa. 2017. 'Is Deference the Price of Being Seen as Reasonable? How Status Hierarchies Incentivize Acceptance of Low Status'. *Social Psychology Quarterly* 80 (2): 132–52. https://doi.org/10.1177/0190272517695213.

Risman, Barbara J. 2004. 'Gender As a Social Structure: Theory Wrestling with Activism'. *Gender & Society* 18 (4): 429–50. https://doi.org/10.1177/0891243204265349.

Rivera, Lauren A., and Andras Tilcsik. 2016. 'Class Advantage, Commitment Penalty: The Gendered Effect of Social Class Signals in an Elite Labor Market'. *American Sociological Review* 81 (6):

1097–1131. https://doi.org/10.1177/0003122416668154.

Robeyns, Ingrid. 'Sen's capability approach and gender inequality: selecting relevant capabilities'. *Feminist Economics* 9, no. 2–3 (2003): 61–92.

———. 2007. 'When Will Society Be Gender Just?' In *The Future of Gender*, ed. Jude Browne, 1st edn, 54–74. Cambridge University Press. https://doi.org/10.1017/CBO9780511619205.004.

———. 2017. *Wellbeing, Freedom and Social Justice: The Capability Approach Re-Examined*. Open Book Publishers. https://doi.org/10.11647/OBP.0130.

Roscigno, Vincent J., Lisette M. Garcia, and Donna Bobbitt-Zeher. 2007. 'Social Closure and Processes of Race/Sex Employment Discrimination'. *The ANNALS of the American Academy of Political and Social Science* 609 (1): 16–48. https://doi.org/10.1177/0002716206294898.

Rosenbaum, Stacy, Linda Vigilant, Christopher W. Kuzawa, and Tara S. Stoinski. 2018. 'Caring for Infants Is Associated with Increased Reproductive Success for Male Mountain Gorillas'. *Scientific Reports* 8 (1): 15223. https://doi.org/10.1038/s41598-018-33380-4.

Roth, Louise Marie. 2004a. 'Engendering Inequality: Processes of Sex-Segregation on Wall Street'. *Sociological Forum: Official Journal of the Eastern Sociological Society* 19 (2): 203–28. https://doi.org/10.1023/b:sofo.0000031980.82004.d7.

———. 2004b. 'The Social Psychology of Tokenism: Status and Homophily Processes on Wall Street'. *Sociological Perspectives* 47 (2): 189–214. https://doi.org/10.1525/sop.2004.47.2.189.

———. 2015. *Selling Women Short: Gender and Money on Wall Street*. Princeton, NJ: Princeton University Press.

Rowlands, Julie, and Rebecca Boden. 2020. 'How Australian Vice-Chancellors' Pay Came to Average $1 Million and Why It's a Problem'. *The Conversation*, 2 December 2020. https://theconversation.com/how-australian-vice-chancellors-pay-came-to-average-1-million-and-why-its-a-problem-150829.

Royal Commission into Aged Care Quality and Safety. 2020. *Experimental Estimates of the Prevalence of Elder Abuse in Australian Aged*

Care Facilities. Adelaide, South Australia: Royal Commission into Aged Care Quality and Safety.

———. 2021. 'Final Report: Care, Dignity and Respect'. https://www.royalcommission.gov.au/aged-care.

Rubery, Jill. 2015. 'Regulating for Gender Equality: A Policy Framework to Support the Universal Caregiver Vision'. *Social Politics: International Studies in Gender, State & Society* 22 (4): 513–38. https://doi.org/10.1093/sp/jxv036.

Saini, Angela. 2017. 'Silicon Valley's Weapon of Choice against Women: Shoddy Science'. *Guardian*, 8 August 2017. https://www.theguardian.com/commentisfree/2017/aug/07/silicon-valley-weapon-choice-women-google-manifesto-gender-difference-eugenics.

———. *The Patriarchs: The Origins of Inequality*. 2024. Boston, Mass.: Beacon Press.

Sandberg, Sheryl. 2010. 'Why We Have Too Few Women Leaders'. Presented at the TEDWomen 2010, December. https://www.ted.com/talks/sheryl_sandberg_why_we_have_too_few_women_leaders?language=en.

———. 2013a. *Lean In: Women, Work, and the Will to Lead*. New York: Alfred A. Knopf.

———. 2013b. 'Why I Want Women to Lean In'. *Time*, 7 March 2013. https://ideas.time.com/2013/03/07/why-i-want-women-to-lean-in/.

Sauer, Carsten, Peter Valet, Safi Shams, and Donald Tomaskovic-Devey. 2021. 'Categorical Distinctions and Claims-Making: Opportunity, Agency, and Returns from Wage Negotiations'. *American Sociological Review* 86 (5): 934–59. https://doi.org/10.1177/00031224211038507.

Sawer, Marian. 2013. 'Misogyny and Misrepresentation: Women in Australian Parliaments'. *Political Science* 65 (1): 105–17. https://doi.org/10.1177/0032318713488316.

Scarborough, William J., Ray Sin, and Barbara Risman. 2019. 'Attitudes and the Stalled Gender Revolution: Egalitarianism, Traditionalism, and Ambivalence from 1977 through 2016'. *Gender & Society* 33 (2): 173–200. https://doi.org/10.1177/0891243218809604.

Schechtman, Marya. 2011. 'The Oxford Handbook of the Self'. In *The Narrative Self*, ed. Shaun Gallagher. Oxford University Press.

Schmitt, David P. 2015. 'The Evolution of Culturally-Variable Sex Differences: Men and Women Are Not Always Different, but When They Are . . . It Appears Not to Result from Patriarchy or Sex Role Socialization'. In *The Evolution of Sexuality*, ed. Todd K. Shackelford and Ranald D. Hansen, 221–56. Evolutionary Psychology. Cham: Springer International Publishing.

———. 2017. 'On That Google Memo about Sex Differences'. *Psychology Today* (blog). 7 August 2017. https://www.psychologytoday.com/intl/blog/sexual-personalities/201708/google-memo-about-sex-differences.

———. 2023a. 'Extensions of Sexual Strategies Theory across Peoples, Cultures, and Ecologies'. In *The Oxford Handbook of Human Mating*, ed. David M. Buss, 1st edn, 66–118. Oxford University Press.

———. 2023b. 'How Can Sex Differences Be Evolved and Culturally Variable?' *Psychology Today*, 5 May 2023. https://www.psychologytoday.com/au/blog/sexual-personalities/202304/how-can-sex-differences-be-evolved-and-culturally-variable.

Schmitt, David P., Anu Realo, Martin Voracek, and Jüri Allik. 2008. 'Why Can't a Man Be More like a Woman? Sex Differences in Big Five Personality Traits across 55 Cultures'. *Journal of Personality and Social Psychology* 94 (1): 168–82. https://doi.org/10.1037/0022-3514.94.1.168.

Schultz, Vicki. 1998. 'Reconceptualizing Sexual Harassment'. *The Yale Law Journal* 107:1683–1805.

———. 2010. 'Feminism and Workplace Flexibility'. *Connecticut Law Review* 42 (4): 1203–21.

———. 2018. 'Reconceptualizing Sexual Harassment, Again'. *The Yale Law Journal Forum*, June, 22–66.

Schwartz, Shalom H., and Tammy Rubel. 2005. 'Sex Differences in Value Priorities: Cross-Cultural and Multimethod Studies'. *Journal of Personality and Social Psychology* 89 (6): 1010–28. https://doi.org/10.1037/0022-3514.89.6.1010.

Schwartz, Shalom H., and Tammy Rubel-Lifschitz. 2009. 'Cross-National Variation in the Size of Sex Differences in

Values: Effects of Gender Equality'. *Journal of Personality and Social Psychology* 97 (1): 171–85. https://doi.org/10.1037/a0015546.

Science News Staff. 2020. 'Researchers Retract Controversial Female Mentorship Paper'. *Science*, December. https://doi.org/10.1126/science.abg2662.

Scott, Linda M. 2020. *The Double X Economy: The Epic Potential of Women's Empowerment.* New York: Farrar, Straus and Giroux.

Seccombe, Wally. 1986. 'Patriarchy Stabilized: The Construction of the Male Breadwinner Wage Norm in Nineteenth-Century Britain'. *Social History* 11 (1): 53–76. https://doi.org/10.1080/03071028608567640.

Serbin, Lisa A., Diane Poulin-Dubois, and Julie A. Eichstedt. 2002. 'Infants' Responses to Gender-Inconsistent Events'. *Infancy* 3 (4): 531–42. https://doi.org/10.1207/S15327078IN0304_07.

Shen, Winny, and Dana L. Joseph. 2021. 'Gender and Leadership: A Criterion-Focused Review and Research Agenda'. *Human Resource Management Review* 31 (2): 100765. https://doi.org/10.1016/j.hrmr.2020.100765.

Sherman, Natalie, and James Clayton. 2023. 'Silicon Valley Bank: Regulators Take over as Failure Raises Fears'. BBC, 11 March 2023. https://www.bbc.com/news/business-64915616.

Shirazi, Talia N., Heather Self, Khytam Dawood, Lisa L. M. Welling, Rodrigo Cárdenas, Kevin A. Rosenfield, J. Michael Bailey, et al. 2021. 'Evidence That Perinatal Ovarian Hormones Promote Women's Sexual Attraction to Men'. *Psychoneuroendocrinology* 134 (December): 105431. https://doi.org/10.1016/j.psyneuen.2021.105431.

Shirazi, Talia N., Heather Self, Kevin A. Rosenfield, Khytam Dawood, Lisa L. M. Welling, Rodrigo Cárdenas, J. Michael Bailey, et al. 2022. 'Low Perinatal Androgens Predict Recalled Childhood Gender Nonconformity in Men'. *Psychological Science* 33 (3): 343–53. https://doi.org/10.1177/09567976211036075.

Shorter, Edward. 1975. *The Making of the Modern Family.* New York: Basic Books.

Shows, Carla, and Naomi Gerstel. 2009. 'Fathering, Class, and Gender: A Comparison of Physicians and Emergency Medical Technicians'.

Gender & Society 23 (2): 161–87. https://doi.org/10.1177/
0891243209333872.

Shutts, Kristin, Mahzarin R. Banaji, and Elizabeth S. Spelke. 2010.
'Social Categories Guide Young Children's Preferences for Novel
Objects'. *Developmental Science* 13 (4): 599–610. https://doi.org/
10.1111/j.1467-7687.2009.00913.x.

Siegel, Reva B. 1994. 'Home As Work: The First Woman's Rights
Claims Concerning Wives' Household Labor, 1850–1880'. *The Yale
Law Journal* 103:146. http://hdl.handle.net/20.500.13051/8808.

Sierminska, Eva. 2018. 'The "Wealth-Being" of Single Parents'. In
*The Triple Bind of Single-Parent Families: Resources, Employment and
Policies to Improve Wellbeing*, ed. Rense Nieuwenhuis and Laurie C.
Maldonado, 51–80. Bristol University Press.

Simpson, Ruth. 2004. 'Masculinity at Work: The Experiences of Men
in Female Dominated Occupations'. *Work, Employment & Society* 18
(2): 349–68.

Sloan, Judith. 2023. 'Why the Gender Pay Gap Theory Just Doesn't
Add Up'. *The Australian*, 11 March 2023.

———. 2024. 'Gender Pay Gap Just Nonsense'. *The Australian*,
27 February 2024.

Smith, Adam. 1776. *An Inquiry into the Nature and Causes of the Wealth
of Nations*. London: Printed for A. Strahan and T. Cadell Jun. and
W. Davies.

Smith, Belinda M. 2008. 'From Wardley to Purvis – How Far Has
Australian Anti-Discrimination Law Come in 30 Years?' *Australian
Journal of Labour Law* 21 (1): 3–29. https://doi.org/10.2139/
ssrn.1005528.

Smith, Subrena E. 2020. 'Is Evolutionary Psychology Possible?'
Biological Theory 15 (1): 39–49. https://doi.org/10.1007/
s13752-019-00336-4.

Smithers, Kathleen, Jess Harris, and Nerida Spina, 2023. 'Australian
unis could not function without casual staff: it is time to treat them
as "real" employees'. 24 April 2023. https://theconversation.com/
australian-unis-could-not-function-without-casual-staff-it-is-
time-to-treat-them-as-real-employees-203053.

Sober, Elliott. 1980. 'Evolution, Population Thinking, and

Essentialism'. *Philosophy of Science* 47 (3): 350–83. https://doi.org/ 10.1086/288942.

Social Metrics Commission. 2023. 'Measuring Poverty 2023: A Report of the Social Metrics Commission'. https:// socialmetricscommission.org.uk/wp-content/uploads/2023/12/ SMC-2023-Report-Web-Hi-Res.pdf.

Soh, Debra. 2017. 'No, the Google Manifesto Isn't Sexist or Anti-Diversity. It's Science'. *The Globe and Mail*, 8 August 2017. https://www.theglobeandmail.com/opinion/no-the-google-manifesto-isnt-sexist-or-anti-diversity-its-science/ article35903359/.

———. 2020. *The End of Gender: Debunking the Myths about Sex and Identity in Our Society*. New York: Threshold Editions.

Soit, Honi. 2022. 'Most Vice-Chancellors Earn Far More than the Prime Minister'. *University World News*, 17 August 2022. https:// www.universityworldnews.com/post.php?story= 20220817142508922.

Sojo, Victor E., Robert E. Wood, and Anna E. Genat. 2016. 'Harmful Workplace Experiences and Women's Occupational Well-Being: A Meta-Analysis'. *Psychology of Women Quarterly* 40 (1): 10–40. https://doi.org/10.1177/0361684315599346.

Sojo, Victor, Cordelia Fine, Holly Lawford-Smith, Ziying Yang, and Karin Verspoor. 2020. 'The "Good, Bad and Merit" Arguments in Australian News Coverage of Workplace Gender Diversity'. University of Melbourne. https://melbourne.figshare.com/ articles/online_resource/The_good_bad_and_merit_arguments_ in_Australian_news_coverage_of_workplace_gender_diversity/ 13011914.

Stanfors, Maria, and Frances Goldscheider. 2017. 'The Forest and the Trees: Industrialization, Demographic Change, and the Ongoing Gender Revolution in Sweden and the United States, 1870-2010'. *Demographic Research* 36 (January): 173–226. https:// doi.org/10.4054/DemRes.2017.36.6.

Stanton, Steven J., Keith M. Welker, Pierre L. Bonin, Bernard Goldfarb, and Justin M. Carré. 2021. 'The Effect of Testosterone on Economic Risk-Taking: A Multi-Study, Multi-Method Investigation'. *Hormones and Behavior* 134 (August). https://doi.org/10.1016/j.yhbeh.2021. 105014.

Steinberg, Ronnie J. 1990. 'Social Construction of Skill: Gender, Power, and Comparable Worth'. *Work and Occupations* 17 (4): 449–82. https://doi.org/10.1177/0730888490017004004.

Sterelny, Kim. 2008. *Thought in a Hostile World: The Evolution of Human Cognition*. Malden, MA: Blackwell.

———. 2014. *The Evolved Apprentice: How Evolution Made Humans Unique*. Cambridge, Mass.; London: The MIT Press.

———. 2019. 'Norms and Their Evolution'. In *Handbook of Cognitive Archaeology: Psychology in Prehistory*, ed. Tracy B. Henley, Matthew J. Rossano, and Edward P. Kardas, 375–97. London: Routledge.

———. 2021. *The Pleistocene Social Contract: Culture and Cooperation in Human Evolution*. New York, NY: Oxford University Press.

Stern, Charlotta, and Guy Madison. 2022. 'Sex Differences and Occupational Choice Theorizing for Policy Informed by Behavioral Science'. *Journal of Economic Behavior and Organization* 202 (January): 694–702. https://doi.org/10.1016/j.jebo.2022.08.032.

Stewart-Williams, Steve, and Lewis G. Halsey. 2021. 'Men, Women and STEM: Why the Differences and What Should Be Done?' *European Journal of Personality* 35 (1): 3–39. https://doi.org/10.1177/0890207020962326.

Stoet, Gijsbert, and David C. Geary. 2018. 'The Gender-Equality Paradox in Science, Technology, Engineering, and Mathematics Education'. *Psychological Science* 29 (4): 581–93. https://doi.org/10.1177/0956797617741719.

———. 2019. 'A Simplified Approach to Measuring National Gender Inequality'. *PLOS ONE* 14 (1): e0205349. https://doi.org/10.1371/journal.pone.0205349.

———. 2022. 'Sex Differences in Adolescents' Occupational Aspirations: Variations across Time and Place'. *PLOS ONE* 17 (1): e0261438. https://doi.org/10.1371/journal.pone.0261438.

Stoker, Janka I., Mandy Van Der Velde, and Joris Lammers. 2012. 'Factors Relating to Managerial Stereotypes: The Role of Gender of the Employee and the Manager and Management Gender

Ratio'. *Journal of Business and Psychology* 27 (1): 31–42. https://doi.org/10.1007/s10869-011-9210-0.

Strassmann, Diana. 2009. 'Not a Free Market: The Rhetoric of Disciplinary Authority in Economics'. In *Beyond Economic Man: Feminist Theory and Economics*, ed. Marianne A. Ferber and Julie A. Nelson. Chicago: University of Chicago Press.

Strazdins, Lyndall, Jennifer A. Baxter, and Jianghong Li. 2017. 'Long Hours and Longings: Australian Children's Views of Fathers' Work and Family Time'. *Journal of Marriage and Family* 79 (4): 965–82. https://doi.org/10.1111/jomf.12400.

Su, Rong, James Rounds, and Patrick Ian Armstrong. 2009. 'Men and Things, Women and People: A Meta-Analysis of Sex Differences in Interests'. *Psychological Bulletin* 135 (6): 859–84. https://doi.org/10.1037/a0017364.

Tait, Amelia. 2020. 'Susan Fowler: "When the Time Came to Blow the Whistle on Uber, I Was Ready"'. *Guardian*, 3 February 2020. https://www.theguardian.com/world/2020/mar/01/susan-fowler-uber-whistleblower-interview-travis-kalanick.

Tatli, Ahu. 2011. 'A Multi-Layered Exploration of the Diversity Management Field: Diversity Discourses, Practices and Practitioners in the UK'. *British Journal of Management* 22:238–53. https://doi.org/10.1111/j.1467-8551.2010.00730.x.

Taub, Stephen. 2024. 'The 23rd Annual Ranking of the Highest-Earning Hedge Fund Managers'. Institutional Investor. https://www.institutionalinvestor.com/article/2doquhk4ghsahyyia26m8/corner-office/the-23rd-annual-ranking-of-the-highest-earning-hedge-fund-managers.

Thompson, William. 1825. *Appeal of One Half of the Human Race, Women, Against the Pretensions of the Other Half, Men, To Retain Them in Political, and Thence in Civil and Domestic, Slavery*. London: printed for Longman, Hurst, Rees, Orme, Brown and Green.

Thomson, Russell, Sarah Hegarty, and Elizabeth Webster. 2024. 'Female Consumer Preferences and Workplace Diversity: Evidence from the Box Office'. Mimeo. Melbourne: Swinburne University of Technology. https://papers.ssrn.com/sol3/papers.cfm?abstract_id=4928137.

BIBLIOGRAPHY

Thornton, Margaret. 2015. 'The Political Contingency of Sex Discrimination Legislation: The Case of Australia'. *Laws* 4 (3): 314–34. https://doi.org/10.3390/laws4030314.

Tilly, Charles. 1998. *Durable Inequality*. Berkeley: University of California Press.

Tomaskovic-Devey, Donald. 2014. 'The Relational Generation of Workplace Inequalities'. *Social Currents* 1 (1): 51–73. https://doi.org/10.1177/2329496513514032.

Tomaskovic-Devey, Donald, and Dustin Robert Avent-Holt. 2019. *Relational Inequalities: An Organizational Approach*. New York: Oxford University Press.

Tomaskovic-Devey, Donald, Dustin Avent-Holt, Catherine Zimmer, and Sandra Harding. 2009. 'The Categorical Generation of Organizational Inequality: A Comparative Test of Tilly's Durable Inequality'. *Research in Social Stratification and Mobility* 27 (3): 128–42. https://doi.org/10.1016/j.rssm.2009.04.004.

Toossi, Mitra, and Leslie Joyner. 2018. 'Blacks in the Labor Force'. US Bureau of Labor Statistics. https://www.bls.gov/spotlight/2018/blacks-in-the-labor-force/pdf/blacks-in-the-labor-force.pdf.

Trarbach, Ericka Barbosa, Leticia Gontijo Silveira, and Ana Claudia Latronico. 2007. 'Genetic Insights into Human Isolated Gonadotropin Deficiency'. *Pituitary* 10 (4): 381–91. https://doi.org/10.1007/s11102-007-0061-7.

Treviño, Linda Klebe, and Katherine A. Nelson. 2011. *Managing Business Ethics: Straight Talk about How to Do It Right*. 5th edn. New York: John Wiley.

US Attorney's Office, Central District of California. 2023. 'Former Wells Fargo Executive Agrees to Plead Guilty to Obstructing Bank Examination Involving the Opening of Millions of Accounts Without Customer Authorization'. Press release, 15 March 2023. Accessed 29 August 2024. https://www.justice.gov/usao-cdca/pr/former-wells-fargo-executive-agrees-plead-guilty-obstructing-bank-examination#:~:text=In%20a%20plea%20agreement%20filed,obstruction%20of%20a%20bank%20examination.

US Bureau of Labor Statistics. 2024. 'Occupational Outlook

Handbook: Registered Nurses'. https://www.bls.gov/ooh/healthcare/registered-nurses.htm.

———. (n.d.) 'Standard Occupational Classification'. Accessed 24 May 2024. https://www.bls.gov/soc/#:~:text=All%20workers%20are%20classified%20into,according%20to%20their%20occupational%20definition.

US Department of Treasury, Office of the Comptroller of the Currency. 2020. No. N20-001: Notice of Charges in the Matter of Carrie Tolstedt, et al. 23 January 2020. https://www.occ.gov/static/enforcement-actions/eaN20-001.pdf.

USA Facts. 2022. 'How Has the Structure of American Households Changed over Time'. https://usafacts.org/articles/how-has-the-structure-of-american-households-changed-over-time/.

Vagni, Giacomo, and Richard Breen. 2021. 'Earnings and Income Penalties for Motherhood: Estimates for British Women Using the Individual Synthetic Control Method'. *European Sociological Review* 37 (5): 834–48. https://doi.org/10.1093/esr/jcab014.

Valian, Virginia. 2014. 'Interests, Gender, and Science'. *Perspectives on Psychological Science* 9 (2): 225–30. https://doi.org/10.1177/1745691613519109.

Virgin Money UK. 2023. 'Gender Pay Gap Report 2023'. https://www.virginmoneyukplc.com/downloads/pdf/Gender-pay-report-2023.pdf.

Vitali, Stefania, James B. Glattfelder, and Stefano Battiston. 2011. 'The Network of Global Corporate Control'. *PLOS ONE* 6 (10): e25995–e25995. https://doi.org/10.1371/journal.pone.0025995.

Wakshlak, Aviva, and Marta Weinstock. 1990. 'Neonatal Handling Reverses Behavioral Abnormalities Induced in Rats by Prenatal Stress'. *Physiology & Behavior* 48 (2): 289–92. https://doi.org/10.1016/0031-9384(90)90315-U.

Walby, Sylvia. 1986. *Patriarchy at Work: Patriarchal and Capitalist Relations in Employment*. Cambridge: Polity Press.

Weaving, Morgan, Thayer Alshaabi, Michael V. Arnold, Khandis Blake, Christopher M. Danforth, Peter S. Dodds, Nick Haslam, and Cordelia Fine. 2023. 'Twitter Misogyny Associated with Hillary Clinton Increased throughout the 2016 U.S. Election

Campaign'. *Scientific Reports* 13 (1): 5266. https://doi.org/10.1038/s41598-023-31620-w.

Weeden, Kim A. 2002. 'Why Do Some Occupations Pay More than Others? Social Closure and Earnings Inequality in the United States'. *American Journal of Sociology* 108 (1): 55–101. https://doi.org/10.1086/344121.

Wessel, Lindzi. 2020. 'After Scalding Critiques of Study on Gender and Mentorship, Journal Says It Is Reviewing the Work'. https://doi.org/10.1126/science.abf8164.

West, Mark, Rebecca Kraut, and Han Ei Chew. 2019. 'I'd Blush If I Could: Closing Gender Divides in Digital Skills through Education'. Paris: UNESCO. https://unesdoc.unesco.org/ark:/48223/pf0000367416/PDF/367416eng.pdf.multi.

Westwood, Sallie. 1998. 'Review: Linda McDowell, *Capital Culture: Gender at Work in the City*, Oxford: Blackwell, 1997'. *Work, Employment and Society* 12 (4): 808–9. https://doi.org/10.1017/S0950017098310272.

Whipple, Dorothy. 1939. *The Priory*. London: Persephone Books.

White, Perrin C., and Phyllis W. Speiser. 2000. 'Congenital Adrenal Hyperplasia Due to 21-Hydroxylase Deficiency'. *Endocrine Reviews* 21 (3): 245–91. https://doi.org/10.1210/edrv.21.3.0398.

Wilkinson, Krystal, Jennifer Tomlinson, and Jean Gardiner. 2017. 'Exploring the Work–Life Challenges and Dilemmas Faced by Managers and Professionals Who Live Alone'. *Work, Employment and Society* 31 (4): 640–56. https://doi.org/10.1177/0950017016677942.

Williams, Joan C., Jennifer L. Berdahl, and Joseph A. Vandello. 2016. 'Beyond Work–Life "Integration".' *Annual Review of Psychology* 67 (1): 515–39. https://doi.org/10.1146/annurev-psych-122414-033710.

Wilson, David Sloan, Eric Dietrich, and Anne B. Clark. 2003. 'On the Inappropriate Use of the Naturalistic Fallacy in Evolutionary Psychology'. *Biology & Philosophy* 18 (5): 669–81. https://doi.org/10.1023/A:1026380825208.

Wittenberg-Cox, Avivah. 2014. *Seven Steps to Leading a Gender-Balanced Business*. Boston, Mass.: Harvard Business Review Press.

Woetzel, Jonathan, Anu Madgavkar, Kweilin Ellingrud, Eric Labaye, Sandrine Devillard, Eric Kutcher, James Manyika, Richard Dobbs, and Mekala Krishnan. 2015. 'The Power of Parity: How Advancing Women's Equality Can Add $12 Trillion to Global Growth'. McKinsey Global Institute. https://www.mckinsey.com/~/media/mckinsey/industries/public%20and%20social%20sector/our%20insights/how%20advancing%20womens%20equality%20can%20add%2012%20trillion%20to%20global%20growth/mgi%20power%20of%20parity_executive%20summary_september%202015.pdf.

Women in Computer Science. (n.d.) 'The Gender Gap: A Quantitative Description'. https://cs.stanford.edu/people/eroberts/cs181/projects/women-in-cs/statistics.html.

Women's Budget Group. 2016. 'A Cumulative Gender Impact Assessment of Ten Years of Austerity Policies'. https://www.wbg.org.uk/publication/a-cumulative-gender-impact-assessment-of-ten-years-of-austerity-policies/.

Women's Budget Group, and Runnymede. 2016. 'New Research Shows That Poverty, Ethnicity and Gender Magnify the Impact of Austerity on BME Women'. https://wbg.org.uk/wp-content/uploads/2016/11/AFS_2016_press_25Nov2016.pdf.

Wong, Julia Carrie, and Kari Paul. 2020. 'California Passes Prop 22 in a Major Victory for Uber and Lyft'. *Guardian*, 4 November 2020.

Wong, Wang I., Vickie Pasterski, Peter C. Hindmarsh, Mitchell E. Geffner, and Melissa Hines. 2013. 'Are There Parental Socialization Effects on the Sex-Typed Behavior of Individuals with Congenital Adrenal Hyperplasia?' *Archives of Sexual Behavior* 42 (3): 381–91. https://doi.org/10.1007/s10508-012-9997-4.

Wong, Yan Ling Anne, and Maria Charles. 2020. *Gender and Occupational Segregation*. Companion to Women's and Gender Studies. Wiley Blackwell. https://doi.org/10.1002/9781119315063.ch16.

Wood, Danielle, Kate Griffiths, and Owain Emslie. (2020). *Cheaper childcare: A practical plan to boost female workforce participation*. Grattan Institute. https://grattan.edu.au/wp-content/uploads/2020/08/Cheaper-Childcare-Grattan-Institute-Report.pdf.

BIBLIOGRAPHY

Wood, Wendy, and Alice H. Eagly. 2002. 'A Cross-Cultural Analysis of the Behavior of Women and Men: Implications for the Origins of Sex Differences'. *Psychological Bulletin* 128 (5): 699–727. https://doi.org/10.1037/0033-2909.128.5.699.

———. 2012. 'Biosocial Construction of Sex Differences and Similarities in Behavior'. In *Advances in Experimental Social Psychology*, 46:55–123. Elsevier. https://doi.org/10.1016/B978-0-12-394281-4.00002-7.

Workplace Gender Equality Agency. 2024. 'Employer Gender Pay Gaps Snapshot'. Australian Government. https://www.wgea.gov.au/sites/default/files/documents/Employer%20Gender%20Pay%20Gaps%20Snapshot_FINAL_1.pdf.

World Economic Forum. 2019. 'Global Gender Gap Report 2020'. https://www3.weforum.org/docs/WEF_GGGR_2020.pdf.

Worsdale, Rosie, and Jack Wright. 2021. 'My Objectivity Is Better than Yours: Contextualising Debates about Gender Inequality'. *Synthese* 199 (1–2): 1659–83. https://doi.org/10.1007/s11229-020-02835-5.

Yamaguchi, Masami K. 2000. 'Discriminating the Sex of Faces by 6- and 8-Mo.-Old Infants'. *Perceptual and Motor Skills* 91 (2): 653–64. https://doi.org/10.2466/pms.2000.91.2.653.

Younger, Barbara A., and Dru D. Fearing. 1999. 'Parsing Items into Separate Categories: Developmental Change in Infant Categorization'. *Child Development* 70 (2): 291–303. https://doi.org/10.1111/1467-8624.00022.

Zawidzki, Tadeusz. 2013. *Mindshaping: A New Framework for Understanding Human Social Cognition*. Cambridge, Mass.: MIT Press.

———. 2018. 'Mindshaping'. In *The Oxford Handbook of 4E Cognition*, ed. Albert Newen, Leon De Bruin, and Shaun Gallagher, 734–54. Oxford University Press.

Zentner, Marcel, and Klaudia Mitura. 2012. 'Stepping Out of the Caveman's Shadow: Nations' Gender Gap Predicts Degree of Sex Differentiation in Mate Preferences'. *Psychological Science* 23 (10): 1176–85. https://doi.org/10.1177/0956797612441004.

Zosuls, Kristina M., Diane N. Ruble, Catherine S. Tamis-LeMonda, Patrick E. Shrout, Marc H. Bornstein, and Faith K. Greulich. 2009.

'The Acquisition of Gender Labels in Infancy: Implications for Gender-Typed Play'. *Developmental Psychology* 45 (3): 688–701. https://doi.org/10.1037/a0014053.

Zucker, Kenneth J., Janet N. Mitchell, Susan J. Bradley, Jan Tkachuk, James M. Cantor, and Sara M. Allin. 2006. 'The Recalled Childhood Gender Identity/Gender Role Questionnaire: Psychometric Properties'. *Sex Roles* 54 (7–8): 469–83. https://doi.org/10.1007/s11199-006-9019-x.

INDEX

INDEX